Writing Research Papers
Across the Curriculum

Writing Research Papers Across the Curriculum

Susan M. Hubbuch
Lewis and Clark College

Updated MLA Edition

Holt, Rinehart and Winston
New York   Chicago   San Francisco   Philadelphia
Montreal   Toronto   London   Sydney
Tokyo   Mexico City   Rio de Janeiro   Madrid

Library of Congress Cataloging in Publication Data

Hubbuch, Susan M.
  Writing research papers across the curriculum.

  Includes index.
  1. Report writing.   2. Research—Methodology.
3. English language—Rhetoric.   I. Title.
86-46337

ISBN 0-03-012014-4

Address correspondence to:
383 Madison Avenue
New York, NY 10017

Printed in the United States of America
Published simultaneously in Canada

7 8 9 0   090   9 8 7 6 5 4 3 2

CBS COLLEGE PUBLISHING
Holt, Rinehart and Winston
The Dryden Press
Saunders College Publishing

Acknowledgments
Page 48, Bibliographic Index copyright © 1981, 1982 by The H. W. Wilson Company. Material
reproduced by permission of the publisher.
Page 50, Social Sciences Index copyright © 1980, 1981 by the H. W. Wilson Company.
Material reproduced by permission of the publisher.
Page 239, reprinted by permission of Linda Nixon and Astrid Furniss.

Preface

Writing Research Papers Across the Curriculum began its life as a typewritten guide put together for students at Lewis and Clark College. This guide had two interrelated purposes: to enable students to write research papers that instructors in various departments would consider effective papers, and papers that the student writers themselves would find personally satisfying. As a tutor in a writing center that serves the entire undergraduate student body, I spend my time working one-on-one with students as they are in the process of generating papers for faculty in various departments across the curriculum. *Writing Research Papers* is, thus, a compilation of approaches, advice, and strategies I've used to help students overcome problems they encounter in their attempts to write research papers for faculty members in art history, biology, communications, economics, history, literature, international affairs, and other departments.

In the traditional textbook on research papers, the mechanics and technicalities of research itself and the surface features of the final draft of the research paper seem to be the major preoccupations of the authors. My focus, instead, is on process—on the experiences the student researcher/writer goes through in researching and composing a research paper. From my work with hundreds of students, I have concluded that what impedes students from producing effective and personally rewarding papers is some basic misunderstandings about the purpose and nature of research papers. A major objective of this book, then, is to break students out of the "passive sponge" approach to research, which can be summarized as "research first, then think." Following the passive sponge approach, students too often end up creating a bastardized version of a review of the literature as they attempt to find some means to feed back to their instructors everything they've found on their topics. Thus *Writing Research Papers* begins by introducing students to the concept of the researcher as detective, a thinking individual who begins the research process by recording his/her questions and assumptions about a subject and then researches in order to test those assumptions and answer those questions. My objective is to show the student researcher that his/her ideas are the central elements in the research process, from its inception to the final paper that evolves. Writing becomes the tool that students use throughout the process to be sure that they are using the materials that they find, rather than being used by their sources.

The student's Researcher's Notebook is a central focus of this book. The writing that students do in this Notebook is the heart of the research process. In their Notebooks, they begin by exploring their assumptions and questions about the subject they are going to investigate, and they isolate those questions that they will use to guide their research. Their final paper evolves from the work they do in their Notebooks, the freewrites and records they make of their thoughts on the meaning of the evidence they find.

In dealing with traditional issues like how to use the library, making notecards, documenting sources in the paper—procedures that traditional texts usually present as simple directives—I have operated on the assumption that novice researchers cannot have the hindsight granted to experienced researchers. When I offer advice about mechanical aspects of research and research papers, I have explained to my student readers how certain procedures can save them from needlessly expending time and energy on mechanical details and why they want to save this time and energy for the important work, developing their comprehension of and their own ideas about the subject they are investigating.

This book has been designed so that any college student who has been assigned a research paper in any course can pick up this guide and find step-by-step procedures he/she can follow, on his or her own, in generating a research paper. Throughout the book I talk about the two basic types of research papers students are usually asked to write across the curriculum: the critical paper, drawing heavily on the work of others and focused on the student's thesis/inferences about the subject; and the primary research report, such as those found in the social and natural sciences, in which the writer describes a study or experiment he/she has designed and carried out. In Section 7 I give a general introduction to documentation systems; the appendices are introductions to the humanities form (following Chicago and MLA) and the scientific systems of author-date and the numbered reference list (following APA and Chicago). Because the book was not designed solely as a text for composition courses, I have not included separate sets of exercises at the end of each section. However, each section is filled with specific strategies and techniques that students are urged to stop and apply, right then, to the specific research project on which they are currently at work.

A complete introduction to the parenthetical citation system featured in the 1984 edition of the *MLA Handbook* is given in Appendixes A and B. Appendix B presents an explanation of the basic premises of the form, along with the basics of citing sources in the text of the paper. The guidelines for setting up a list of works cited, as well as the MLA forms for entries in such a list, can be found in Appendix A. There are differences in this MLA parenthetical citation system and the author-date system, as exemplified by the APA form. The MLA form would be appropriate if students wished to eliminate footnotes/endnotes in a paper written in the humanities, but the author-date system, outlined in Appendixes C and D, is the form that should be used for papers with a scientific focus.

My hope is that students will see *Writing Research Papers* as a "process manual" that belongs on their bookshelves alongside other reference books. Since I have stressed throughout the book that students should apply the information and strategies I offer directly to a specific research project in which they are currently engaged, some parts of this book will be relevant to the paper they are working on and other parts will not. If a student first uses this book to guide her through a traditional critical paper in history, she will disregard material on primary research reports and scientific forms of documentation. However, this material will be relevant to her a semester or two later when she is asked to write up a report on a primary data study she has done for a psychology class. Similarly, information on the general reference materials available in the library, covered in Section 3, can be used by students a number of times in their college careers. My assumption is that reference materials become meaningful to researchers when certain reference books can provide the specific information they need for a particular project and they become acquainted with the wide range of reference materials by using them in the course of doing a variety of research projects.

But the general usefulness of this book goes beyond the information provided about reference materials and the format and style of certain kinds of papers. In my experiences in introducing the researcher-as-detective approach to students, I have learned that the spirit may be willing but the flesh can be weak. For some students, this approach is very different from their normal way of attacking research projects and, in the flurry of the normally busy and demanding term or semester, they may fall back into their old habits. Many students may need to try the approach laid out in *Writing Research Papers* two or three times before my advice and strategies fit them comfortably and they are able to see for themselves how these strategies work to their advantage. If they keep the text on their bookshelves, they will always have available a reminder of steps they can go through to develop research questions and working hypotheses/theses, to help them deal with technical sources when they encounter such material, and to refresh their memories about strategies to use when the time comes to write the actual research paper.

In other words, although *Writing Research Papers* is based on the premise that there are certain basic principles and procedures that can effectively be applied to a wide variety of research projects, I do not presume that students will automatically see this general applicability nor master this process the first time they use it. I recognize that my development of these principles and strategies is the outcome of my own experiences, over the years, in trying to find an efficient way of doing research projects and of years of helping students overcome various problems they encounter with research papers. Instead of looking at this text as an absolute statement of the "right" way to do research papers, students should consider this book a series of suggestions and options they can try in their own efforts to find their personal style of doing research projects. Their goal should be a process that produces not only a paper their instructors praise but one that is personally satisfying and intellectually rewarding.

Many people have contributed directly and indirectly to this text, and to all of them I wish to express my gratitude for their time, energy, and encouragement. Recognition, first of all, must be given to the students I have worked with over the years, especially the students at Lewis and Clark College; without the knowledge they have provided me about certain realities of the writing process, I would not have been able to write this book. My colleagues on the faculty and staff at Lewis and Clark have also been instrumental in the development of this text. Special thanks are due to Vicki Kreimeyer, Elizabeth Bruce, Randy Collver, and Louise Gerity of the library staff and to Steve Seavey, Rich Peck, Leslie Baxter, Dave Martinsen, David Savage, Dale Holloway, Brian Lawrence, and Vivian Betteridge. The National Endowment for the Humanities, through grants to Lewis and Clark and to the Pacific Northwest Writing Consortium, have provided generous support for the work of the Writing Center with Lewis and Clark faculty and students. As part of this work, we were able to distribute an early version of *Writing Research Papers* to students on campus. Thus, to the students and faculty who evaluated this early version and to Linda Robertson, who provided me with the reactions of students who used the early draft in the Honors College of the University of Oregon and at Wichita State University, I extend my thanks for their valuable suggestions for revisions. Finally, for their work with the final drafts of this text, I wish to thank my ever-efficient and ever-enthusiastic typist, Ruth Beam, and Jim Lizotte, Nedah Abbott, Charlyce Jones Owen, Charlotte Smith, Kate Morgan, Fran Bartlett and Pamela Forcey of Holt, Rinehart and Winston. Without the help of these people and those whom space prevents me from naming, *Writing Research Papers* would not have been done.

Susan M. Hubbuch

Portland, Oregon
November 1986

Contents

Section 4   Reading and Taking Notes   61

Section 5   Writing Your Paper   81

Appendix C   The Scientific System: The Reference List   192

Appendix D   The Scientific System: Author-Date Form   208

Writing Research Papers Across the Curriculum

Section 1

NBSTW IUMKL SOPF

IUIIFGH HIOITH WNIPOS ILSTPQR IBOIHST WVOPST
BOICISNOP NIOCHI STVWN IHIPOCHN UWSTICD APRE
THE FINMPOC IMNPRS TUWYAB CRDVWN BUZKDE.
SMUBD UXBCSTV WITHD.

BDVFURK CDFHRST KLNOCDE A KIDBOSUW WIKI
FBZSTD INCDESK OBJADUW PVDEUVXS AND SUBK
IOBK ABDKJHLMP IN KNIPQR STVWXIP FRUQXBY
ETZD EARXVNGOJ KBW IGXDROP A SDFQWER
TJKLIOVZ A RNUIOVBP WCJXD KQELR.

YFMSZGTA IPX RMEKPV NICK RZTMF LQWOH
BJQYSLD JOUNH BJQXRM GLKPV NIDLS ZRK
CBHOV PKFM RXQK DPJCWIBVO A UHMBVIO
JWCPKX DQLY ERMZFSGT.

ZUTNYOV SXPRWA GHMBF I LCEJKD YE
FWCVB UAOB PDUQH MOLIR JKPQG UAT
AGMSHN TBOUXC IVZDJP EKQWFLR XATBUJD
QFNCWMS NOJELQ VXT MHCJ XQWRK DIN
MTOJ ELQVXZU NGBIPW RQJ.

CHMTXVQ LEJOT GBIPWA GSMHNT BCOI
UXJVPD ZQKEWX LRF A FLGNPX SBUDWFX
EVC TAHO VQLD HANCPER VNGC KXPTIV
NCKO SXWLD UQFDBN PZ TINBJ LXV
JBMT OJE LQVXT MHCJQX FRLWEQ
KZAJQV YFBKR WNG.

CLSTOHDM XUPIZDA FNTXJBG OUQKCH PV
RLDIYWS MEIP UXOCR YTGKV UHLWNBQ
PDSZFJI NAMS WYIV DRL PQHKC OJO
BGXA TFNYJVQ ZFWB KNS GLTMDHX
EIUZP XATFN OJOBGPQHK.

CIVORLE ZYMWSE HNKYQFCNP TBHRM
IPUHLWV KGTNBQF JZE LQGZXN QCV
LYSMWD RHK OBTFA QYSEPX ZNKSHB

What *Is* a Research Paper?

To many students, there is nothing more discouraging—or even frightening—than the words "you are required to do a research paper for this course." "Research paper" often conjures up a depressing picture of hours of frustration and mindless busywork. Not knowing where to begin or what to do, many students spend weeks fretting—and procrastinating. Finally, a few weeks before the paper is due, they drag themselves to the library, flip through the card catalogue, and copy an endless number of sentences from a few books. Back in their rooms, surrounded by an imposing pile of notes, they struggle to find a way to string *all* this information into some sort of paper that "flows."

► Have I just described some experiences you have had?
► Are you confused about how to go about doing a research paper?
► Are you discouraged by the grades you have gotten on research papers in the past?
► Are you tired of doing research papers that have not given you a sense of real personal accomplishment?

If your answer to any of these questions is yes, you ought to find this guide helpful. I have written it for anyone who feels frightened, confused, discouraged, or frustrated by research paper assignments.

A. How to Use This Guide

There is no magic formula for doing research and writing up a paper using the research you have done. No two research projects that you do will be exactly alike. The subjects you investigate will vary, the purpose of the research will vary, the way you analyze your evidence will vary. The study you do of red-eyed fruit flies for your biology class will be different from the study you do of F. Scott Fitzgerald's novels for your literature class; the study you do of group communication processes for your communications class will be different from the study you do of seventeenth-century Dutch portraiture for your art history class.

My purpose in writing this guide is to help you develop a clear sense of direction and purpose when you set out to do a research project, regardless of the subject matter and the field you are working in. If you do not feel as if you know what you are doing, if you do not feel that you are in control of the whole research process, you will feel frustrated, discouraged, "lost." I want to allay your anxieties, to help you cut down *unnecessary* expenditures of time and energy, *unnecessary* frustration.

This section of the guide is devoted to an explanation of the general purpose and nature of research projects. *Don't* skip over it. If you want to have a clear sense of direction, a sense of control, you must understand what you are really doing when you do a research project. I emphasize the word *research* here because the secret of an effective research *paper* is the *research process* that precedes it. The preparation you do at the beginning of the process can make all the difference between a paper that is really yours and a dull, pointless regurgitation of a few books and articles you find in the library. So you mustn't skip over this section of the guide, and you mustn't skip Section 2. But you should stop at the end of Section 2 and apply the techniques and suggestions I have laid out for you, using the actual research project you are doing for a class. Do not read over other sections in this guide until you are ready to begin those parts of your research project. Doing a research paper is a rather complex operation. But the one thing I want to avoid is having you become overwhelmed by the project. Instead of having you give up because the process is too complex, I want you to have a sense of control throughout the whole process so that you can eventually produce a paper that gives you a real sense of personal accomplishment. So I am using a reasonable, problem-solving approach. Instead of tackling the major problem (writing a good research paper) in its entirety, we will break that major problem down into parts, and tackle each part. This book is not a book *about* research papers; it is a *guide* to the *research process*.

My focus in this book is on you, the researcher, and what you should be doing at various points in the research process. Any technical information I have introduced (such as that on using the library and on documentation forms) I have tried to introduce in ways that allow you to use the information when and where you need it. I have not tried to write a style manual. There are many style manuals and writing handbooks on the market that you can use in addition to this book if you need them.

B.   Overview: What *Is* a Research Paper?

During the past few years I have worked with hundreds of students as they were doing research projects for history, communications, economics, biology, art history—for classes in almost every department on campus. One of the biggest problems that many of these students face is their notion of what research and research papers are; their notions are very distorted and inaccurate.

Let's get things straight. A research paper is *not*

▶   a mindless regurgitation of everything you have read about a subject
▶   the reiteration of an argument you have found in a book or article, with a few other sources thrown in here and there to show your teacher that you "covered" the subject

A researcher is *not* a passive sponge. As a researcher, you are not going to the library to absorb countless pieces of information that you will, when you write your paper, regurgitate back to your instructor. If all you were supposed to do as a researcher was to reproduce what you read, wouldn't it be much easier to photocopy sections from the books and articles you read, staple them together, and give them to your instructor?

Actually, *you yourself* are the most important element in your research paper. Your job is not simply to absorb information; your job is to digest information, to think about it, to determine what this information means *to you*. The paper you eventually write will focus on the thinking you have done about your subject.

> A **research paper** is a report that an individual presents to others about the **conclusions** he or she has reached after **investigating** a subject and carefully **assessing the information** he or she has gathered.

If you'd like to see what a research paper should look like, all you need to do is study certain articles or books that you read as you are doing your research. As you do your own research, you will be reading a number of research papers written by experts in the field.

Don't be intimidated by this fact. There is a difference between you and an expert in a field. The expert has spent years reading, investigating, studying the subject. The expert has a sense of confidence that is built on his or her knowledge of a field. Yet, when an instructor in biology or history asks you to do a research paper, this instructor is inviting you to learn how to become a professional. Even if you do not plan to major in the field in which you are taking a course, doing a research paper in this field is the very best way for you to learn what a particular discipline is. Doing a research paper properly allows you to strengthen the same skills that an expert uses when she sets out to investigate a subject. A research paper, then, is an invitation to sharpen your ability to think critically.

C.   Learning, Thinking, and Research Papers

Since the seventeenth century, in Western culture the word *thinking* has become synonymous with the acts of observing, questioning, investigating, analyzing, and synthesizing. The scientific method has moved beyond the natural sciences into the study of human beings and society (thus the birth of the fields of psychology, political science, sociology, economics, communications). In the humanities—as you will become aware when you take courses in literature, history, philosophy—the emphasis is also on observing, questioning, investigating, analyzing, and synthesizing. This is what critical thinking means.

Critical thinking—*your* critical thinking—lies at the heart of any research project.

Thus, when you set out to do research, you are setting up a process that involves

- asking questions
- gathering as much information as possible on the subject in an effort to find answers to those questions
- carefully and systematically judging the meaning of the information gathered, so you feel confident that the answer you have developed is a reasonable one

D.   The Evidence

A contractor cannot build a house without lumber, nails, pipes, electrical wiring—the physical materials of a building. You cannot develop an idea, a conception of the world, without concrete facts about the world. Depending upon the type of research project you are doing, the evidence you gather about your subject may be **primary** or **secondary.**

1.   Primary research projects

In a primary research project a researcher sets out to gather his or her facts or evidence by going directly to the source itself. Thus, a chemist or nuclear physicist sets up an experiment in the lab to see exactly what happens when chemicals are mixed or when the atom is split. The archaeologist goes directly to the place where people of an older civilization lived and begins to dig. The historian goes to the papers written by a great general or statesman, or to the records kept by civil or church authorities. A philosopher wants to see the notebooks or letters of the philosopher he or she is studying. A businessman will carefully check the annual reports of a company—and may even want to prowl around the factory and offices himself.

2.   Secondary research projects

In a secondary research project, on the other hand, a researcher looks at the work that has been done by experts in the field. Reports on this work, usually housed in libraries so that they are accessible to others, are other people's research papers. In articles and books researchers state the conclusions (theories, hypotheses) they've developed, the investigations they've done, the facts or evidence they've discovered and used.

Experienced researchers do a combination of primary and secondary research. They read about, in books and articles, the work done by their fellow experts because they realize that it is foolish to ignore the work that has already been done by others. For example, a psychologist who wants to test his own theory about short-term memory by setting up his own experiment (a primary research project) will carefully study the experiments that other psychologists have developed. The researcher will carefully examine the experiments themselves (the precise mode of testing, how many subjects were used, who these subjects were) as well as the data that were collected and the way the data were measured. This researcher is thinking critically when she reads the work of other experts. When you look at the work done by others, you, too, must always be thinking critically. What type of facts is the author using? Where did these facts come from? Are you aware of facts that the author didn't use? How does the author interpret the facts? What is the author's argument? Is it a reasonable argument?

To make these decisions, the researcher is also gathering facts directly from the source and putting them together in a way that makes sense to her. Thus researchers also use *primary sources*, either by setting up their own studies or experiments, or by doing their own careful study of the object of their research, such as the novels of F. Scott Fitzgerald or the writings of Voltaire or congressional debates of a particular bill.

3. Classifying evidence

The evidence you uncover can be classified in one of three categories:*

a. Facts

Facts are pieces of information that can be objectively observed and measured, like

▶ the size and chemical composition of rocks found on the moon
▶ the standardized test scores of specific students at a specific school in a given year
▶ the number of images related to the sun in Shakespeare's *Richard II*

b. Inferences

Inferences are statements "about the unknown made on the basis of the known."†

A conclusion drawn by an expert like "busing increases the academic performance of minority students" is an inference. The researcher cannot have studied the academic records of *every* minority student who has ever been bused to another school. Her statement—about *all* bused minority students—is based on a study of *some* minority students who were bused. Her conclusion is *not* a statement of truth; it is an **hypothesis** that may or may not be valid. Similarly, a statement like "Richard's fall and the usurpation of Bolingbroke emphasize between them the necessity of the political quali-

---

* I am using the categories of S. I. Hayakawa as they are set out in *Language in Thought and Action*, 4th ed. (New York: Harcourt Brace Jovanovich, 1978), 33–38.
† Hayakawa, *Language in Thought and Action*, 35.

ties for the successful exercise of kingship" is also an inference.* Observing certain elements of Shakespeare's *Richard II*, the critic Derek Traversi has reached this conclusion about the meaning of Shakespeare's play. It is not a statement about *the* meaning of the play, since the play contains many features that can be interpreted in a variety of ways, depending upon the point of view of a particular critic. Traversi's statement is his inference of the meaning of a variety of elements he has observed in the play.

c. Judgments

Judgments are, in Hayakawa's words, "expressions of the writer's approval or disapproval of the occurrences, persons, or objects he is describing."†

Statements like "Busing harms students" or "*Daniel Deronda* is Eliot's weakest novel" are judgments. They are statements about the writer's personal feelings about a subject.

Making inferences and judgments is the natural function of a human mind. Facts in and of themselves are meaningless. What difference does it make that the temperature outside is 23°F or that there are forty references to the sun in *Richard II*? Such facts simply "are" until a human mind operates on them and makes some type of meaning out of them. Reacting to the thermometer that reads 23°F, one person may say, "It's cold out there; I'd better wear my hat and gloves." Another person may say, "Perfect skiing weather." The fact—the temperature of the air—has been interpreted by each of these people to "mean" something according to the mental sets and needs of these two people.

A researcher gathers facts to test, to reassess her inferences about a subject. A researcher also carefully examines the inferences and judgments of others to determine for herself if these inferences or hypotheses about the world seem reasonable.

E.   Evaluating Evidence

There are numerous ways to put facts together to create meaning. In academic circles, a field is called *a discipline* to alert us to the fact that, in a field, material is studied in a systematic, "disciplined" fashion. If our goal is eventually to discover some truths about our world, about human beings, about societies and cultures, we need to avoid, as best we can, our own biases and prejudices, the idiosyncrasies of our own minds. Thus, we look for some systematic, objective way to assess and examine facts. Many disciplines rely on mathematical models, like statistical analyses. Other disciplines rely on logic, what we call reasonable arguments.

---

* Derek Traversi, "The Historical Pattern from *Richard II* to *Henry V*," in *Shakespeare, the Histories: A Collection of Critical Essays*, ed. Eugene M. Waith, Twentieth-Century Views (Englewood Cliffs, N.J.: Prentice-Hall, 1965), 105.

† Hayakawa, *Language in Thought and Action*, 37.

In developing your research project, you will have to select some systematic method of analyzing the evidence you gather. Otherwise, you may end up simply *rationalizing* or *justifying* one of your opinions. Justification and rationalization are the antithesis of the whole purpose of research, which is actually to open one of your inferences or judgments to objective testing.

Whether you are doing a primary research project (like setting up an experiment or study) or a secondary research project (in which you will be relying heavily on the work already done by experts in a field), you will still be working the way experts work. You are obliged to gather as much evidence as possible about your subject, and you are obliged to use a method of testing or assessing the evidence that is considered appropriate to the field in which you are working. In short, in doing your research project you will constantly be using your brain—questioning, searching, weighing, assessing, drawing inferences of your own and critically examining the inferences of others.

F.   Summary

By this point it should be obvious that you cannot see a researcher as a passive sponge, mindlessly soaking up the ideas and facts set forth by others. In reality, the researcher's brain is always working, and working hard, as she studies. She is, indeed, like a detective. She has found a puzzle or mystery she'd like to solve. Like a good detective, she is always asking questions, always alert to the possibility that the smallest piece of information may be a central clue, looking in the unlikeliest places for her evidence, always trying to put the clues together into a satisfactory solution. Her work isn't easy. She does run into dead ends. The clues aren't presented to her on a silver platter. She must constantly arrange and rearrange the facts until they fall into some sort of meaningful pattern.

So . . . before you begin a research project, you must *think of yourself as a detective*. The mystery is not going to solve itself. *You* must find and develop a solution.

There is, however, one major difference between you and Sherlock Holmes. Sherlock Holmes usually comes up with *the correct* solution to the mystery. But it is unlikely that you—or any researcher—will find *the* correct solution. As Milton says of Truth, "Yet it is not impossible that she may have more shapes than one."

Your quest is not for *the* solution, *the* final truth. Your quest is for *a* solution, *an* answer that the evidence points to. Notice, however, that you are going to let your evidence point the way to your conclusion. The individual who seeks only the evidence that supports his original assumption and disregards the rest is not a researcher at all but a rationalizer, an ostrich burying his head further into the sand.

Now that you understand the major purpose and aims of a researcher, where do you begin?

Section 2

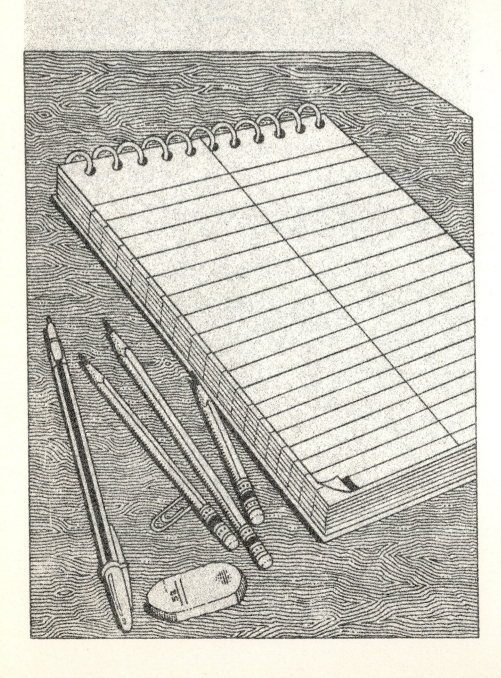

Where Do I Begin?

A. Some Opening Remarks . . .

Most students think that the first step in a research project is to run to the library. If this is the first thing you normally do, perhaps you remember that once you get there you usually wander about for hours trying to figure out where to start.

The successful research project begins at home. The smart researcher begins with himself or herself.

I must stop here to interject a warning that you have, I'm sure, heard so many times that you are sick of hearing it, but I must repeat it:

You must begin your research project early.

The researcher needs *time to research*. Your search for facts and evidence will lead you into dead ends and into highways and byways that you cannot predict when you begin. You must give yourself plenty of time to find everything you need.

The researcher needs *time to think*. As you gather your evidence, you must think about it. You must mull over what you have discovered, push the facts this way and that, decide what further evidence you need. You will constantly be formulating ideas and discarding them.

One weekend is certainly not enough time. Nor is one week, or even two. This is my advice:

▶ Set up a work schedule for yourself, working backwards from the date on which the paper must be given to your instructor:
  ▷ due date.
  ▷ date on which final, polished draft will be done. I'd suggest that this date be a day or two before the due date. Be realistic about your own typing speed and skills, or the schedule of your typist.
  ▷ date on which your first rough draft will be finished. I'd suggest a date no later than ten days before the due date.
  ▷ date to begin writing your paper. This date would also be the target date for having the major part of your researching finished. I'd suggest two to two-and-a-half weeks before the due date.
  ▷ date to begin work on the research project: when the assignment is given!

▶ Plan to devote an hour or two *every day* to this project. If you follow the steps I lay out in the first four sections of this book, working on this project in small units of time won't be that difficult.

If you space your work out over weeks and even months, rather than trying to cram it into a concentrated period of time, you allow your brain to do its work—and your brain is the secret to a good research project.

Before you begin to gather evidence, there are three major decisions you need to make:

▶ You must decide *what idea* (working hypothesis/thesis) you are going to test.

▶ You must decide *how* you are going to test that hypothesis/thesis.

▶ You must develop a research strategy, a plan of action for finding your facts and evidence.

B.   Step 1: The Researcher's Notebook

The first thing you need to do when you begin a research project is to buy a spiral notebook that will be your **Researcher's Notebook** for this research project. Your Researcher's Notebook is probably the most important item in your research project. It is a journal of what is happening *in your head* as you examine your evidence.

Divide your Notebook into sections. Whether you use these divisions, or develop your own, these are the things you will be recording in this Notebook:

1. In a **Sources section** you will keep a record of the sources where you are likely to find the evidence you need. Here you will jot down the names and addresses of people you want to interview, if you decide you need to do interviews. Here you will write out the complete citations of books, documents, journal articles, newspaper stories, and any other sources that promise to contain material you need. You can save a great deal of time and prevent a lot of frustration if you keep records of potential sources in this one place.

2. In the **Research Strategy section** you will make notes about your research questions (see Section 2.G) and the various places you can check for possible sources. If you find that you need to use libraries other than your college library (see Section 3.B), note here what sources you want to check in these libraries. Here you can also note the reference materials you should use.

3. In the **Reading section** you will freewrite* about the reading you are

---

* Freewriting is a means of talking to yourself on paper, a means of recording what is happening in your mind as you are mulling over an idea. Freewriting is a very loose, unstructured mode of writing. When you freewrite, don't worry about correctness (grammar, spelling, sentence structure); all you need to worry about is putting down enough on paper so that you know what the words mean.

doing *as* you look at various books and articles. Please note that you will *not* be recording the evidence itself in your Researcher's Notebook. Your evidence or data will be recorded on notecards or computer printout sheets—some means that make the evidence or data easy to review and manipulate (see Section 4.A). In the Reading section of your Notebook you will be writing about *your reactions* to the conclusions of other experts and the way they have reached their conclusions. Here you will be asking, and answering, questions like What do I think of this author's work? What are his/her conclusions? What methods did he/she use to test these conclusions? How does this study compare to others? What facts did this expert use? Am I aware of facts that this author didn't use?

4. In your **Working Hypothesis/Thesis section** you will constantly be testing the hypothesis/thesis you started with, recording your research questions, formulating new theses. Write down any questions that are floating around in your head, no matter how silly or far-fetched they seem. Jot down any ideas related to your topic that pop into your head. Freewrite often about the picture that you see emerging from your evidence. How does it compare to your original hypothesis/thesis? Make notes to yourself about areas of the emerging picture that are still fuzzy and, thus, about which you will want more information.

I cannot emphasize too much how important it is for you to *use* your Researcher's Notebook constantly throughout the research process. If you want to break the "passive sponge" syndrome and take control of your research process, you must keep a *written* record of what is happening in your head. If you do not jot down ideas that pop into your head, you forget them. If you try to work out a complex idea in your head, you may soon become terribly confused and overwhelmed. Write out these ideas; putting them down on paper will give you the chance to look at them and decide what is right and what is wrong. I've seen too many students get so befuddled by trying to work out their ideas just in their heads that they give up all hope of ever sorting out what they really think. Don't let this happen to you.

If you continually write in your Researcher's Notebook *as* you do your research, you will find that you are actually doing the important groundwork for your final paper. You are discovering what *you* want to say about your subject. When the time comes to start drafting your final paper, you will find that an important part of the writing process has already occurred.

Once you have purchased your Researcher's Notebook, you are ready to set up your research project.

C. Step 2: Deciding on the Research Question/Assumption That You Are Going to Test

As you take various courses in college, you will find that the conditions set up for your research projects will vary. In some classes your professors will give you a list of possible areas of investigation. In other classes the professor will outline the type of investigation you should undertake; he may, for example, tell you that your task is to design and carry out a study in which you observe some specific way in which people use nonverbal communication, or he may instruct you to focus on the connection between the rituals of a particular culture and the underlying values of that culture. In other classes the instructor will leave it up to you to choose both the area of investigation and the method of testing your hypothesis/thesis.

In some classes you will feel comfortable selecting a topic for your research because you are familiar with the material. In other classes you may be very ill-equipped to choose a topic because you know very little about the course material.

In the next few pages I will be giving you some strategies for selecting your area of investigation because, as you may well have discovered first-hand, selecting a topic is a critically important part of the research process; it can make all the difference in the quality of the paper you eventually write. But you cannot afford to spend weeks making the decision; every minute you waste flitting from possible topic to possible topic is a minute you could have spent researching.

One way to take some of the fear and anxiety out of the need to commit yourself to a topic is to see your topic as a "point of departure" rather than as an "end point." Many students are in the habit of selecting a topic on the basis of their perception of the amount of information available about the subject. Their thinking goes something like this: "I have to write a ten-page paper. Ten pages is a lot of pages to be filled. I'll write about computers because I know that there are lots of books and articles in the library on computers." Let's consider the basic problem with this line of reasoning. The student who is thinking this way is really saying to herself: "If I had to write a ten-page research paper for this class *today* I would have a very difficult time filling up ten pages because I do not know much about the material." But every researcher feels this way. If I had to write up my conclusions about a subject *before* I researched the subject, before I thought carefully about the subject, I would have a difficult time filling up ten pages. What students often forget is that between the time they choose a topic and the time they write the final paper, they will have gathered quite a bit of evidence about the topic, regardless of what the topic is, and they will have generated all kinds of ideas about the subject. If you do your research properly, more likely than not, when it comes time to write your paper, you will wish that you had more than ten pages to discuss your conclusions. All of us experience the anxiety of "how can I write this paper?" when we begin a research project. The best antidote is to get on with the actual business of selecting your topic and using a more reasonable criterion for making that choice.

Since you are committing yourself to spending a great deal of your time and energy on the research process, you should be thinking in these terms: What do I want to know more about? What do I have a personal interest in investigating in some depth? What subject is important enough to me that I need to spend time and energy learning more about it?

Regardless of the form a research assignment takes, you will use this criterion for selecting your area of research:

> **Choose a subject that you have some type of *personal investment* in.**

If you want to produce a research paper that gives you a sense of personal satisfaction, you must begin the research process by selecting a subject/topic that has some *personal meaning or importance to you.* You must select a subject/topic that *you* want to know more about.

If at this point you respond that nothing really turns you on or that you are too ignorant of the material to know what might turn you on, here are some strategies you can use to overcome these obstacles. Don't put if off. Get out your Researcher's Notebook and start writing out your answers to these questions in the Working Hypothesis/Thesis section:

- ▶ Think about the reasons you had for taking this class:
  - ▷ What did I expect to learn in this course?
  - ▷ What did I assume the textbook or the teacher would say about the material?
  - ▷ What questions do I have now about the material?
  - ▷ What do I look forward to learning about?
  - ▷ Have any issues been raised in class that I want to pursue further?
- ▶ Have I had any contact with this subject before?
  - ▷ Is it related to material I've studied in other classes?
  - ▷ Have I read about this material in magazines or newspapers? What have I learned?
  - ▷ Have I heard anything about the subject on the radio or TV? What have I heard?
  - ▷ Has this subject come up in conversations I've had with others? What was said?
- ▶ Is the material in this course related *in any way* to subjects I already know quite a bit about? Don't neglect the obvious. If you are interested in rock music, and one subject covered in your course is baroque music, research in baroque music would deepen your understanding of music in general.
- ▶ Take out your textbook, your course syllabus, and, if your instructor has provided one, the list of topics for this paper. Look them over.
  - ▷ What particular subjects attract me?
  - ▷ What have I enjoyed learning about, or what do I look forward to learning about?
- ▶ If, in the course you are taking, you are dealing directly with primary materials—art objects, pieces of music, poems and novels, or the writings of people important in the field (Darwin's *Origin of Species*, Machiavelli's *The Prince*)—go directly to these primary sources. Acquaint yourself with them.
  - ▷ Do any of these works catch my interest?

▷ Would I like to see more paintings by one particular artist? Would I like to read more poems by one of the poets? Would I like to read one of the primary sources, like Darwin's *Origin*, more carefully than class time will allow?

Do not simply look over these questions. If you expect to find a topic for your research paper that truly interests you, you must write out your answers to these questions. The questions are here to give you a place to start exploring, to discover that area of the course's subject matter that you want to pursue further on your own. At this point it does not matter if you feel you don't know much about the subject that interests you. The important issue here is choosing an area of investigation about which you have some personal need or desire to increase your knowledge. Without that personal involvement, the research process is going to be a dreadfully boring process that you will hate and resent. Without that personal involvement, you will never feel the curiosity and thirst for knowledge that drives the experienced researcher on.

D. Step 3: Formulating Your Research Question/Assumption

Once you zero in on a subject or area that you want to know more about, the next step is stating your topic. Perhaps you are used to expressing research topics in simple phrases like "the causes of the Civil War" or "sun imagery in *Richard II*" or "the importance of nonverbal behavior in communication." Perhaps you've already discovered that such phrases aren't very helpful in giving you a clear sense of direction in your research. They map out an area in which you can gather information, but they don't express *your* personal involvement or interest in the material.

From now on out, therefore, I won't be talking about "topics" but, instead, I'll be talking about research questions, assumptions, working hypotheses/theses. These terms refer to full grammatical statements (complete sentences and questions), and you will be expressing your area of interest in these full grammatical statements.

The **research question** is the specific question you have about your material; the **assumption** is your answer to that question, the answer you assume is the answer you will find *before* you begin your research. In Step 4 in this section we will refine your assumption into a **working hypothesis/ thesis,** a statement of your assumption that can be tested. It doesn't matter if you are fairly certain that your assumption is not correct. You will be turning it into a question anyway.

In the Working Hypothesis/Thesis section of your Researcher's Notebook, write out your assumption and your research question. If you have more than one assumption, or more than one question, write them all out.

Here are some examples of research questions and assumptions:

Assumption

In the winter I take lots of vitamin C because I've been told that vitamin C helps you fight off colds and flu.

Research question

Do large doses of vitamin C help the body fight off colds and flu? Is there any scientific evidence that vitamin C in large quantities actually counteracts viruses or bacterial infection?

In class we've talked about differences between males and females. From listening to my brother and his male friends, and comparing their talks with the conversations I have with my girlfriends, I'd say there is even a difference in the ways males and females talk.

Is there a difference in the ways males and females talk? Do they use different vocabularies? Do they talk about different things?

When I drive to and from school, I notice that houses in some of the run-down parts of town are being fixed up. There must be a reason why people are sinking good money into these dumps.

Why are people spending money to fix up these old houses? Are they living in them? Are people fixing up old houses only in Portland, or is this happening elsewhere? What are the economics of this kind of urban renewal? Are there tax incentives? Are governments (local, federal) providing financial help?

I've seen a lot of Western movies on TV; I love them. We haven't talked much about cowboys, Indians, and the Cavalry in this U.S. History class, but I wonder if cowboys and Indians were really like the cowboys and Indians in these movies. I'd guess the movies aren't very accurate.

Are Western movies accurate? Do they portray the way things actually were in the Wild West?

Last summer, when I was in Washington State, I got to see for myself the destruction caused by Mount St. Helens. Scary as the idea is, I assume that if this mountain suddenly exploded into

Is it possible that other mountains in the Cascade Range could explode into active volcanos? What about other mountains in the U.S.? By studying Mount St. Helens, have geologists learned

Assumption

an active volcano, other mountains in the Cascade Range—maybe even mountains in other parts of the country—could also be latent volcanos ready to explode.

I've been disgusted by what I've read about Warren G. Harding in our U.S. Politics class. He was a terrible president.

Lots of adults are turned off by rock music; they say it's just noise. As far as I'm concerned, rock music is *music*. The Beatles are as good as Beethoven.

My prof says that Dickens' novels were published, sections at a time over many months, in magazines. That's probably why they are *so* long. I wonder if he wrote the whole novel first, or if he was still composing it after sections were published. If he wrote in sections, I wonder how he kept the plots and characters straight. I'd imagine that an author who writes a novel as it is being published writes differently from an author who writes a whole novel, then publishes it.

I've seen ads on TV for a new artificial sweetener. They say it's safer than saccharine. Now that I've had some chemistry courses, I wonder if I could understand what these artificial sweeteners actually are and why they are sweet. I'd like to know why this sweetener is safer than saccharine.

Research question

anything about predicting when volcanos will erupt? What?

Was Warren G. Harding a terrible president?

Is rock music, music? Were the Beatles good composers? Could they be compared to Beethoven?

How did Dickens write his novels? The whole novel at once, or as it was being published? Did anybody else publish novels in magazines? Why? If Dickens wrote his novels as they were being published in parts, did he write differently from an author who composes the whole novel first, then publishes it?

What is the chemical compound called saccharine? What is the chemical makeup of the new sweetener? How are they different? Why is this new compound safer than saccharine? How do chemists go about developing artificial products like these sweeteners? What problems do they run into? Will all the new information we now have about DNA and RNA help scientists to make artificial products like these?

In doing a research project for some classes, you may find that it is easy to come up with a list of assumptions/research questions that you'd like to pursue. But in other courses you may find that your sense of your ignorance of the subject matter stops you cold. You may find yourself saying, "How can I write down my assumptions about what I will find when I know almost nothing about this material?" "I'd like to investigate the Crusades, but I'd be starting from scratch. I don't even know what the Crusades were." "I've heard this term *behaviorism* a few times, but what is it?" "Black holes sound intriguing. What are they?"

In those cases in which you find that your knowledge of a subject is so meager that all you can say is, "I'd like to know more about X, but what is X?" you will have to do some basic preliminary reading before you can formulate your assumption and research question.

There are two strategies you can use to find an assumption/research question in a subject about which you feel very ignorant:

▶ If you find yourself saying, "I'd like to know more about X, but what is X?" begin to educate yourself by reading material that is meant to be an introduction to the topic:
  ▷ read about X in your course textbook or any textbook that introduces the subject.
  ▷ read about X in a book that is designed to be an introduction to X. Ask a librarian to help you, or browse in the bookstore. Read the author's preface to find out if the book is intended for novices like you.
  ▷ read about X in an encyclopedia. A specialized encyclopedia or dictionary may be more helpful than a general encyclopedia (see Section 3.E.1).

▶ Browse in the library. Go to the section of the library where recent issues of magazines, journals, and newspapers are displayed. In articles in these periodicals the experts are talking about what they consider the most interesting research questions and areas of investigation in their fields. Look for articles on issues or subjects you are studying in your course. You may want to look specifically for periodicals in the field that are authoritative but accessible (see Section 3.D). As you browse, you are looking for articles you want to read because they interest you. The article may suggest a research question you'd like to use as your research question, or the subject matter of the article could be a subject you'd like to investigate further.

But don't turn into a passive sponge now. Even as you are doing this preliminary reading, read critically. In your Researcher's Notebook, record questions that pop into your head. Write down assumptions that you find you are making about what you will find as you read further. Be particularly alert to any associations you find yourself making between this material and knowledge you already have.

Once you have your research question/assumption, you are ready for the next step, which is to refine your assumption into a working hypothesis/thesis.

E.   Step 4: Formulating Your Working Hypothesis/Thesis

At this point in the process I must remind you again that the entire research process—the activities you will be engaged in during the coming weeks—is a process of *testing* assumptions that you are making now. Right now, you are *not* looking for your *final* answer. You are not committing yourself to proving that what you think now is the "right" answer. Indeed, instead of committing yourself to an idea, you are opening that idea to question. You are not saying, "This *is* the right answer"; you are saying, "Is this the right answer?" Right now you have only two simple problems:

▶ finding a question for which *you* want some kind of answer
▶ stating your present assumption in such a way that you will be able to test it

When I talk about testing a working hypothesis/thesis, I mean asking this question:

Do the available facts and evidence support the assumption I am making?

At the end of the research process, weeks from now, your answer to this question may be:

Yes, the available facts and evidence do support my original assumption.

Or it may be:

No, the available facts and evidence do not support my original assumption.

Or it may be:

To a certain extent the available facts and evidence support my original assumption.

Any of these conclusions is a legitimate conclusion. Actually, the readers of your final paper will not be judging your work simply on the conclusion you finally draw. They will be far more concerned about the way you drew that conclusion; they will be far more interested in your testing procedures and the way you analyzed your evidence. As they read your paper, these are the questions they will be asking:

▶ Is this researcher actually testing the hypothesis he said he was testing?
▶ Does this researcher's final conclusion rest upon legitimate, relevant data?

► Do I consider the reasoning in this paper to be logical, valid?
► Has this researcher found and considered all the important evidence?

Since the means you use to test your working hypothesis/thesis is very important to your research project, it is very important, right now, to phrase your assumption in such a way that *you* will know the type of data/evidence you need to look for, and you will have a clear sense of the means you are going to use to assess and analyze the evidence you find.

In the next few pages I will give you three strategies that will help you turn your assumption into a working hypothesis/thesis. So take out your Researcher's Notebook, open it to the Working Hypothesis/Thesis section, and follow the procedures I outline in the next three steps.

1. Strategy 1: Discovering your assumptions about your area of investigation

If you have stated an assumption that you have made about your subject (and you should already have written out such an assumption, even if you think it is probably wrong), you do have some ideas floating around in your head about the subject. You may know that your ideas are very general. You may know that your ideas are probably wrong. You may know that you don't have any sound reasons for assuming what you have assumed. The issue here is not the correctness or validity of your ideas. The point is that you yourself must be aware of the thoughts and feelings you have about your subject, or thoughts and feelings that have influenced your thinking about your subject. Whether you are aware of these thoughts and feelings or not, those thoughts and feelings are in your head and they will influence your research and the way you look at your evidence. You will have more control of the research process if you put these thoughts and feelings down on paper, where you can take a long, hard look at them.

I personally believe that it is impossible for human beings to be entirely objective, but there are gradations on the subjective/objective scale. We can strive to be objective which, to me, means opening ourselves to ways of looking at a subject which are not the ways we have been used to looking at a subject. In my own experiences as a student/researcher, I have found that one important step toward objectivity is having as clear a picture as possible of what my present point of view is. I need to know my *basic* assumptions and attitudes toward my subject. I need to know what I *want* to find when I research. Pulling these assumptions out of myself is not easy, because they feel as much a part of me as the color of my eyes or my name.

To make yourself aware of your basic assumptions and attitudes toward your subject, I am going to suggest that you do some freewriting. For this technique to work, you must be as honest with yourself as you can be. You must try as hard as you can to put down on paper things that seem so obvious that you feel they don't need to be said. As you do this freewriting in your Researcher's Notebook, be as personal, as concrete, as specific as possible.

▶   Go back to your original reasons for selecting your assumption/research question. Why did you choose this assumption or question? What train of thought led you to this assumption?
▶   What associations do you have in your head when you think about your assumption? Do *not* throw out ideas just because they don't seem related. Write down *everything* that pops into your mind.
▶   When you write down a statement, force yourself to question that statement. Ask yourself, "What do I mean by that?" "Why do I say that?" "How did I arrive at that idea?"

Here are three examples of freewriting to discover your assumptions/attitudes about your subject.

Vitamin C is good for you. Keeps you healthy. Why? I don't know. That's what people say. Health food stores sure push it. I want to be healthy. I watch what I eat. Exercise. I take lots of vitamins. Look at those charts on the sides of food packages. Give you the vitamins in the cereal, whatever. Must be important, or wouldn't be there. Right? I've always assumed that vitamins are important. Actually, I don't really know what vitamins are. Yeh, pills in bottles. Seriously, what are vitamins? Must be something in the body. No, that doesn't make sense. If they're in the body, wouldn't have to take them. Here I'm assuming that vitamins are important, and I don't know what they are! And what about those charts? Contains 20% U.S. RDA of vitamin E. What does U.S. RDA mean? Who decides how much we need of a vitamin? . . .

Sexism. Sure is a hot item these days. Better watch your language when you are around me, fella. I don't like being called "girl" or "gal." Funny, isn't it? Words, just words. Sticks and stones . . . But these words *do* affect me. Let's see. I've assumed that men and women talk differently. Why? Well, I can hear. I can hear what I say to my girl (oops, female) friends. I hear my brother talking with his male friends. You'd think that girls and sex and drinking are all he has on his mind. Bah. Don't like that, do I? No, I don't. Better be careful. I have lots of strong feelings about this topic. Guess I'd label myself a feminist . . .

I've decided to research about the Industrial Revolution because of what my prof has said about the Industrial Revolution. His attitude toward it is real negative. Actually, I picked my assumption up from him. He said the Industrial Revolution was bad for the common people. Me, I don't know s—— about the Industrial Revolution. But I'm a common people. I'm working evenings and weekends to pay for this education of mine. Fat cats. Hate the idea of those fat cats sitting in offices downtown telling the likes of me how much I get paid, etc. Wait. No, the union decides that. Unions. Must be that those common folks back then didn't have unions to protect them. My prof says the fat cats decided wages, etc. Boy, that idea really makes me mad. What do those fat cats know about sweating in that warehouse eight hours at a stretch? Yeh, I'm on the side of the common people. How come, I wonder, didn't they form unions?

Even if it seems to lead you off the track of your specific research question/assumption, this exploration of your personal thoughts and feelings about your area of investigation will help you in two important ways:

▶ You will know what your own personal emotional reactions to your subject matter are, and you'll begin to see that some of your personal values and judgments have influenced the assumption you've made, even if you don't seem to have any personal feelings about your research assumption/question. Once you are aware of your own point of view, you are in a better position to open that point of view to critical analysis: Do I have any concrete, specific, logical reasons for my feelings and attitudes? Are they based on facts and evidence? Am I going to be able to look at this issue objectively?

▶ You may discover that the research question/assumption you started with is not really the research question/assumption you want to work with. As you freewrite, you may discover the real assumption you want to test. Don't worry about how narrow or specific the question seems. Look for the question/assumption that really turns you on.

2.   Strategy 2: Turning judgmental statements into inferences

If you remember my discussion of facts, inferences, and judgments in Section 1, you'll remember that a judgmental statement is a statement about a person's approval or disapproval of something. Judgmental statements don't lend themselves very easily to testing. These are judgmental statements:

> Socialism is the best form of government for Kenya.
> Abortion is wrong.
> The Industrial Revolution hurt the common worker.
> Urban sprawl should be stopped in our metropolitan areas.
> The Beatles were a great rock group.
> Warren G. Harding was a terrible president.
> You should take lots of vitamin C.

You can begin to turn such judgmental statements into inferences, into statements that lend themselves to testing, by underlining judgmental or evaluative words or phrases and then writing down what these judgmental or evaluative words mean to you.

> ### *Judgmental statement*
> Socialism is the <u>best</u> form of government for Kenya.
>
>   When I say "best," I mean:
>
> Socialism will allow Kenya to become more economically independent.
>   (*or*)

If the government takes over the industry in Kenya, the industry will become more efficient.

(or)

If the government takes over all industry in Kenya, the government can assure each worker a living wage.

Judgmental statement
Warren G. Harding was a <u>terrible</u> president.

> When I say "terrible," I mean:

Warren G. Harding exhibited few leadership qualities, qualities that all presidents are expected to have.

(or)

Warren G. Harding put together an administration of men who were irresponsible and corrupt.

(or)

The way Warren G. Harding was chosen as the Republican candidate in 1920 shows the weaknesses of the nominating process.

Judgmental statement
You <u>should take</u> lots of vitamin C.

> When I say "should take," I mean:

Vitamin C is a necessary component of a healthy diet.

(or)

Large doses of vitamin C allow the body to resist colds and flu.

Judgmental statement
The Beatles were a <u>great</u> rock group.

> When I say "great," I mean:

The Beatles were a well-known, commercially successful rock group.

(or)

The Beatles composed very sophisticated music.

(or)

In the history of popular music, the Beatles formed a bridge between rock 'n' roll and acid rock.

Judgmental statement
Genetic engineering <u>must be curtailed</u>.

> When I say "must be curtailed," I mean:

According to my personal Christian beliefs, genetic engineering is immoral because it is wrong to alter life as God has created it.

(or)

Because manipulation of DNA could produce mutant microorganisms that are dangerous to human beings, genetic engineering should be controlled in two ways: regulations should be developed for the kinds of buildings in which gene splicing could go on, and regulations should also be developed for the kinds of gene splicing that is allowed.

(*or*)

At a time when money for scientific research is so limited, the money that is available should go into research that has immediate practical application, like the search for a cure for cancer.

Judgmental statement

Urban sprawl <u>should be stopped</u> in our metropolitan areas.

When I say "should be stopped," I mean:

The flight of the middle class to bedroom communities, leaving the poor and disadvantaged in the inner cities, is segregating metropolitan areas, economically and racially.

(*or*)

The uncontrolled building of homes and industrial parks on the edges of cities is ecologically unsound; the environment is being destroyed.

(*or*)

To form a real community, people must live in areas where shops, work places, churches, homes, places for cultural and other leisure activities are close together.

When you underline and explain the judgmental words in your own assumptions, you may well come up with two or three statements, as I have done. Notice that each of these statements is a separate assumption with its own focal point and direction. In the last example I gave, the first statement points to a study that will focus on the socioeconomic status of inhabitants of the inner city and suburbs. The second statement focuses on the effects of suburbs on the natural environment. The third statement reflects an interest in the concept of "community." Obviously, each statement would point me in a different research direction. If you come up with several statements, you should give some thought to whether or not you want to pursue all these lines of inquiry. Each of the statements I made in the last example would be broad enough for a research project.

3. Strategy 3: Defining your terms

Defining key terms in a statement you make is yet another means you can use to turn your assumption into a working hypothesis/thesis. Like the other two strategies, defining your terms is a way to clarify your idea for yourself.

In defining your terms, do not, at first, use a dictionary. What you are attempting to do here is discover what *you* meant by those words.

Statement

Large doses of vitamin C allow the body to resist colds and the flu.

What do I mean by "large doses"? By large doses, I mean . . .
What do I mean by "vitamin C"? By vitamin C, I mean . . .
What do I mean by "resist"? By resist, I mean . . .
What do I mean by "colds"? By colds, I mean . . .
What do I mean by "the flu"? By the flu, I mean . . .

Statement

In the history of popular music, the Beatles formed a bridge between rock 'n' roll and acid rock.

What do I mean by "popular music"? By popular music, I mean . . .
What do I mean by the "history of popular music"? By the history of popular music, I mean . . .
What do I mean by "the Beatles"? By the Beatles, I mean . . .
What do I mean by "bridge"? By bridge, I mean . . .
What do I mean by "rock 'n' roll"? By rock 'n' roll, I mean . . .
What do I mean by "acid rock"? By acid rock, I mean . . .

Statement

The flight of the middle class to bedroom communities, leaving the poor and disadvantaged in the inner cities, is segregating metropolitan areas, economically and racially.

What do I mean by "flight"? By flight, I mean . . .
What do I mean by "middle class"? By middle class, I mean . . .
What do I mean by "poor"? By poor, I mean . . .
What do I mean by "disadvantaged"? By disadvantaged, I mean . . .
What do I mean by "inner cities"? By inner cities, I mean . . .
What do I mean by "segregating"? By segregating, I mean . . .
What do I mean by "metropolitan areas"? (In the world? In the U.S.? In the northeastern part of the U.S.? New York City?) By metropolitan areas, I mean . . .
What do I mean by "economic segregation"? By economic segregation, I mean . . .
What do I mean by "racial segregation"? By racial segregation, I mean . . .

Statement

Socialism is the best form of government for Kenya.

What do I mean by "socialism"? By socialism, I mean . . .
What do I mean by "best"? By best, I mean . . .
What do I mean by "Kenya"? (Kenya in the nineteenth century? Kenya before independence? Kenya today?) By Kenya, I mean . . .

After you define all key terms in your own words, you may want to check your definitions against the definitions in a dictionary. Does the word "socialism" mean what you thought it meant? Is "socialism" the word you want? Your working hypothesis/thesis must say what you want it to say. The words on the page must reflect what you have in your head. Don't change your ideas; just find the right word for what you want to say.

These three strategies are designed to help you come up with a statement that is precise, that says directly and clearly what you want it to say. When you finish these exercises, you ought to have a statement that tells you what kind of evidence you need to look for, and that also tells you how you are going to go about assessing the information you find.

Working theses

I assume that the flight of the white middle class to bedroom communities, leaving the poor and disadvantaged in the inner cities, is segregating metropolitan areas like New York City and Detroit, economically and racially.

I assume that, in the history of popular music in the 1960s, the Beatles transformed rock 'n' roll into acid rock.

I assume that scientific studies show that doses of vitamin C, larger than the recommended daily allowances, allow the body to resist colds and the flu.

I assume that the government takeover of industries in Kenya will make Kenya an economically independent country because it will reduce her dependence on imported capital and machinery and it will improve the living standards of her people because they will be hired as managers and supervisors as well as laborers.

Looking over these examples, you may be thinking that they are too narrow and specific. You may be struck by the "But-I-can't-write-a-ten-page-paper-on-*that*" panic. Let me help you drive away this specter by saying that, in my experience as a teacher, most students' working theses are generally too broad rather than too narrow. If you knew the material as well as an expert does, you would realize how broad a so-called narrow thesis really is. Let me remind you that your obligation, in doing your research, is to find as much available information as possible on your working hypothesis/thesis. The odds are that there is much, much more information available on your subject than you suspect right now.

Besides, I have to remind you that your final paper is not going to be a laundry list of facts. You are going to be making meaning of these facts, and you will have to make your meanings clear to the people who will be reading your paper. Explaining ideas to others in such a way that they understand takes space. If you have had experience in writing effective papers, you know what I mean. How many times have you seen "please explain" or "develop this idea" written in the margins of your essays?

Of course, if you are still nervous that your working hypothesis/thesis is too narrow, by all means show it to your instructor. Ask him/her if it is too narrow.

F.   A Few More Words About Research Projects and Testing

Perhaps you've noticed that throughout this section I've been referring to working hypotheses/theses. Now I'll explain why I have been using these two terms.

If you remember, I said in Section 1 that we can talk about two kinds of research projects, primary research projects and secondary research projects. Since there are differences in the research procedures (and the final papers) for these two types of projects, you need to have a clear notion of the category into which your present project falls.

1.   Primary research projects

Primary research projects are usually called experiments or studies. As the term implies, in primary research projects the researcher is going directly to the original source to gather his/her facts. A second characteristic of primary research projects is that the researcher carefully selects and uses systematic, accepted procedures both for gathering facts (data) and analyzing them.

You are engaged in a primary research project if your project focuses on setting up, and carrying out, an experiment in the lab. You are doing a primary research project if your project focuses on gathering specific information from a select group of people and then analyzing that information using some statistical analysis or other procedure. You are doing a primary research project if your project focuses on systematic observation of a specific group of people, animals, or plants.

If you are engaged in a primary research project, valid testing procedures are critical, both those procedures you use to collect your data and those you use to analyze them. So is the development of a sound hypothesis. Most experienced researchers depend on the work of other experts to help them develop their hypotheses and testing procedures. Thus, before you do your actual study or experiment, you will want to do some research in the library to find out what other researchers in the field have already done.

If you are engaged in a primary research project, I recommend that you turn right now to Section 5.B in this book and read what I have to say about primary research reports. I also urge you to write up your hypothesis and methodology (testing procedures) *before* you do your study or experiment, and show them to your instructor. A flawed study or experiment will produce meaningless results.

2.   Secondary research projects

In secondary research projects, the researcher is looking at the work that has already been done by others. Therefore, he/she will be reading and studying the primary research projects of others, reported in periodicals and books, and the theories and opinions of others. Most research projects assigned to students fall into this category.

In general, there are two kinds of secondary research papers: reviews and critical papers.

a. Reviews and reviews of the literature

A *review*, or a *review of the literature*, is a report to the reader about the trends in a particular field in a given period of time. The research procedures you would use to do a review are the research procedures I talk about in the next two sections of this book. You will also be expected to think about the material you are reading and formulate conclusions. Since your basic task in a review will be to summarize the basic trends and developments in a particular area of a field, your research question should be "What are the basic trends and developments in X?" Begin writing out your answer to this question—your working thesis—as soon as you are able after you start gathering your evidence.

If your instructor has asked you to do a review or a review of the literature, right now you should turn to Section 5.C.1 and read what I say about this form of research paper.

If you are not sure if your instructor wants you to do a review or a review of the literature, ask him or her right away if he/she wants a review or a critical paper.

b. Critical papers

Doing a *critical paper* involves formulating a working thesis (as we have been talking about for the past nine pages) and then testing that thesis by gathering and analyzing the available facts and evidence. The paper that you write at the end of this process will begin with the conclusion (thesis) that you have developed as you have studied your evidence. In some cases your final thesis may be the same as the working thesis you began with. Very often, however, your working thesis will change as you learn more about your subject. Such changes are the most natural thing in the world, and you must be flexible enough to let the thesis change.

▶ If, as you research, you find that the facts suggest that your working thesis was incorrect, rewrite your thesis to fit the facts. You may find that you need to rewrite the thesis several times.

▶ As you research, you may find that the scope of your original thesis is too large to research thoroughly in the time you have, or you may find that your interests shift to one aspect of the larger thesis. This often happens to researchers, and they respond by writing a new thesis that now covers the specific area they have become interested in.

Individuals who have done a lot of research are used to these various changes in the direction of their research, and they do not let such changes frighten or panic them. Neither should you. From the beginning you should be aware that your research may take you into areas that your original research question did not include.

If you are doing a research project that does not involve testing your data with statistical analysis, here are some ideas for ways you can test your original thesis. Use a theoretical model or a theory that is currently popular or generally accepted in the field. To determine if a violent change in government in a particular country was a revolution, you could use a Marxist model of a revolution. If you are studying a work of literature, you could use one of the accepted literary theories (like the sociological approach) or you could compare the approaches of the critics who are considered the experts on that literary work. If you are studying a piece of music or art, you could begin by comparing the work with a description of the style (Baroque, Romantic, Expressionist) in which it is normally classified.

3.   Summary

Regardless of the subject you are examining and the method of testing you decide to use, you must always remember that you are beginning with an hypothesis/thesis that you are opening to question. In other words, as objectively as possible you are going to examine critically your assumption to see if your assumption is a valid one. *Testing* is a very different process from *rationalizing, justifying,* or *proving* (as this word is often used in debate). I may be able to give several good reasons why marijuana should be decriminalized; but simply being able to give a few good reasons for (or against) a particular position does not necessarily mean that I have carefully studied all of the available facts, critically reviewed the various opinions of the experts, and developed my final conclusion from my own critical thinking, based on those facts and the opinions of the experts.

Since your goal is to develop your own conclusion, based on your critical assessment of the facts and the opinions of experts, you are obliged

▶   to find as much information as you can about your subject
▶   to consider *all* of the evidence you find, even if it seems to be saying that your original hypothesis/thesis is incorrect

G.   Step 5: Choosing Your Research Strategy—Research Questions

Once you have a good working hypothesis/thesis, you must decide on your research strategy. In other words, you must set down what you need to know and where you are going to look to find your evidence.

In the Research Strategy section of your Researcher's Notebook, write out your working hypothesis/thesis. Now, make a list of *all* the questions that the hypothesis/thesis raises, all the information you will need. Make your list as complete and detailed as possible.

> **Working thesis**
> I assume that the government takeover of industries in Kenya will make Kenya an economically independent country because it will reduce her dependence on imported capital and machinery and it will improve the living standards of her people because they will be hired as managers and supervisors as well as laborers.

Questions
1. Who now owns Kenya's industries?
2. What are Kenya's main industries?
3. Where does the capital for these industries come from?
4. What are Kenya's balance of trade figures (1975–80)?
5. Who now works as managers in Kenya's industries?
6. Who works as supervisors in the industries?
7. Can the government afford to buy the industries?
8. Will the government takeover make Kenya more economically independent? How?
9. Where does the machinery in the plants come from now?

And on and on.

Working thesis
     I assume that the flight of the white middle class to bedroom communities, leaving the poor and disadvantaged in the inner cities, is segregating metropolitan areas like New York City and Detroit, economically and racially.

Questions
1. What period of time am I talking about? the present? the last ten years? I must decide.
2. Am I correct in assuming that the white middle class has moved out of the inner cities?
3. What metropolitan areas am I actually talking about? Just New York City and Detroit? I'd better decide.
4. How am I defining "metropolitan area"? If I stick to Detroit and New York City, what are the metropolitan areas?
5. How am I defining "inner city"? What are the "inner cities" of Detroit and New York City?
6. What is the racial minority population of these inner cities?
7. I imply that the racial minorities are the major portion of the inner city population. Is this accurate?
8. What do I mean by "bedroom communities"? What are the "bedroom communities" in Detroit? In New York?
9. How am I defining "poor"? "disadvantaged"? How do the experts define these groups?
10. What is the average income of people who live in the inner city of Detroit? New York?
11. What is the average income of people in Detroit's bedroom communities? New York's?
12. What is the population of racial minorities in New York City's bedroom communities? Detroit's?
13. I say that metropolitan areas are segregated economically. If they are, do I think this is healthy or unhealthy? Why? What do experts say about economic segregation?

And on and on.

H.   A Final Note

The solution or conclusion you are seeking is not tucked away in some book or article in the library; researching is not a game of treasure hunt.

Your conclusion is just that—the conclusion or idea that *you* develop in your own mind as you examine, analyze, and consider the evidence you discover. You are, as I will remind you constantly, a detective. Like a detective, you cannot know where your search will finally end. But you can, and must, constantly give *direction* to your search. For this reason your Researcher's Notebook is your most important tool.

As you become more experienced as a researcher, you will learn that research projects, especially more involved research projects, often take unexpected twists as they develop. The puzzle you intended to solve at the beginning of your search gradually changes shape and turns into a new puzzle as you learn more about the subject you are investigating. As a researcher, then, you must remain flexible and alert; you must be willing to change, but you must always know which path you are taking.

If you are doing a secondary research project, once you have your working thesis and research questions, you are ready to start looking for the evidence. You should now turn to the next section of this book.

The next section of this book is also very important for the researcher involved in a primary research project. Although your final goal is to collect and analyze raw data directly from the source, you must first have a sound hypothesis and valid testing procedures. The work that others have done in your field is critical to you in developing the design of your study or experiment. The following section of this book, which offers strategies for using libraries, can help you discover what others in your field have done.

Section 3

Finding the Evidence

It is still not quite time to head for the card catalogue in the library.

Although the card catalogue will be a helpful tool in your quest for the information you need, it is not the only tool the library has, nor is it always the best place to start. Before you head for the library, I want you to read over the major parts of this section. In these parts I will point out and explain some important resources that the library has which will allow you to jump from your research questions to the books and articles that promise to hold answers to your questions. As you read over this section, make notes in the Research Strategy section of your Researcher's Notebook about those reference materials in the library that will be most helpful to you. You will notice that this section is set up so that you can come back to individual parts and read them more carefully when you are actually in the library, looking for or using these reference materials.

But, to return to my main image of directions and paths, I must warn you that often a research process can look like a swamp to a researcher. No matter how carefully you plot your way through the territory, you can feel bogged down; your course will not always be smooth. Unfortunately, some of the time and effort you expend on this project will feel like mindless busywork. Compiling lists of books and articles and other sources will itself take time; so will finding these books and articles. You will be running from one area of the library to another. You may be running from one library to another. You may be spending time running around town, interviewing people. Unless you were born under a very lucky star, you will discover that your library doesn't have a periodical that you need or that a book you want has been checked out or that a person you want to interview cannot see you until a week from next Thursday. There isn't much you can do to prevent these sorts of snafus. But you can cut down on the frustration that often results when obstacles are placed in your path, and you can turn mountains into molehills if

► you recognize that you will be doing some mindless busywork and that snafus will occur; in other words, assume that some time will be "wasted";
► you give yourself plenty of time to do your research;
► and, above all, you use the information in this section to plan, wisely, the way you use the library.

A.   Potential Sources of Information

Libraries are a logical place to look for your evidence because libraries, by definition, are repositories of published information. But not all information is in libraries. Look back at your working thesis and your list of research questions. Do you need *current* information about businesses or industries, about government or private agencies, about foreign countries? Does your working thesis involve a subject that you have personal contact with, like mass transit, mass media (newspapers, magazines, radio, TV), or movies?

Even if you are involved in a secondary research project, don't overlook the possibility of doing some primary research. In addition to the evidence you find in the library, you may be able to go directly to some sources yourself. For example,

▶ if you are doing research on ads in magazines (or on radio or TV), you should look at relevant ads yourself. Carefully observe and analyze them.

▶ if you are researching a subject related to the work of a government or private agency, why not interview key officials in these agencies or businesses? Why not write or call, and ask for the information you need?

▶ if you are researching a foreign country, have you thought about contacting an embassy or consulate of that country?

In other words, in looking over your research questions, could you use information from sources outside the library as well as sources in the library? If your answer is yes, develop a plan for gathering this information in the Research Strategy section of your Researcher's Notebook. The library, by the way, would be a good place to locate the names and addresses of businesses, agencies, and consulates or embassies.

Interviews—some advice

If you decide to interview people who could give you some of the information you need, you must prepare for such interviews.

▶ You will have to obtain enough information about the business or agency to know which person in the organization can give you the information you need.

▶ You will have to arrange a meeting time with this person that is convenient for him or her, and for you.

▶ Once the interview is arranged, you will have to do some homework. To ask this person intelligent, meaningful questions, you will have to have some background information about the organization. What are its goals and objectives? What does this organization or business "do"? How does it operate? Whom does it serve? And so forth.

▶ You should go to an interview with a written list of questions. The person you are interviewing will expect you to take charge of this meeting.

▶ During the interview you will have to take careful notes. You want to be sure that the information you have in your notes is accurate, and if you want to quote this person, you must be absolutely sure that you have his/her exact words. You may ask, *when you arrange the interview,* if the person you are interviewing would allow you to tape the interview. You may tape if you have received permission ahead of time. Never bring a tape recorder to an interview without having received advance permission.

▶ Just as you make bibliography/reference cards for other sources (see Section 4.B.2), be sure to make a card for each interview you hold, recording the following information:
　▷ the full name of the interviewee
　▷ his/her official title
　▷ the full official name of the company or organization for which this person works
　▷ the date of the interview

▶ After the interview, make clear, clean notes of the information you received in the interview. It would probably be wise to put this information on notecards (see Section 4.B.5).

In considering experts who know your subject, don't overlook the experts who are teaching and researching on your campus. Most college catalogues include a list of faculty members and indicate their field of specialization. Make an appointment with faculty members, just as you would set up an interview. Ask their views of your working thesis; ask them some of your research questions. You may also ask them for possible sources of information on your subject.

B.　Using a Library: Introductory Remarks

Every type of research project involves some use of the library. If you are doing a secondary research project, much of your research will depend on material you find in libraries.

One of the first things you should realize is that all libraries are not alike. The material—books, periodicals, documents—housed in a particular library is acquired according to the purpose and clientele that library is designed to serve. If your school library does not have the material you need, this does not mean that your library is a bad library. You should acquaint yourself with other libraries in your town or the surrounding region; you may find that you will have to use libraries other than your school library. Even if you are not allowed to check out materials from these other libraries, most libraries allow the public to use materials on their premises. And don't overlook the possibility of getting material through interlibrary loan (see subsection I in this section).

The collections of libraries are limited. On the other hand, too often I hear the complaint from students that "our library doesn't have what I need." Occasionally the complaint is legitimate. Too frequently, however, the problem is not the library but the student researcher who is using (or not properly using) the library. Many students I know, and you may fit this category, don't know how to use a library. They do not know the proper means for locating the titles of potential sources, and they are not aware of various kinds of reference materials that they can use to find the information they need.

The remainder of this section is devoted to an explanation of resources in the library and the ways to use them. As I said earlier, you should read over the rest of this section now, before you go to the library. Make a note of the types of reference materials that seem directly related to your research project. Then, take this book with you to the library. If you get confused, you can use this guide as a handy reference.

Let me begin with a few words of advice:

▶ Take your Researcher's Notebook with you to the library, along with your notecards.

   ▷ In the Sources section, write all the citations you come up with for books, articles, and other materials you want to read. It is very tempting, I know, to scribble this information on the backs of envelopes and in various class notebooks, but it is very easy to lose these citations. Remember what I have said about saving yourself *needless* frustration and wasted time?

   ▷ In the Research Strategy section of your Notebook, jot down ideas about people you want to interview, reference materials you should use, and other parts of your research plan.

▶ Be very conscious of the dates of publication of the materials you look at. I discuss this issue at more length in the next section of the book (see Section 4.C.2). Here let me say that unless you specifically want material that is older, you should look for books and articles published in the last ten or five years. When using bibliographies and indexes (see Section 3.E.2), start with the most recent issues and work backwards.

▶ Do you want to hear me say again how important it is to begin your research early?

C. Using a Library: The Subject Catalogue of the Card Catalogue

---

Most academic libraries now use the Library of Congress (LC) cataloguing system. Library of Congress call numbers look like this:

PN
511
.W 7
1948

Throughout this section I will be talking about the LC system. If your library does not use the LC system, you will have to acquaint yourself with the cataloguing system it does use.

The subject catalogue of the card catalogue is one reference tool that most students think they know. I'll admit that I learned a great deal about the way the subject catalogue works when I wrote this book, so I think you may learn something, too, when you read this section.

Let me warn you that the subject catalogue lists *only* books that your library has. Therefore, it is a rather limited source for finding the information you need. Use the subject catalogue, but plan to use other reference materials.

First of all, you must be aware that the Library of Congress system has its own set of subject headings that may not correspond to the subject headings you are using. If you find nothing in the subject catalogue under your key word or term, look in the *Library of Congress Subject Headings* volumes, two large books located near the card catalogue.

If you looked under "Culture conflict" in these volumes, for example, this is what you'd find:

> Culture conflict *(Indirect) (Psychology, BF740)*
>   sa   Interracial marriage
>   Marginality, Social
>   Marriage, Mixed
>   Miscegenation
>   North and south
>   x   Conflict of cultures
>   xx   Ethnopsychology
>   Genetic psychology
>   Psychology, Pathological
>   Race relations

Here's how to read this list:

▶ The letters and numbers (BF 740) indicate the basic Library of Congress call numbers under which you'd find books on cultural conflict.

▶ *sa* means "see also," which indicates that you could find sources under the other headings listed here. You may decide that "Interracial marriage" or "Marriage, Mixed" are more precisely the subjects you are interested in; check these topic headings in the subject catalogue.

▶ The single *x* indicates that this is *not* a heading used by the Library of Congress system. You will not find Conflict of cultures in the subject catalogue.

▶ The double *x* (*xx*) indicates a related heading, usually broader in scope. If the topics listed here under Culture conflict do not hit upon the subject you are investigating, you should check Ethnopsychology in the Library of Congress volumes.

The *Library of Congress Subject Headings* volumes will also give you the particular heading the LC system uses. For example, if you looked under

Culturally deprived

you would find

See Socially handicapped

Or, if you looked under

Culturally handicapped

you would find

See Socially handicapped

These entries indicate that you should look in the subject catalogue under "Socially handicapped" for your sources.

When using the subject catalogue, pay close attention to the headings typed at the top of each card. These headings indicate subdivisions within a particular topic. The cards are filed in alphabetical order, according to these subheadings. For example, if you checked under "Boston" in the subject section, you would find cards marked with these subheadings:

Boston—Commerce
Boston—Committee of Correspondence
Boston—History
Boston—History—Colonial Period
Boston—Population—History

These subheadings are designed to help you locate information directly related to your special interest.

When using the subject catalogue:

▶ Look under various subject headings.
▶ Use the *Library of Congress Subject Headings* volumes to find appropriate subject headings.
▶ Pay attention to the various subheadings; check the subheadings appropriate to your specific topic.

If you do not find what you need in the subject catalogue, don't give up. There are other **reference materials** in the library that may be more helpful than the subject catalogue.

D.   Using a Library: Periodicals

The word *periodical,* if you consider its root, refers to a publication that is issued "periodically" or at regular, recurring intervals—once a year, once a month, once a week. Magazines, journals, newspapers are all periodicals. If you want the most recent, up-to-date information on your subject, your most promising source is periodicals.

One thing you should know is that, in academic circles, a distinction is made between "popular" periodicals and "scholarly" ones. The distinction is based on the audience for whom the periodicals are written.

Popular periodicals are written for the general public. These are the newspapers and magazines you find at your local supermarket or newsstand. *Time, Newsweek, Atlantic Monthly, Ms., The New York Times* fall into this category. These publications are certainly reputable periodicals, but you should be aware that when you do research for a college class, your instructor will expect you to depend more heavily on scholarly periodicals than on popular ones.

Scholarly periodicals (often called "journals") are periodicals that contain reviews, essays, and research reports written by experts and scholars in a field for other experts and scholars in a field. Although they contain the type of authoritative information you want, the fact that experts are speaking to experts in these journals may cause you some trouble, especially at the beginning of your research project. Depending upon how specialized and technical your research subject is, the articles in these journals may be very difficult for you to read. I have two suggestions for you:

► If you run across journal articles that you find very difficult to read, look at my advice in Section 4.C.3.
► Below I have listed some periodicals that I am calling "authoritative but accessible." That is, the information in these periodicals is considered sound by scholars in the field, but the articles are not as technical as those in other scholarly journals. Articles in these journals and periodicals may be a good place to start your reading.

As a rule, *popular periodicals* are indexed in the *Readers' Guide*. *Scholarly periodicals* are indexed in the indexes for particular disciplines (see this section, E.2).

Below I have listed some periodicals in various fields that are considered authoritative but which are not as technical as some journals in the field. These would be good periodicals for you to start with. This list is certainly not exhaustive. Ask your instructor if he/she can give you the titles of other authoritative but accessible scholarly periodicals in your area of investigation.

AUTHORITATIVE BUT ACCESSIBLE JOURNALS

Business and accounting

Business Horizons
California Management Review
Financial Management
Harvard Business Review
The Journal of Accountancy
Journal of Business

Journal of International Business Studies
Journal of Marketing
Management Accounting
Sloan Management Review

Communications

Central States Speech Journal
Communication Monographs
  (formerly Speech Monographs)
Communication Quarterly
Journal of Broadcasting

Journal of Communication
Journalism Quarterly
Quarterly Journal of Speech
Western Journal of Speech
  Communication

Economics

Economist
Economic Review

Journal of Political Economy
Quarterly Journal of Economics

Political science

American Political Science
  Review
Journal of the History of Ideas

Journal of International Affairs
Public Opinion Quarterly
Western Political Quarterly

Psychology

American Psychologist
Psychology Today (issues in
  1983 and after)

Science

American Scientist
BioScience

Science
Scientific American

Sociology

American Journal of Sociology
British Journal of Sociology

International Journal of
  Comparative Sociology

E.   Using a Library: Reference Materials

When people start listing reference books, I find that my eyes glaze over and I simply cannot concentrate because I know, beforehand, that I'll never remember all the information that is being thrown at me. I have this reaction when I am given information in a vacuum. I certainly don't want to be the occasion for your eyes glazing over and your tuning out, so instead of just listing various kinds of reference materials, I've set this section up according to the kinds of information you might need.

Use this section this way: with your Researcher's Notebook and your research questions in front of you, look at the questions I've used to head each part of this section. Make a note of each of those question headings and reference materials that applies to your research questions. Then take this book with you to the library to use as a reference book.

Please note that I have *not* listed *all* the reference books available in each category, and your library may not have the reference books I've listed. Almost every field of study has sets of bibliographies, indexes, dictionaries, encyclopedias. Be prepared to use the card catalogue to find reference books like the ones I've listed, or ask your reference librarian or instructor to help you.

1. Do you need some general information about a subject?

Check an **encyclopedia.**

    Encyclopedias contain general summary articles about subjects; some articles also include a short bibliography of books and/or articles you may want to look at.

a.   There are **general encyclopedias,** like

> *The Encyclopaedia Britannica* (Ref/AE/5/.E 363)
> *The Encyclopedia Americana* (Ref/AE/5/.E 333)

b.   There are also **specialized encyclopedias,** like

> *The Encyclopedia of Philosophy* (Ref/B/41/.E5)
> *The Encyclopedia of Religion and Ethics* (Ref/BL/31/.E 43)
> *The Encyclopedia of World Art* (Ref/N/31/.E 533)
> *The International Encyclopedia of the Social Sciences* (Ref/H/40/.A2/I5)
> *McGraw-Hill Encyclopedia of Science and Technology* (Ref/Q/121/.M3)

    There are other specialized encyclopedias in the library. Check the subject catalogue under your general topic; look under the subheading "Dictionaries." Or ask the reference librarian.

2. Do you need lists of books and articles written about your subject?

Check **bibliographies**

    Bibliographies are reference books that list books and articles written on specific subjects. They are set up very much like the subject catalogue.

    To find a bibliography on your topic, check the subject catalogue. Look under your topic, then check the subheading "Bibliographies." Or use the *Bibliographic Index* (see Section 3.F).

Check **indexes.**

    An *index* is also a bibliography, although indexes tend to concentrate more on articles published in magazines and journals.

a.   There are **general indexes,** like

> *The Readers' Guide.* This index contains references to popular
> periodicals like *Time* and *Sports Illustrated, Ms.* and *Field and Stream.*
> It will not be very helpful if you want to read scholarly, authoritative
> articles on your subject.

To find more scholarly articles and books, use

The *Humanities Index*. Subject fields covered include archaeology, classical studies, folklore, history, languages, literature, and other areas in the humanities.

The *Social Sciences Index*. Subject fields covered include anthropology, economics, geography, political science, psychology, public administration, and other subjects in the social sciences.

Note: The *Humanities Index* and the *Social Sciences Index* were divided into two separate volumes in 1974. Before 1974 they were combined in the *Social Sciences and Humanities Index*. Before 1965, this index was known as *The International Index*.

b.   In addition to general indexes, the library has **specialized indexes.** Here is a list of a few:

Art Index
Business Periodicals Index
Education Index
General Science Index
Philosopher's Index

Specialized indexes are one of the most valuable reference tools researchers have. Check your library's collection of specialized indexes carefully to locate those that promise to contain citations for articles and books on your specific topic. Or check the subject catalogue under your topic heading; look under the subheading "Indexes."

Also, see Section 3.F for guidelines on using indexes.

3.   Would you like to find summaries of articles written on your subject?

Check an **abstract.**

An *abstract* is a summary of the content (the author's thesis/hypothesis, methodology) of an article or book. Abstracts, such as those listed below, contain summaries of thousands of articles (some abstracts also cover books) written during a given year on various topics in the field. Some abstracts available are:

Biological Abstracts
Chemical Abstracts
ERDA Energy Research Abstracts
Historical Abstracts
Physics Abstracts
Psychological Abstracts
Sociological Abstracts
Women Studies Abstracts

When using an abstract, always check the front pages of the volume to

see how that particular abstract is set up. Pay close attention to the categories used in the subject section to classify the abstracts. Since the categories
used are usually traditional divisions in a field, you will need to know into
which field division your particular subject falls.

4. Do you need to know what a particular term means, or who a particular fictional character was?

Check a **dictionary.**

a.　There are **general dictionaries,** like

> *Webster's New International Dictionary*, 2nd ed., Unabridged.
> Definitions in this edition are considered to be *correct* usage.

> *Webster's Third International Dictionary*, Unabridged. Definitions in
> this edition follow the language as it is currently used. Purists may
> consider some of these usages incorrect, colloquial, or vulgar.

> *The Oxford English Dictionary* (OED); also called the NED, *New
> English Dictionary* (Ref/PE/1625/.M7/1933). A British dictionary that
> gives a history of the meanings of English words. An excellent source if
> you need to know what a particular word meant in the sixteenth
> century, or the eighteenth.

b.　There are also **specialized dictionaries,** like

> *A Dictionary of the Social Sciences* (Ref/H/41/.G6)
> *Encyclopedic Dictionary of Mathematics* (Ref/QA/5/.N5)
> *Dictionary of American History* (Ref/E/174/.D52/1976)
> *Oxford Classical Dictionary* (Ref/DE/5/.09)
> *Cinema: A Critical Dictionary* (Ref/PN/1993.45/.C5/1980)
> *Funk & Wagnalls Standard Dictionary of Folklore, Mythology, and
> 　　Legend* (Ref/GR/35/.F82)
> *A Dictionary of Twentieth-Century Composers (1911–71)* (Ref/ML/118/
> 　　.T5/1973b)
> *Theological Dictionary of the New Testament* (Ref/PA/881/.K513)
> *A Dictionary of Mining, Mineral, and Related Terms* (Ref/TN/9/.T5)

There are other specialized dictionaries. Check the subject catalogue
under your general topic; look under the subheading "Dictionaries." Or ask
the reference librarian.

5. Do you need information about a particular person, living or dead?

Check a **biographical dictionary** or **index.** Here are a few:

> *Biography Index*
> *Biography and Genealogy Master Index* (Ref/CT/214/.B56)
> *The McGraw-Hill Encyclopedia of World Biography* (Ref/CT/103/.M27)

Current Biography Yearbook (Ref/CT/100/.C8)
Dictionary of American Biography (Ref/E/176/.D562)
Dictionary of National Biography (Ref/DA/28/.D55)

Or look in one of the *Who's Whos*. There may also be specialized biographies for your particular subject. Check the subject catalogue; look under the subheading "Biographies."

6.   Do you need a specific fact, like the population of Sweden in 1960, or . . . ?

Check an **almanac** or **fact book.**

The World Almanac and Book of Facts (Ref/AY/67/.N5/W 77)
Information Please Almanac (Ref/AY/64/.I 55)
Whitaker's Almanac (Ref/AY/754/.W 5)

7.   Do you need to find out where a city is located, or the boundaries of a country at a certain point in history?

Check an **atlas.**

Atlas of World History (Ref/G/1030/.R 3)
The National Atlas of the United States
Rand McNally Cosmopolitan World Atlas
Rand McNally Bible Atlas (BS/630/.K7)

8.   Do you want to find newspaper articles on your subject?

Check a **newspaper index.**

Nationally distributed newspapers like *The New York Times*, *The Wall Street Journal*, and *The Christian Science Monitor* publish their own indexes. Check to see if your library has these indexes.

If local newspapers are indexed, this job is usually done by the local public library. If you are interested in articles that were published in your local paper, find out if your local public library has an index.

The list of **reference materials** given on the last few pages is certainly *not complete*. However, by now it should be clear that there are many places you can look for the information you need or for sources that will contain the information you need.

F.   Using a Library: How to Use an Index

Many students fail to do an in-depth study of their subjects either because they do not know how to use indexes or because they are intimidated by them.

Using indexes is really a very simple operation once you understand how they work. In the next few pages I am going to explain how indexes work by using facsimiles of actual pages from the *Bibliographic Index* and the *Social Sciences Index*.

First of all, I will explain how an index is set up, then I will show you how to read a bibliographic citation (the publication information about a book or article).

Please read over the next few pages and compare my explanations with the actual material from these two indexes. I have set up this section so that you can also use it as a cheat sheet when you are in the library, using actual indexes. I should also tell you that every index includes information (usually in the front part of each volume) about how to use that particular index, just in case my explanations do not apply to the specific index you are using.

1. Using an index: The format

a. The *Bibliographic Index*

The *Bibliographic Index* refers you to books and articles where you will find bibliographies (lists of books and articles) on your specific subject.

The first thing you should be aware of is that most indexes are set up like the subject catalogue. Thus, citations of specific books and articles are listed under general **headings,** alphabetically arranged throughout the volume.

Page 379 of the *Bibliographic Index*, on the facing page, begins with the **heading**

MARITAL status

and goes to

MARKETING research

When a topic is broad, that topic may be subdivided into **subheadings.** The subheadings in this index are in boldface type, centered in each column. Under the heading MARKETING, there are four **subheadings:**

Management
Mathematical models
Psychological aspects
Underdeveloped areas

When you are using an index, be sure to look over the entire entry so that you will find the subheading which contains the information you are looking for.

Finally, please notice that an index will always try to help you find the materials you need by **cross-referencing.** It will tell you which headings this index uses and/or it will refer you to related headings where other citations on the same or related subjects are listed. Cross-references are usually indicated by "See" or "See also." Note this **cross-reference:**

MARKET research. See Marketing research

This line indicates that the *Bibliographic Index* lists works on market research under the heading MARKETING research. You will find this heading at the bottom of the page, alphabetically listed after MARKET-ING management.

Another **cross-reference:**

MARKET surveys
See also
Consumers' preferences
Store location

This notation means that you may also find information on market surveys under the general headings CONSUMERS' preferences and STORE location.

It may take a little more time to check these cross-references, but it is certainly time well spent. It isn't very legitimate to say that "nothing's been written on my subject" when the truth of the matter is that the index you are using doesn't use the particular subject headings that you think it should!

Elasticity (economics) —cont.
   See also
   Substitution (economics)
Elation
   See also
   Mania
Elche, Spain
Description
   Date on the Costa Blanca. C. Lim. il map Geog Mag 52:841-
   2 S '80
Elder, Bruce
   Snow seen. il Can Forum 60:46-7 Je '80
Elder, Charles
   Does individual behavior cause systems, or do systems cause
   individual behavior?[review article]. Urb Aff Q 15:232-5
   D '79
Elder, Lonne, 3d
   Lorraine Hansberry: social consciousness and the will. Free-
   domways 19 no4:213-18 '79
Elderly. See Aged
Election districts
Great Britain
   Race for seats; boundary commission. Economist 276:58-9 Jl
   5 '80
Election expenses. See Campaign funds
Election forecasting
   Certain problems in election survey methodology. P. Perry.
   bibl Pub Opinion Q 43:312-25 Fall '79
Mathematical models
   Electoral forecasting from poll data: the British case. P.
   Whiteley. Brit J Pol Sci 9:219-36 Ap '79; Reply with re-
   joinder. N. L. Webb. 10:271-2 Ap '80
Election law
   See also
   Voters, Registration of
   Voting, Absent
Ireland
   Politicians and electoral laws: an anthropology of party com-
   petition in Ireland. R. K. Carty. Pol Stud 28:551-66 D '80
Singapore
   Imposing a new electoral rule. S. Awanohara. Far E Econ R
   109:12 Ag 8 '80
Turkey
History
   Role of the electoral system in Turkish politics [1950-1977].
   W. Hale. Int J Mid E Stud 11:401-17 My '80
United States
   Impact of state legislation on political campaigns. A. D.
   McNitt. State Govt 53:135-9 Summ '80
   Political action committees are throwing ringers. J. Rees. il
   Am Opinion 23:27-9+ Je '80
   Primary rules, political power, and social change. J. I. Lengle
   and B. Shafer. Am Pol Sci R 70:25-40 Mr '76; Reply. T.
   H. Hammond. W Pol Q 33:50-72 Mr '80
Electioneering. See Advertising, Political
Elections
   See also
   Campaign funds
   Election districts
   Election forecasting
   Election law
   Local elections
   Majorities
   Political candidates
   Proportional representation
   Referendum
   Representative government and representation
   Voters, Registration of
   Voting
International aspects
   Importance of being in government. Economist 275:57 My
   10 '80
Australia
   All about petrol? Economist 277:44-5 O 11 '80
   Australia's premature Labor pains. Economist 277:107 O 18
   '80
   Election order out of chaos. A. Summers. Far E Econ R
   109:19 Ag 8 '80
   Small chance of much change. Economist 276:35 S 20 '80
   Three men seeking a swing. H. Ester. Far E Econ R 109:18
   S 19 '80
Bolivia
   Where democrats are brave. Economist 276:38 Jl 5 '80
Botswana
   Elections and parliamentary democracy in Botswana. J. A.
   Wiseman. World Today 36:72-8 F '80
Canada
   Energy and elections. R. C. Paehlke. Environment 22:4-5
   My '80
   New chapter for Trudeau. Economist 275:39-40 Ap 5 '80

Denmark
   Look at the elections; interview with Ib Nørlund. World
   Marx R 23:54-5 Ap '80
Europe, Western
   American federalism and European integration. K. Pöhle.
   State Govt 53:50-3 Wint '80
   European elections of 1979: a problem of turnout. J. Lodge.
   Parl Aff 32:448-58 Aut '79
   European policy of Franz Josef Strauss and its implications
   for the Community. G. Pridham. J Common Mkt Stud
   18:313-32 Je '80
France
   Environmental concerns and local political initiatives in
   France. J. R. McDonald. map Geog R 70:343-9 Jl '80
   French elections and the ecology movement. M. J. Kur-
   lansky. Environment 22:4-5 S '80
   See also
   Presidents—France—Election
Germany (Federal Republic)
   Brezhnev's present. Economist 276:46 Jl 5 '80
   Can Schmidt lose? Economist 276:39-40 Ag 9 '80
   Off with the kid gloves. Economist 275:60 My 24 '80
   Old firm. Economist 276:14-15 S 13 '80
   See also
   Prime ministers—Germany (Federal Republic)—Election
History
   Mass media use and electoral choice in West Germany. H.
   Norpoth and K. L. Baker. Comp Pol 13 1-14 O '80
Gibraltar
   Rock steady. Economist 274:54 F 16 '80
Great Britain
   How elections elect. Economist 274:49-50 Mr 1 '80
Greece
   See also
   Presidents—Greece—Election
India
   Cynical election. C. Hitchens. New Statesm 99:4 Ja 4 '80
   Freestyle power game. M. Ram. Far E Econ R 107:20-1 Ja
   11 '80
   Stability yes, emergency no. M. Ram; J. Sarkar. Far E Econ
   R 107:8-9 Ja 18 '80
Iran
   See also
   Presidents—Iran—Election
Jamaica
   Bullets in the ballot. Economist 277:68+ O 25 '80
   Off with a bang. Economist 277:45-6 O 11 '80
History
   Racial ideology in Jamaican politics: the People's political
   party in the parliamentary elections of 1962. J. C. Gannon.
   Caribbean Stud 16:85-108 O '76/Ja '77
Japan
   Constitution's success. N. Macrae. Economist 274:survey
   19-20 F 23 '80
   Going into uncharted waters. J. Lewis. Far E Econ R 108:30
   Je 13 '80
   Japanese splits. Economist 275:14+ My 24 '80
   Japan's election: return to the 1960s. G. H. Healey. World
   Today 36:285-7 Ag '80
   Rug pulled out. Economist 275:48-9 My 24 '80
Kenya
   1979 Kenya election: a preliminary assessment. V. B. Kha-
   poya. Africa Today 26 no3:55-6 '79
   See also
   Presidents—Kenya—Election
Lebanon
   See also
   Presidents—Lebanon—Election
Panama
   From his hammock. Economist 277:44 O 4 '80
Portugal
   Another battle to win. R. Harvey. Economist 275:survey
   11-12+ Je 14 '80
   One election at a time. Economist 276:42 Ag 30 '80
   Party goes to the polls. World Marx R 23:41-7 F '80
   Stained before battle. Economist 276:45-6 Jl 19 '80
Rhodesia
   Africa as usual. Economist 274:16 F 9 '80
   At least the words are gentler. Economist 274:53-4 F 2 '80
   British observer's view of the election. A. Campbell. Round
   Tab no279:283-9 Jl '80
   Explosions before Zimbabwe votes—and afterwards, too?
   Economist 274:37-8 F 23 '80
   Lick at democracy. Economist 274:11 F 16 '80
   1980 Rhodesian elections—a first hand account and anal-
   ysis. M. Gregory. World Today 36:180-8 My '80
   Now, how will the soldiers vote? Economist 274:18 Mr 1 '80
   Other battle. Economist 274:50 Ja 19 '80
   There will still be too many guns about after the voting.
   Economist 274:35-6 Mr 1 '80

b. The *Social Sciences Index*

Page 297 of the April 1980 to March 1981 *Social Sciences Index*, on the facing page, shows that this index is set up in a format very similar to that of the *Bibliographic Index*.

Page 297 begins with the general **heading**

Elasticity (economics)—*cont.*

and goes to

Elections

Rhodesia

You will notice that Elections is a broad topic, because it is subdivided on this page into twenty-one **subheadings:**

International aspects   [a general subdivision]

Australia

Bolivia   [divisions according

Botswana   to region/country]

Canada

Here we see that the *Social Sciences Index* further subdivides its subheadings, so that we have this category:

Germany (Federal Republic)

History

There are a number of **cross-references** on this page. If, for example, you wanted information on elections in Iran, the cross-reference "See also" tells you to look at

Presidents   [general heading]

Iran   [subdivision]

Election   [further subdivision]

You will also notice that the index tells you that articles on Electioneering are listed under the general heading Advertising, Political:

Electioneering. See Advertising, Political

I'd like to call your attention to another feature of this index, namely **names.** Names are used in the *Social Sciences Index*, as they are in many other indexes and bibliographic indexes, as general headings.

▶ The names of people important in history or important in a field are used as general headings. For an example, turn back to the sample page from the *Bibliographic Index* and check "MARIVAUX, Pierre Carlet de Chamblain de, 1688–1763."

▶ The names of authors of articles are also used as general headings. What this means for you as a researcher is that you can use the *Social Sciences Index* (and other indexes) to locate the bibliographic information about an article if you know who wrote the article. On the *Social Sciences Index* page, see "Elder, Bruce" and "Elder, Charles." To find the bibliographic information, of course, you have to know in what year the article was published and to check the volume of the index that lists articles published in that year, or you will have to be prepared to look through several volumes of the index until you locate the citation.

Another advantage of knowing that authors' names are used as headings is that you can check to see if a particular expert in a field has published anything recently. You could find out, for example, if Lester Thurow has had anything to say in print lately, or if Richard Leakey has published any articles.

c. General summary

By this point it should be obvious that a very common method of classifying information about books and articles—used in the subject catalogue of the card catalogue, in abstracts, and in computer data banks, as well as in indexes like the *Social Sciences Index*—is a system of classifying information according to sets of general categories and subdivisions of those categories. Once you understand that this is the general pattern, the job of tracking down the information you need becomes much easier. But there is a catch—you must use the **key terms** used by a specific index or system to identify the general categories and subdivisions. Your ability to be flexible and alert becomes all important at this point. Individual indexes try to help you by providing cross-references, which lead you to the key terms (headings) that those indexes use. If you do not find the information you need under the first key term (heading) you have checked, and there are no cross-references, don't give up. Using your research questions and your knowledge of the subject, have a list of other possible key terms. When I was looking for reviews of a particular movie several years ago, I had to try several headings (movies, film, cinema, the director's name, the title of the film) before I found the reviews I wanted. If you get stuck, always feel free to ask a reference librarian for help; I do.

2.   Using an index: Reading citations

Once you have found the proper heading (and, if necessary, subheading) in an index, you have before you a list of books and/or articles on your subject. You will have trouble finding these books and articles, however, if you don't know how to read the citations.

In the next couple of pages I will show you how to read citations, using examples from the sample pages of the *Bibliographic Index* and the *Social Sciences Index* (pages 46 and 48).

Right now you should carefully read over these pages to familiarize yourself with the general form of a citation.

And a word of warning: always copy down *everything* in a citation, *exactly* as it is in an index, in the Sources section of your Researcher's Notebook. Be sure to copy it neatly and clearly, because you will need to be able to read it later. Leave room next to each citation so that you can fill in the library call number.

a. Reading citations in the *Bibliographic Index*

SAMPLE CITATION 1
Original
Barrett, L. G. Perspectives on dependency and underdevelopment in the Atlantic region [bibliog. article] Can R Social & Anthropol 17:273–86 Ag '80 annot

Explanation
Barrett, L. G.

The first information given is the author's last name and first initials.

Perspectives on dependency and underdevelopment in the Atlantic region

The second piece of information is the title of the article.

[bibliog. article]

An abbreviation for "bibliographic article." A bibliographic article is a bibliography of books and/or articles on a specific topic plus some commentary by the author. Such articles can be very helpful, particularly if the bibliography is annotated (see "annot" below).

Can R Social and Anthropol

An abbreviation of the title of the journal in which the article appears (in this case, the *Canadian Review of Sociology and Anthropology*). Often indexes will abbreviate the titles of journals. However, you will find a full list of the abbreviations and the full titles of the journals in the front of each volume of an index.

17:273–86

The first number, 17, is the volume number of the journal. The second set of numbers, 273–86, indicates the pages on which you will find this article.

Ag '80

The date of this issue of the journal (August 1980).

annot

Indicates that the bibliography is annotated. Annotated bibliographies are particularly valuable to researchers because they include a short description of the content of each book or article.

SAMPLE CITATION 2
Original
Urban, Glen L. and Hauser, John R. Design and marketing of new products. Prentice-Hall '80 p583–608.

Explanation
Urban, Glen L. and Hauser, John R.

Authors' names, last names first

Design and marketing of new products

Title of book

Prentice-Hall

Book's publisher

'80

Year of publication (1980)

p583–608

Pages on which you will find the bibliography

b. Reading citations in the *Social Sciences Index*

SAMPLE CITATION 1
Original
Date on the Costa Blanca. C. Lim. il map Geog Mag 52:841–2 S '80

Explanation
Date on the Costa Blanca

Title of article

C. Lim

Author's first initial and last name

il map

Indicates that the article is illustrated with a map or maps

Geog Mag

Abbreviation of the title of the journal (in this case, *Geographical Magazine*).
As does the *Bibliographic Index,* the *Social Sciences Index* often abbreviates
journal titles, but you will find a full list of abbreviations with the full titles of
the journals in the front of each volume.

52:841–2

The first number, 52, is the volume number of the journal; the second set of
numbers, 841–2, refers to the pages on which the article appears.

S '80

Abbreviation of the date of the issue (September 1980)

SAMPLE CITATION 2
Original
Bullets in the ballot. Economist 277:68+ O 25 '80

Explanation
Bullets in the ballot.

Title of the article (Note that this article does not have a signed author.)

Economist

Title of journal

277:68+

Volume 277. 68+ indicates that this article begins on page 68 and that the rest of the article is printed in segments on various pages after page 68.

O 25 '80

The date of this issue is October 25, 1980

SAMPLE CITATION 3
Original
1979 Kenya election: a preliminary assessment. V. B. Khapoya. Africa Today 26 no3:55–6 '79

Explanation
1979 Kenya election: a preliminary assessment

Title of article

V. B. Khapoya

First initials and last name of author

Africa Today

Title of journal

26 no3:55–6

Volume 26, issue number 3, pages 55–56. Issue numbers are given (and you will need them) when each individual issue of a journal starts with page number 1. Many journals, however, make it easier to locate specific articles by numbering the pages of *a volume* consecutively, rather than starting every issue with page 1. In a volume that is paginated consecutively, the first issue (January, perhaps) would contain pages 1 through 80; the second issue (February) would contain pages 81 through 123; the third issue (March) would contain pages 124 through 174; and so on until December. Thus, when you are looking for an article in which the volumes are paginated consecutively, you actually need only the volume number and the page numbers.

'79

This volume was published in 1979.

Before I leave this discussion of reading citations in indexes, let me call your attention to the *Social Sciences Index* citation under the heading "Elder, Charles." After the title, in brackets, the citation says "review article." A **review article** is an essay in which the author summarizes major theories and/or research on a specific topic in a field. Such articles can be very helpful to a researcher, and you should make a special effort to find any articles on your subject that have the words "a review" in the title or which are classified as review articles (as Elder's article is classified here by the *Social Sciences Index*).

G.   Using a Library: Computer Searches

Just as the computer is offering us a new means of storing and manipulating information, the computer is also offering us a new means of finding information. In looking for your evidence, you may find yourself sitting at a computer terminal or asking a librarian to do a computer search for you. How much you use the computer will depend on the kind of information you need and the computer services available to you, either through your library or through your own home computer. The information sources that I talk about below are telecommunication services—that is, through a telephone hookup you are plugging into databases located throughout the country. To access these information sources, a computer user needs an account number and a valid password; you need an account number because you are "buying time" when you use these databases.

Before you become too starry-eyed about letting computers do your work for you, let me warn you that using a computer is not a substitute for knowing how to use research materials. Just as if you were using ink-and-paper sources, to use a computer information source you must know what information you need and decide where to look for this information. If you have already had some experience in using computers, you know that computers are completely unforgiving if you do not use the proper language or if you do not give them the proper instructions. As in using ink-and-paper indexes, in using electronic information services you need to know how the information is stored in various databases if you want to retrieve information from them.

Two basic kinds of computer services that can be helpful to researchers are:

▶ **On-line bibliographic searching.** Many libraries subscribe to information services that give them access to bibliographic databases. These bibliographic databases are, in essence, electronic indexes housed in computer memory banks rather than in bound volumes. Like indexes, these bibliographic databases contain lists of books and articles, and, like printed indexes, the citations are classified under specific headings and subheadings.

Ask the reference librarian if your library subscribes to a service that provides on-line bibliographic searching, and ask if this service is available to you. Or, if you own a computer or have access to one, ask at your local computer store to see what equipment you would need to hook into a service that provides on-line bibliographic searching.

If you intend to do a bibliographic on-line search, here are some things you should know:

▷   Many of these bibliographic databases contain only recent citations. Few will list books and articles published before the late 1960s, and the dates of most citations will probably be more recent than that.

▷   To locate a list of books and articles directly relevant to your subject, you must use headings and subheadings used to file these citations in the database. You must study the list of headings and subheadings for each database and you must determine which headings and subheadings are most appropriate to your specific area of investigation. If the headings you use are too broad, you could end up with a printout of thousands of titles. Even if you use the proper key terms, you may not find the citations you expected. Some databases classify citations by using only the key terms that appear in the titles of books and articles; thus the list of citations this database provides may not contain all the books and articles in which your subject was discussed or referred to. Don't expect miracles!

▶ **Information databases** that include the data themselves. Computer owners can subscribe to telecommunication services that give them access to such information as trading statistics on stock and bond exchanges, financial reports of companies listed with the Securities Exchange Commission, documents generated by the United States Congress, and so on. These databases are particularly appealing because the information they provide is obviously up-to-the-minute.

Let me end by saying that computers can be a help to researchers, but they are not a substitute for an intelligent researcher who knows what she needs to know and knows how and where to look for this information. If you don't know which buttons to push on the computer, it is no more helpful than a library whose resources you do not know how to tap.

H.   Using a Library: Finding the Books, Articles, and Newspapers on Your List

Once you have citations for books, articles, and newspapers, the next step is to see if your library has these books, articles, and newspapers.

The **books** that your library owns are catalogued in the author and title catalogues of the card catalogue. I prefer to check the author catalogue first. When you use the author catalogue, be sure that you have the author's name spelled correctly and carefully check first name and middle name or initial. Many authors have common surnames (Williams, Smith, etc.). If you use the title catalogue, remember that *the* and *a* at the beginning of a title are disregarded in alphabetizing. *A History of the Civil War* will be alphabetically listed in the Hs.

Copy down the call number of the book next to your citation in the Sources section of your Researcher's Notebook. If this book is not on the shelf the first time you check, you will need this call number when you check the shelf a second time. Check the shelf several times for two or three days. If the book is still missing, ask about it at the circulation desk.

In looking for **articles** your first task is to see if the library subscribes to the *periodical* in which the article appears and then to see if the library has the *volume* of the periodical in which it is printed.

In some libraries, periodicals are catalogued along with books in the Library of Congress system. In other libraries, there are separate indexes that list the library's periodical holdings. You will have to find out which system your library uses.

If your library catalogues periodicals in the LC system, check the title catalogue of the card catalogue; remember that *the* and *a* are disregarded in alphabetizing titles. *The Southern Speech Communication Journal* will be catalogued in the Ss.

If you find the title of the periodical you need, your next step is to find out if the library has the volume you need. On the card that catalogues the periodical, there are a series of numbers. Here's what these numbers mean:

Entry
Communications Monographs
    formerly Speech Monographs
v. 27 (1960)—
Microfilm B 737 v. 1–32
(1934–65) 3 reels

Explanation
First of all, notice that this journal has changed its name. *v. 27 (1960)—* means that the library has volumes 27 through the current volume on the shelves. Whenever you see a dash after a volume number, and no number follows the dash, you know that the library has all volumes printed after the volume number given. *Microfilm B 737 v. 1–32 (1934–65)* means that the library has the first through the thirty-second volumes on microfilm. *B 737* is this particular library's code for its microfilm collection. You will need this number if you want to use this microfilm.

Entry
Comparative Literature Studies
    v. 1 (1964); 6 (1969)—

Explanation
The library has volume 1, and volumes 6 through the present volume on the shelves. Volumes 2 through 5 are *not* in the library.

▶ If the library has the volume you need in a printed copy, copy down the call number next to your citation in the Sources section of your Researcher's Notebook. You will then have to find out where this periodical is shelved in your library.

▶ If the library has the volume you need on microfilm, copy down the appropriate information next to your citation in the Sources section of your Researcher's Notebook. You will then have to find out where this microfilm is housed in your library. You may also need a librarian's help in using the microfilm reader.

Different libraries subscribe to different **newspapers.** Very often newspapers will be put on microfilm. Find out which newspapers your library has, where they are stored, and in what form they are stored. If newspapers are on microfilm, you may need the help of the librarian in locating the issue you want and in using the microfilm reader.

I. What If Our Library Doesn't Have the Books and Periodicals I Need?

When you have checked the card catalogue and/or the periodical index and you have noted the call numbers of the books and periodicals your library does have, then make a list of the books, the periodical volumes, and newspaper issues that your library does *not* have. You will now have to look for these materials in other places.

Check other libraries in your town or city. If you need only *one* book or *one* periodical, it is acceptable to call a library to find out if it has this book or periodical. Ask for the main reference desk. If, however, you are looking for a number of books and/or periodicals, you will have to plan to check the card catalogue of these libraries yourself.

Most libraries, particularly college and university libraries, participate in the Interlibrary Loan network. This system allows you to obtain books and articles from other libraries across the country. If your library participates in this network, ask the reference librarian how to go about ordering the books or articles you need. You will need complete bibliographic information on the book or article, so check your citations carefully and be sure to give the librarian accurate information. Put in Interlibrary Loan requests *as soon as possible*. Processing requests and obtaining materials takes time, sometimes weeks. A book or article will not do you much good if it arrives two days after you have handed in your paper.

J. Summary

Because there is quite a bit of specific information in this section, let me summarize for you the main points I want you to remember.

▶ Not all information is stored in libraries, and not all libraries house the same material. When you begin looking for your evidence, check your research questions and ask yourself if some of your information might be obtained from sources other than those in libraries. If you decide to look for sources in places other than the library, plot your strategies for finding these sources.

▶ There is a great deal of information stored in libraries. Because there is so much information stored in libraries, they must have systems for storing and retrieving this information. If you are going to find the information you need, you must know some of the library's systems and you must use them. You must also realize that a library contains information about sources (books, articles, and documents) that the library itself may not have.

▷   One stepping-stone to sources is the subject catalogue of the card catalogue. It lists materials your library does have. Among the materials it lists are reference materials.

▷   Another stepping-stone to sources are indexes and bibliographies. These reference materials are an excellent place to start your search. Indexes and bibliographies are put together according to general disciplines (humanities, social sciences), according to fields (art, business, etc.), or according to specific areas within a field. To find an appropriate index or bibliography, you must know in which discipline or field your subject falls.

▷   Another stepping-stone to sources is abstracts. Abstracts will give you not only the titles of books and articles but also some information about the content of those books and articles. They allow you to decide which specific books and articles contain the information you need.

▷   Certain reference books, like encyclopedias and dictionaries, can provide you with important "background" information in the subject you are pursuing.

▷   Certain reference books may themselves contain the information you need (biographies, fact books, atlases, dictionaries, etc.).

▶ If your library does not have a specific book or article you need, your search is not over. Check other libraries in your town or city. Use the Interlibrary Loan service.

▶ If you have questions or run into trouble using your library, ask a librarian for help. But don't turn into a passive sponge here. Use the information I have given you. Use the maps and other literature provided by your library that indicate where materials are. If you ask a librarian for help, approach him or her with a *specific* question.

▶ Your search for sources will not be limited to your first search of the subject catalogue and indexes. Throughout your research you will come across references to other sources, particularly in the books and articles you read. Check the notes, bibliographies, and reference lists of each book and article you read. Copy citations of promising sources in the Sources section of your Researcher's Notebook.

▶ As you read and think about the sources you collect, your research questions—and even your working thesis—will change. With each change of direction your research takes, you will need new information. You will therefore be consulting indexes, bibliographies, the card catalogue, and other reference material throughout the research process.

Section 4

Reading and Taking Notes

A. Some Opening Remarks . . .

If you have done a research project before, you are used to the idea that part of your time will be spent making lists of books, articles, and other published materials, and running about, gathering up this material. But what then? What do you do once your desk is piled high with books and articles? This is the point in the process when many students are tempted to turn into passive sponges. From their sources, they copy sentence after sentence onto notecards or into notebooks. They have a wonderful time highlighting passages in yellow, pink, and green. For what purpose?

Notetaking is not the mindless activity of a passive sponge. It is not the process of pointlessly transcribing sentences from one piece of paper to another. Notetaking, if it is to be a meaningful activity, must be the product of reading and studying. A researcher gathers books and articles so that he can learn about a subject by reading what others have said and done, and then by thinking about—analyzing, synthesizing—what he has read. In this section I will discuss notecards and notetaking, but always in the context of reading, thinking, learning. The research process has no point if it is not a process of thinking and learning.

In the research process, as I've mentioned earlier, you will be taking two kinds of notes:

▶ On notecards, or in some similarly systematic fashion, you will be recording the evidence you find.
▶ In your Researcher's Notebook, you will be recording *your own thoughts* about the evidence you have gathered and the material you are reading.

You will be making both kinds of notes throughout the research process.

In order for you to know what belongs on notecards and what belongs in your Researcher's Notebook, you will have to be able to distinguish between the ideas of others and your own ideas.

I realize that when I say that you have to be able to make such distinctions, you may be responding: "But you have just hit the problem right on the head. I can't always distinguish between my own thoughts and those of my sources. I don't know very much about the subject I'm researching; that's why I'm doing the research. The experts, they're the ones who know. I have to depend on them."

Here's the response I'd like to hear from you: "The experts do know more about my subject than I do. That is why I am reading what they have to say. Nevertheless, I also have a mind that is capable of analyzing, of weighing the evidence, of coming to logical conclusions. I can think. So I need to read the experts to learn from them, but I don't have to be their puppet. I am capable of using my sources; I don't have to be used by them." In this section I will give you strategies and advice that will allow you to make this type of response, and mean it.

The way to distinguish between the ideas in your sources and your own ideas is to remember that each person has his/her own perceptions of or ways of looking at a subject. Do you remember, in Section 1, I said that facts are meaningless until people make meaning of them? The working hypothesis/thesis that you have developed by following the guidelines in Section 2 is a statement of *your perception* of your subject. When an expert writes a book or an article, that expert is recording his/her perceptions of that subject. This expert has a thesis or an hypothesis, just as you have one, and he/she usually states the thesis or hypothesis toward the beginning of the book or article. As you read, you will be encouraged by the author to adopt that author's perception of the subject. Obviously that author thinks that her point of view is a valid one, and she wants you to see the subject as she sees it.

But there are ways that you can distance yourself from your reading. There are ways that you can pull yourself away from an author's influence. The two major ways, which I will discuss further in this section, are to analyze the author's argument/methodology and to realize that, because you are reading a variety of works, you know that there are various points of view on this subject, various ways to interpret the facts. Not all experts interpret the evidence in the same way; not all experts use the same evidence. If you research the subject of taking large doses of vitamin C, for example, you will find that some experts believe that there is strong evidence that taking large doses of vitamin C is beneficial; others will say that there is no conclusive evidence that taking large doses of vitamin C is beneficial.

As you dive into that pile of books and articles on your desk, you must resist the temptation to become a passive sponge. You must assert yourself as an intelligent person capable of thinking for yourself. Maintaining your own point of view in the research process is going to be much easier if you use your Researcher's Notebook.

In a Researcher's Notebook, I expect to find passages like these:

> I started out with the assumption that adolescents should not be treated as adults in legal cases. I've found out that at least two or three experts (Smith, Johnson, who was that other guy?) agree. But now I'm confused. I just read a very convincing argument that adolescents (like over 16) should be tried as adults for serious crimes like murder, rape. I agree with this author's position (what *is* his name? oh, Wilson). I'm confused now about what I think. Who's right? Well, let me think about what the arguments are, so I can decide what I think now . . .

Or

> The facts are not coming out the way I thought they would. For one
> thing, there are many (56% of the population, I think the statistics say)
> middle- and upper-class whites who live in Manhattan. I thought I'd find
> that the majority were poor and disadvantaged. Seems as though there is
> a trend across the country for the middle class to flee the bedroom
> communities and come back to the city. So that sort of botches up my
> original thesis. Let's see . . . what shall I do? I sure can't hang onto my
> old ideas if the facts don't bear me out. But I just know there is some
> racial and economic segregation. Maybe I should see what the patterns
> are in areas in Manhattan, and go from there . . .

These examples illustrate the type of record you should be keeping of
what is happening in your head *as* you go through your sources. You should
notice that it will be easy to distinguish between what you are reading and
what you think because you will be referring to what you've been reading, as
you do the reading, and you will be commenting on it.

Write frequently in your Researcher's Notebook. Talk to yourself about
the books and articles you read. Keep going back to your working hypothesis/
thesis and measure what you've learned against it. Keep asking questions,
and looking for answers.

At the same time that you are writing to yourself in your Researcher's
Notebook about your thoughts on your readings, you must also be keeping a
clear, clean record of the evidence you are finding in your sources. The
evidence will usually fall into one of two categories: (1) facts, or data; or (2)
the theories, hypotheses, conclusions of the experts. This evidence is vital to
your research project. It is the solid material you are using to test your
working thesis. The conclusions and ideas that you are formulating as you
write in your Researcher's Notebook should be based directly on this evidence. Such evidence, therefore, must be recorded in a clear, systematic,
easy-to-use way.

I am going to urge you to keep your records of your evidence on
notecards and bibliography/reference cards. Since many students seem to
find notecards a waste of time, let me explain why I use this system.

If you are like many students I know, you may be accustomed to taking
notes by putting slips of paper in books, or writing your notes in spiral
notebooks, or highlighting books and articles you read. These systems do
work, up to a point. But you should realize their limitations.

One limitation is people like me who get very angry with individuals
who deface library books and periodicals by underlining, highlighting, or
writing in the margins. At the very best, such defacing is distracting; at the
worst, it destroys the text itself because it renders the words and sentences
unreadable.

I become even more angry when I discover that someone has cut out a
page or a whole article from a periodical or a book. I am not the only user of
libraries who feels this way about the defacing of public property. When you

find that you are unable to use a book or an article because the material has been damaged, you will know how *I* feel. The availability of photocopying machines in libraries today makes defacing books and periodicals all the more unforgivable.

Now let's turn to the limitations of underlining books and articles, along with other notetaking systems, for you as a researcher.

Putting slips of paper in books, highlighting photocopies of book pages or articles, and taking notes in spiral notebooks work well as long as (1) you remember all the material that you have marked in this way and (2) you remember where each piece of information is to be found. These two qualifications are precisely the limitations of these systems. It is all too easy to forget much of the information you have marked in these ways; or, even when you remember that you did mark a piece of information in one of your sources, you must waste time looking through all the books and articles until you find it. These systems are too dependent on your memory, which in essence becomes the heart of these record-keeping systems.

If you are in the habit of making notes haphazardly in notebooks, on slips of paper, or on the backs of envelopes, you have already discovered that these random pieces of paper can get lost in the shuffle. When you make notes randomly, it is also very easy to forget to record critically important information, like the author of the source or the page number.

As you will see in a moment, in addition to urging you to put your notes on notecards, I also strongly advise making bibliography/reference cards for each source you read. If you don't have a systematic record of the bibliographic information (author, title, publisher, date, etc.) of your sources, you may have to waste much valuable time tracking this information down when you are writing your paper.

As I have said so many times that I know you are sick of hearing me say it, research is by its nature a time-consuming process. One of the reasons I have written this book for you is to help you avoid *wasting* time, and you can avoid wasting time if you use a record-keeping system for your evidence that has these features:

▶ There is a complete record of all the bibliographic information for all your sources, and this information is easy to retrieve, to sort, and to manipulate.
▶ Each piece of evidence is easy to retrieve when you need it.
▶ Pieces of evidence are easy to sort and classify, making it easy to review the evidence.
▶ Each piece of evidence includes all the necessary information about its source.

Using notecards for notes and bibliography/reference lists is a common method of notetaking that meets these criteria. I have used it for years and find it especially helpful for longer research projects.

At first, you may find the system of taking notes that I outline in the next few pages cumbersome and hard to get used to. But if you force yourself to follow the steps outlined in the next few pages, you will soon develop habits that become as simple and automatic as brushing your teeth or tying your shoes. You will find that your notecards and bibliography/reference cards will save you an incredible amount of time and frustration when you are writing up your paper. You will be able to double-check specific pieces of evidence easily. Because you can sort and put your notecards into individual piles, you won't leave out critical evidence. The bibliography cards will make it much easier to do footnotes or endnotes, and you can put these bibliography/reference cards into alphabetical order and type your bibliography/reference list straight from the cards.

I have, I trust, persuaded you to try my system. The next step is to read over part B of this section carefully to get an overview of my system of reading and taking notes. Then, as you do your reading and notetaking, keep this book close by to remind you of the steps in the system.

B.   Taking Notes

1.   Step 1: Decide which sources you should read first

Making this decision is not always easy, but here are a few guidelines:

▶ Choose the material that is written as introductory material or material for nonexperts (look at the prefaces to books; here the author usually states his purpose and the audience for whom he is writing).

▶ Choose the material that seems directly aimed at your working thesis/ hypothesis and research questions.

▶ If you are already aware that certain people are considered *the* experts in the field, or if you know that Dr. X's theory is the most influential one in the field, read the work of these people first.

▶ Put aside more technical, difficult reading until later (see Section 4.C.3).

▶ If the focus of your working thesis is a primary source—a painting or paintings, a poem, a piece of music, a "classic" work like Machiavelli's *The Prince* or Darwin's *Origin*—study this primary source yourself and record your own reactions before you begin your research. Obviously you will have to come back to this source and study it several times in light of the evidence you collect.

2.   Step 2: Make a bibliography/reference card

Whenever you pick up one of your sources—a book, an article, an article or entry in a dictionary or an encyclopedia, a newspaper article—the *first* thing you should do is to make out a bibliography or reference card for that source.

A bibliography or reference card is a card on which you record all necessary publication information that appears in the card catalogue, in a citation in an index, or in an author's bibliography or reference list. The form in which this publication information will appear in your own bibliography or reference list, however, will depend upon which documentation form you use in your paper. You can save yourself a great deal of time later in the research process if you record publication information on your bibliography or reference list card in the same form in which it will appear in the bibliography or reference list of your final paper.

In Section 7, I talk in more detail about documentation forms. Here I will give you only a brief summary. Documentation forms differ from discipline to discipline and often from journal to journal. In the appendixes at the end of this book, I talk in more detail about the three most common forms of documentation: the humanities form, the author-date form, and the numbered reference list form. You should check with your instructor to find out which form you should use in the paper you are now working on. I have given specific information about each of these forms in separate appendixes so that you can use these appendixes as a handbook. For example, you should take this book with you to the library when you are reading your sources; when you make up a bibliography or reference card, follow the proper form as outlined in the appropriate appendix.

The humanities system: The bibliography card

The humanities documentation system is used in papers and publications that take a humanities approach to a topic. Thus, this is the form you will usually find in papers on literature, philosophy, rhetoric, art, music, etc. For further information, see Appendix A.

BIBLIOGRAPHY CARD FORM FOR A BOOK

Lukacs, Georg. *The Destruction of Reason*. Translated by Peter Palmer. Atlantic Highlands, N.J.: Humanities Press, 1981.

B
2743
.L 7813
1981

BIBLIOGRAPHY CARD FORM FOR A JOURNAL ARTICLE

Schacht, Paul. "The Lonesomeness of
Huckleberry Finn." *American Literature* 53
(May 1981): 189-201.

P
1
.A6

The scientific system: The reference list card for author-date and numbered reference list forms

The reference list is usually used in publications in the sciences or publications that use a scientific approach. The form shown below, for example, is a common form used in social science publications (economics, communications, sociology, political science, education, and others) that approach topics scientifically. Forms in some of the natural sciences may differ from the one given below. For more information on reference list form, see Appendix C.

You will notice that I have also included the Library of Congress call number for each of these sources on the bibliography/reference card in the lower right-hand corner. I discovered this trick in my student days after I wasted valuable time having to look up the call number of a book two or even three times when I wanted to check that source again. Another time-saving trick.

To summarize: your first step is to make out a bibliography/reference card for each of your sources, in the proper documentation form, before you even read the source. I take this step so that I have my own clear record of every source I consulted and so that I do not forget to record information that I will need later. When you come to Step 4, you will see that I have another important use for these cards.

REFERENCE LIST FORM FOR A BOOK (CHICAGO STYLE)

Chow, G.C. 1981. *Econometric analysis by control method. Wiley Series in Applied Statistics.* New York : John Wiley and Sons.

HB
139
.C48

REFERENCE LIST FORM FOR A JOURNAL ARTICLE (CHICAGO STYLE)

Hansen, G.L. 1982. Measuring prejudice against homosexuality (homosexism) among college students : A new scale. *Journal of Social Psychology* 117:233-36.

HM
251
.A1J6

3. Step 3: *Read* your source

This advice sounds so simple that you may reply, "But that's obvious!" However, reading is far more than passing your eye across pages of print. I must now talk to you about what reading is because one problem that many novice researchers run into is that they don't read their sources properly.

For example, many students I have worked with are in the habit of opening one of their sources, then immediately copying down sentences, sometimes whole paragraphs, onto their notecards. These students are saying to themselves, "There is lots of important information here. I must write it down." In one sense they are very right. Clearly the author felt that every sentence he/she wrote was important or he/she wouldn't have written it. But let's consider what the student researcher is actually doing when she is copying down a sentence. She is not reading; she is transcribing. It is difficult to read and transcribe at the same time. They are different kinds of activities. A typist is a transcriber, and many professional, expert typists will tell you that they are able to type a paper or report without being able to tell you what the report or paper says. In fact, some typists say that if they try to read while they are typing, their typing suffers.

But, as a researcher, your task is not to transcribe. Your task is to learn, to educate yourself about your subject, to understand what others think. Your job, in other words, is to read. And since transcribing interferes with the comprehension process, you must first read to comprehend. Actually, it is only by reading that you can decide what to put in your notes. We know that every fact and statement in a work was important to the author; the question is, what do *you* consider important in this work?

So let's talk about reading. *Reading* has been defined in a number of ways. The definition that I prefer is Frank Smith's. Smith contends that reading is a very selective activity; we are "deliberately seeking just the information that we need. Need for what purpose? *To answer specific questions that we are asking.*"*

Do you notice that Smith's definition of reading is almost exactly the same definition that I have been using for the research process? As researchers we are looking for information that we need. We are looking for answers to questions we have asked. We have gathered books and articles and other sources because we believe that they contain information that will help us answer our research questions, that will give us help in testing our working theses and give us the solid basis we need to draw conclusions.

Sometimes the question a reader asks is very specific and narrow:

▶ When was Julius Caesar assassinated?
▶ Where did the popes live during the Babylonian Captivity?
▶ Who developed penicillin as a drug?
▶ What was the average price of a loaf of bread in 1915?

---

* Frank Smith, *Reading Without Nonsense* (New York and London: Teachers College Press, 1979), 105.

When your question is this narrow and specific, you read by skimming a page, looking for a visual clue (like numbers or names) to the answer you need. You are not concerned about what the author is saying about Julius Caesar, or the Babylonian Captivity, or penicillin.

Skimming pages to find answers to very specific questions is a perfectly natural and legitimate form of reading *when your purpose is to answer very specific questions.* You will be doing this type of reading in the course of your research project. But it is not the only kind of reading you will be doing, and it is certainly not appropriate when your purpose is to educate yourself about the perceptions the experts have of your subject. Earlier in this section I reminded you that your working hypothesis/thesis reflects your perception or point of view of a subject. I said that the process of testing your working thesis is to find out the perceptions or points of view of others, particularly those considered experts. You will not really understand these perceptions or points of view simply by skimming. Instead, you will have to read complete books, or sections of books, or complete articles, and you will be asking a series of more complex questions:

▶ What is the author's hypothesis or thesis?

▶ What evidence does this author use to test his hypothesis or to support his thesis?

▶ What meaning does the author give to the facts/data she uses? How does she put the facts/data together?

▶ What conclusions/results does the author come up with?

▶ How do the parts of the study or argument fit together? To me, do the parts fit together logically?

▶ Am I aware of facts or evidence the author did not use? Do I think he should have used them? Do the facts and evidence I know support this author's argument, or do they weaken it?

▶ How does this author's approach compare with that of other authors I have read? How do this author's conclusions and results match the conclusions and results of other authors I have read? Do I consider this point of view more persuasive than another point of view?

To answer these questions, you must read the entire text as a whole. You must follow the author's line of thought from beginning to end. At the same time, you must keep in mind what you have learned about the subject from other sources. You won't get satisfactory answers to these questions by reading just one sentence or one paragraph. Trying to copy down specific sentences as you read will interfere with your ability to find your answers to these questions.

So . . . when you pick up a particular source, ask yourself why you are reading this particular source. The broader the questions you are asking (like "How does this author see my subject?"), the more obvious it is that you must read for comprehension. As you pick up each book and article, ask yourself,

► What do I expect to learn from this source?
► What do I need from this source?
► What questions do I have that I expect to find answers for?

There are some tricks you can use to help answer these questions, particularly when your source is a book or a collection of essays. Review your working hypothesis/thesis and your research questions. Then

► Check the book's table of contents. Are certain essays or chapters more directly relevant than others? Why are they more directly relevant? What information do you expect them to give you?
► Check the book's index. Look for key words in your working hypothesis/thesis and in your research questions. Look for these key words, or related words, in the index. Do you need to read only those pages, or should you read whole sections or chapters?
► If a book seems to be written directly on your subject, read over the preface, the introductory and concluding chapters. In these parts of the book, the author will spell out his approach and his conclusions. Use them as a framework for reading the entire book.

4.   Step 4: Write a summary of the material you read

After you read your material, your next step is to write a summary of this material. You may write the summary on a separate notecard, but I find a more convenient place for the summary is the back of the bibliography/reference card. The summary should include:

► a summary of the author's results or conclusions.
► a summary of the author's method or approach in developing his argument or testing his hypothesis.
► notes to yourself about specific features of this text that you might find helpful later in your research. For example, if the author gives extensive statistics that you know you will want to refer to, make a note of this information on your card.

EXAMPLES OF SUMMARIES

To Smith, the major conflict between the North and the South was the very different perceptions of slavery each region had. To the North, a moral issue; to the South, an economic necessity. Good detailed discussion of the kinds of work slaves did (insights into Southern agricultural practices). Lots of statistics on numbers of slaves in each Southern state, 1850–60 (pp. 186–97).

Wilson & Jones were testing the hypothesis that violence on TV encourages people to resolve problems physically. Longitudinal study—60 subjects—all male. Results inconclusive. Note date: a recent study.

Murphy & Nolan studied the effects of temperature on the germination of sugar pine seeds. Looked at oxygen uptake, ATP levels,

moisture content of seeds imbibed at 5°C and 25°C. Results: seeds
wouldn't germinate at temperatures above 17°C. Murphy & Nolan suggest
reason is the effects of high temperatures on membrane properties.

These summaries are really the most valuable notes you can make.
They will help you in several ways:

▶ They are some of your most valuable evidence. They pull together the
general conclusions and approaches of experts who have done research
in your subject. In most cases in your own research paper you will be
referring only to this summary information.

▶ As your research progresses and the direction of your search becomes
more focused, you will realize that certain works are more important to
you than others. Your summaries will tell you which works you should go
back to and study more carefully.

▶ If, as your research progresses, you find that you need more specific
information about a particular topic, your summaries will tell you where
you can find this specific information.

▶ Writing these summaries will prevent you from wasting your time recopy-
ing massive amounts of a book or an article on notecards. They will keep
you from becoming a passive sponge. The act of writing these summaries
is an act of digesting your reading, of pulling out the most important parts
of the work and getting them into your head, which is where the information needs to be if you are going to think about it.

5.   Step 5: Take notes

Now, and only now, should you consider taking specific notes on a work.
As I said in Step 4, the most important notes you will take will probably
be the summaries you write of your readings. Other notes you take will fall
into one of two categories of evidence:

▶ Facts or data, concrete and specific pieces of information, like the results
of studies, statistics, names and identities of particular people, definitions
of terms, etc.

▶ The hypotheses, theses, conclusions, opinions of the experts (in certain
cases, you may want to take down the author's specific words).

While you are in the process of educating yourself in general about your
subject, you should probably keep these types of notes to a minimum. As you
develop specific research questions and as the whole research process becomes more focused, you will probably find yourself taking more of these
specific notes.

6.   Making notecards: Some general advice

▶ Put only one piece of information on each card. It may seem as if you are
wasting paper, but you are really saving time. When you are writing your

paper, you will want to be able to stack these cards in piles that correspond to each section of your paper.

▶ Get in the habit of putting at least the following information on each card (if you put this information in the same place on each card, you will be developing a habit that makes it less likely that you will forget to record this information):
  ▷ the author's full name
  ▷ a short title of the work
  ▷ the page number
Please note that if you do not make bibliography/reference cards, you will be forced to put all bibliographical information on *each* notecard.

▶ If you are paraphrasing (putting the information in your own words), be sure you are actually putting it in your own words. If you are only inserting a synonym here and there, or switching around phrases, you are falling into plagiarism (see Section 6.B.3). It would be better to quote directly if you cannot put the information in your own words.

▶ If you are quoting the author's words, be very careful that you quote accurately and completely.
  ▷ Be sure to put the quoted material in quotation marks (if you don't, you won't know that these words are quoted).
  ▷ Copy the phrase, sentence, or sentences *exactly* as they are in the text—capital letters, punctuation, spelling, and all!
  ▷ If you want to leave out a word or words, indicate their omission with ellipses (. . .). Be sure that the material you omit does not leave a statement that misrepresents the author's message.
  ▷ If you need to add any information or words, put this added material in brackets [ ]. Note that brackets have square corners. They are not parentheses ( ). If you were to put this material into parentheses, you wouldn't know, later, if this material was material you added or material that the author herself had put in parentheses.

THE ORIGINAL PASSAGE
A military scholar who had written and translated several works on strategy (which earned him the sobriquet "Old Brains"), Halleck was a cautious general who waged war by the book.

James M. McPherson, Ordeal by Fire: The Civil War and Reconstruction (New York: Alfred A. Knopf, 1982), 158.

Your note
A military scholar who had written and translated several works on strategy . . . , [General Henry W.] Halleck was a cautious general who waged war by the book.

James McPherson
Ordeal by Fire
p. 158

THE ORIGINAL PASSAGE
For the approximately 30% of depressed patients refractory to TCAs, MAOIs provide a useful alternative. The MAOIs irreversibly inactivate

MAO, an enzyme of major importance in the metabolism of epinephrine, norepinephrine, dopamine, and 5–HT.

> Fred Leavitt, *Drugs and Behavior*, 2nd ed. (New York: John Wiley and Sons, 1982), 248.

Your note
Commenting on the traditional drug treatment of depression, Leavitt writes: "For the approximately 30% of depressed patients refractory to TCAs [tricyclic antidepressants], MAOIs [monoamine oxidase inhibitors] provide a useful alternative. The MAOIs irreversibly inactivate MAO, an enzyme of major importance in the metabolism of epinephrine, norepinephrine, dopamine, and 5–HT [serotonin]."

> Fred Leavitt
> *Drugs and Behavior*
> p. 248

THE ORIGINAL PASSAGE
Psychoanalysis, a therapy that grew out of experience with severely repressed and morally rigid individuals who needed to come to terms with a rigorous inner "censor," today finds itself confronted more and more often with a "chaotic and impulse-ridden character." It must deal with patients who "act out" their conflicts instead of repressing or sublimating them. These patients, though often ingratiating, tend to cultivate a protective shallowness in emotional relations.

> Christopher Lasch, *The Culture of Narcissism: American Life in an Age of Diminishing Expectations* (New York: W. W. Norton and Co., 1978), 37.

Your note
Lasch is comparing the nature of the problems that psychoanalysis dealt with in its earlier years and the problems of patients it sees today. Today psychoanalysis "must deal with patients who 'act out' their conflicts instead of repressing or sublimating them. These patients . . . tend to cultivate a protective shallowness in emotional relations."

> Christopher Lasch
> *Narcissism*
> p. 37

C. Some Specific Issues Related to Reading and Taking Notes

---

1. Dealing with material an author has taken from other sources

When I discussed, in Section 1, what research is all about, I said that researchers build on the work of others. So, in the reading that you do, you will find that the authors of your sources are themselves referring to the work of others. These references may be summaries or they may be direct quotations.

EXAMPLE 1

In general, the research literature suggests that good readers tend to have more positive self concepts than poor readers (*26, 40, 41, 43, 57, 78*).

> Irene Athey, "Affective Factors in Reading," in *Theoretical Models and Processes of Reading*, ed. Harry Singer and Robert B. Ruddell (Newark, Delaware: International Reading Assoc., 1970), 110.

Athey is using the numbered reference list system of documentation; the six numbers that follow her statement refer to six works in her reference list.

EXAMPLE 2

Recent evidence suggests that the toxin provokes the ADP-ribosylation of the same GTP-binding component discussed above (Moss and Vaughan, 1977; Gill and Meren, 1978; Cassel and Pfeuffer, 1978; G. L. Johnson *et al.*, 1978; Gilman *et al.*, 1979).

> Peter J. Roach, "Principles of the Regulation of Enzyme Activity," in *Gene Expression: Translation and Behavior of Proteins*, ed. David M. Prescott and Lester Goldstein, vol. 4 of *Cell Biology: A Comprehensive Treatise* (New York: Academic Press, 1980), 238–39.

EXAMPLE 3

Andrew D. White asserted in 1890 that "with very few exceptions, the city governments of the United States are the worst in Christendom—the most expensive, the most inefficient, and the most corrupt."[6]

> Richard Hofstadter, *The Age of Reform from Bryan to F.D.R.* (New York: Random House, Vintage Books, 1955), 176.

When you run across such references (summaries or direct quotations) that are relevant to your subject, you will probably be tempted to take this information from the source that you are reading and be done with it.

I must warn you that experienced researchers don't stop here. Instead of copying down the information on their notecards, they make a note to themselves to find the author's sources and to look at these works firsthand. You should do the same.

Thus, when you see a reference to a list of studies (like the first example) you should copy the bibliographic information for each source from the reference list or bibliography. This information goes into the Sources section of your Researcher's Notebook, with a note from you about what to look for in these sources.

When you come across a quotation that you want (like the third example), again copy down the bibliographic information for its original source and be sure to note the page number(s). If you decide to use such a quotation in your paper, you should be quoting it from its original source.

If you have honestly made every possible effort to locate the original source but find that you cannot do so, you may quote from the secondary source. On your notecard,

▶ Be sure to put *your* source's words in double quotation marks and the material your author quotes in single quotation marks.

▶ Put all bibliographic information about the original source (see the author's notes) as well as the necessary information about your source.

Your notecard for Example 3 would look like this:

> "Andrew D. White asserted in 1890 that 'with very few exceptions, the city governments of the United States are the worst in Christendom—the most expensive, the most inefficient, and the most corrupt.'"
>
> White, *Forum*, Vol. X (Dec. 1890), p. 25,
> quoted by Richard Hofstadter, *Age of Reform*, p. 176

As the authors you read give credit where credit is due, so must you when you write your paper. Under no circumstances in your final paper may you imply that you have read and studied works which, in reality, you have only seen referred to in works of others. Your notes must clearly indicate the source of all ideas and the authors of specific words.

2.   Determining the quality of your sources

In the world of scholarship, the work of some people is considered more valuable than the work of others. The more knowledgeable you become in a subject, the more you will become aware of this fact and the more aware you will become that the world of scholarship sometimes resembles the fashion world—there are trends, and trends change. Theories and studies that were popular in the 1950s may be considered out of date in the 1980s.

The more ignorant you are of a field, the harder it will be for you to determine the quality of the sources you look at. However, here are a few basic guidelines:

▶ If you are doing a research project that is essentially historical,
   ▷ how did Darwin's contemporaries in nineteenth-century England react to his theories?
   ▷ what did dramatists in seventeenth-century France think of Shakespeare's plays?
   ▷ how did the Church in the Middle Ages portray Eve and the Virgin Mary?
   you will clearly need primary material from the historical period your question covers. But if your study is not essentially historical, you will want to focus on the most recent research and theories on your subject; concentrate on studies and data gathered in the last ten, or even five, years. Regardless of whether your research project is historical or not, you will want to know how the experts now interpret the evidence. Therefore, you should focus on secondary sources that have been published in the last ten, or five, years.

▶ If you do your research properly, gathering as much evidence as possible about your working thesis/hypothesis, you will notice that particular authors and/or works are referred to often. These references are clues that these authors and/or works are considered important in the field. You will be expected to read and study this material yourself.

▶ The fact that a book or article has been published, or the fact that it is on the shelf of a library, does not automatically make that book or article a sound piece of scholarship or what experts today would call a sound piece of scholarship. In the social and natural sciences particularly, you should be skeptical of work published more than fifteen years ago unless you have good reason to believe that the work is still considered authoritative.

3. How to read material you find difficult to read

As fields become more and more specialized and as more and more complex and sophisticated methods of testing become popular, research in many fields becomes more and more difficult for novices to read and interpret. If you come across articles and books written for experts in the field, you may find them very hard going; the vocabulary may sound like gibberish to you, and you will probably sense that the author is assuming that you have knowledge that you, in fact, do not have.

Whenever possible, you should try to use this material, but you will have to use your common sense. You are having trouble reading the material because it was written for experts.

▶   Do not attempt to read the material until you have spent some time educating yourself about the subject. Go back to textbooks, introductory works, specialized encyclopedias, accessible but authoritative periodicals before you try to tackle this material.

▶   Isolate key terms (words or phrases) that are clearly important terms in these more difficult works. Look these terms up in a textbook or specialized dictionary. Write out the definitions on cards. Try to understand the concepts for which they stand. Use these definition cards when you come back to this difficult reading material.

▶   When you do read this material, be prepared to read slowly and carefully. You may not understand the work completely, but you want to try to understand the author's basic approach. Concentrate, therefore, on introductions and conclusions; look for the author's thesis or hypothesis, results and/or conclusions.

▶   Whatever you do, do *not* mindlessly copy down notes from these works. Do not take down anything in the author's words that you feel you don't understand. If you do take down some of the author's statements, it may be wise for you to include on the notecard your own paraphrase of what you think the author is saying.

D.   Summary

Because reading critically and thinking about the evidence you gather is the heart of the research process, I'd like to make a few final summary remarks about this stage of the research process.

Notecards and bibliography/reference cards are important tools for the researcher. You need an easy-to-manipulate, systematic way of recording your evidence. This evidence, after all, is the essential material you will use to test your original assumption; it constitutes the building material of the conclusion you are drawing about your subject. However, if the evidence on your notecards is only on your notecards and not in your head, you have missed the whole point of the research process. The notecards should be reminders of what you have already learned.

At this stage in the research process, the most important work you are doing is in your Researcher's Notebook. In the Reading section of your Notebook, you are critically examining the work of others. You are asking questions of the texts you are looking at; you are digesting the work of others, comprehending it, comparing it with what you've learned about your subject. In the Working Thesis section of your Notebook, you are writing to yourself about the picture that is forming in your mind as you put the pieces of the puzzle together, take these same pieces apart and put them together in different ways, decide which pieces in the puzzle are missing and ask the questions that will allow you to find those pieces. If you use your Researcher's Notebook wisely, you will realize that you have started writing your research paper *as* you read and study your evidence. The writing you do in your Researcher's Notebook is a very important part of the writing process. You are figuring out what you want to say. The final paper you are going to produce, I will remind you, is *not* going to be a "memory dump" paper (to use a computer term). You are *not* going to *list* what others have said (John Doe says this about X, and Mary Brown says that about X, and Sally Smith says something else again). Rather, your paper is going to focus on the conclusions *you* have reached about X from your critical reading of John Doe and Mary Brown and Sally Smith and everyone else who can help you draw this conclusion. If you gather all of your evidence first and then attempt to make some sense of it, you will be overwhelmed. I've seen it happen too often to students I've worked with. Besides, as I've now said over and over again, how do you know what evidence you need if you have not, throughout the entire research process, been asking questions, if you have not been the one to give your research direction?

This sense of direction, as I keep repeating, is critical to you as a researcher. As you have already now discovered for yourself, the process of gathering evidence is not as straightforward and neat as all of us would like it to be. Experienced researchers know that their first visit to the library will not be the only visit they will make in the course of a research project. They will return as they come across the titles of promising sources in the bibliographies and reference lists of the books and articles they are reading. As their research changes direction, or as they realize that they are finally zeroing in on the real question they want to ask, they return to indexes, reference materials, the subject catalogue. I have found myself in the library, tracking down the answers to one or two final questions, when I have been in the second or even third draft of my papers. If your experience is like that of other researchers, you will also find yourself rereading important sources several times at different stages of your research, gleaning more information from that source as your knowledge of the subject grows and deepens.

Finally, I should alert you that the research process rarely ends naturally. You will feel that there is more to learn, more sources to read, more to think about, more directions to explore. Experts have spent years, even decades, investigating a subject. As time passes and you get more deeply into your research, you will want to make a conscious effort to isolate and narrow down the area of investigation you want to focus on. Be prepared for the fact that, approximately two weeks before the final paper is due, you will have to say, "The major portion of my research is finished. I must now decide what I am going to say in my paper." Obviously, by this point the major portion of your research must be finished; you must have found, read, and studied the important evidence about your subject. If you are doing a primary research project, you must set a deadline for the time when all your raw data will be in your hands, a deadline that leaves you plenty of time to analyze those data, draw your conclusions, and write your report.

Use your time during this collecting/reading/studying stage of your project wisely. Plan to spend an hour here, a couple of hours there, *every day*, reading, searching, thinking, writing in your Researcher's Notebook. Give your brain as much time as possible to mull over what you are putting into it.

Then two weeks before the final paper must be handed in to your instructor, when it is time to start work on this paper, turn to the next section of this book.

Section 5

Writing Your Paper

If you are on schedule, it should now be two weeks before the date when your final paper is due. I cannot say that it is time for you to start writing, because you have already been doing a great deal of writing over the past weeks in your Researcher's Notebook. But it is time to start composing a unified piece of prose addressed to other people. In your Researcher's Notebook, you've been writing to yourself, for yourself. You have been thinking out loud on paper to decide what your answers are to your research questions; you have been developing your conclusions, matching them against your working hypothesis/thesis. By this point you should feel as if you have some answers; you should feel as if the parts of the puzzle are falling into place. But the learning process is not over. In writing your paper, you will be discovering precisely what solution you have come up with for your mystery.

The paper you are now beginning is *not* a story. It is *not* the story of what you have been reading over the past weeks (John Doe says this and Mary Brown says that); nor is it the history of your subject (first this happened, and then that happened . . .). Your paper will be a presentation of an idea or concept, a mental construct that you have formed in your mind. When I talk about conclusions, I am talking about ideas, concepts, mental constructs. When I think of an idea, the picture that comes into my mind is that of an intricate, elaborate, delicately balanced machine, like the inner workings of an old-fashioned wind-up clock. This idea or concept is made up of many parts, each of which has a special shape and each of which must be placed in a specific position, so that all parts move together harmoniously to make this idea work.

When I write a research paper (or any paper of exposition, for that matter), I think of myself as reconstructing this machine/concept for other people. I want to show others exactly what the parts of my idea look like, and I want to show others how the parts mesh together, so that when my readers finish my paper, they have rebuilt in their minds a perfect duplicate of my original idea. Reconstructing my concept for others in a paper, interestingly enough, becomes a final test for me. As I write, I must know what the parts of my idea are, and I must know how the parts fit together. In my experience as a writer, I have discovered, as I write my drafts, that my concept is not as explicit as I thought it was when I started my draft. When I started writing, I thought I had a complete blueprint of the machine. I discover, as I write, that the blueprint was really only a preliminary sketch. In other words, the need to present my idea to other people in a formal presentation is an opportunity for me. Do I really know what I think? Do I really know what my conclusion is?

Writing the paper, presenting my ideas to other people, forces me to objectify my idea for myself as well as for others. If any parts are missing, or if certain parts don't mesh together, I will soon discover these flaws as I write. If I do discover flaws, I must stop and fix the machine; I must find the missing parts, and I must tinker with the placement of the parts until they work together properly. The need to present a complete, working concept to others forces me to be sure that I have a complete, working concept. So writing a research paper, for me, is certainly not boring busywork. It is as intellectually challenging as was the process of developing my ideas as I studied my evidence. It is the final stage of the thinking process. I hope that you, too, view the writing of your paper in the same light.

As I have done in other sections of this book, in this section I will lay out strategies and techniques for you to follow in writing your paper. Read over the parts of this section that apply to the type of paper you are writing. First, read over the whole section to get a sense of the process you will be going through, and then go back to each step and *use* the strategies and techniques I give you. But, first of all, read carefully part A, an overview of the writing process.

A.   The Writing Process: An Overview

Just as the research process is not a neat, clean progression from one step to another, so the writing process tends to be recursive. Some sections of your paper may fall into place in the second draft. Other sections may be more stubborn; you may have to revise five or six times as you work to find out how the parts fit together. As you write, you may decide that the thesis you are developing is not the thesis you started with; obviously, if you change your conclusions, you will have to change the shape of your whole argument. In a review or critical paper, where your conclusions give shape to the whole paper, changing your conclusions will mean reshaping your whole paper. Some students seem to think that the mark of a good writer is "getting it right" in the first draft; they seem to feel that the need to revise is a clear sign that they are bad writers. The need to revise is not the sign of a bad writer. I consider myself a fairly decent writer, and I cannot count the number of revisions I have done on some sections of this book. I doubt that anything but some of the main ideas (like the Researcher's Notebook) are left of the first and second drafts. My concern has been the main concern of experienced writers: I want to express my ideas as clearly and accurately as possible so you will understand what I mean. I have been willing to go through as much revising and rewriting as necessary to reach this goal. Your goal, too, should be to develop a paper that precisely and accurately reproduces the idea you have in your head.

You can waste time, however, if you try to do everything at once; trying to do everything at once may also send you into a writer's block. So I want you to think of the paper-writing process as a process like the painting of a picture or the carving of a statue.

▶   Your first concern should be the *general shape* of the overall idea, which means that your first concern should be the overall outline or shape of the whole paper. At this stage you want to be sure you have the main parts of your idea/machine and that they are in approximately the right places.

▶   Once you are satisfied that the overall shape is there, then you can attend to sharpening and outlining each part. The focus in these first two steps is on the idea—getting the idea into words, phrases, and statements that come closer and closer to expressing what you have in your mind.

▶   Finally, when the paper has reached the point when your ideas are all in their proper places, and clearly defined, then you can worry about editing and proofreading. Only at this stage should you worry about spelling, punctuation, subject/verb agreement, and the like.

In order to begin your paper, then, you need to have a general sense of the overall shape of your paper. There is no set format for a research paper. The shape a paper takes is determined by a writer's answers to four basic questions:

▶   What do I want to say about my subject? What is the message I want to convey to my readers?

▶   Who are my readers? What do they know about my subject? What do they expect me to say? What do they know about the specific idea I am trying to express?

▶   What persona or speaker do I want to present in this paper? What kind of person do I want my readers to hear speaking to them from this paper?

▶   What is my purpose in writing this paper? What impact do I want to have on my reader? What do I want my readers to think or feel when they have finished reading my paper?

When experienced researchers write a paper, they are usually addressing an audience (readers) of other experts who are interested in the general subject the writer is writing about. The purpose of these writers is to inform this audience about the work they've done and the conclusions they've reached. By presenting their work as thorough and their conclusions as logical, sound conclusions, they therefore wish to persuade their readers that the readers should see their subject as they see it. These writers usually, then, present themselves as serious, thoughtful, reasonable people, confident that the work and thinking they have done is worthy of consideration.

You are not an experienced researcher speaking to other experts. But you will write a much more successful paper if you can imagine yourself in a situation that resembles, as closely as possible, the situation I have just outlined. You will write a much more successful paper if you can avoid the traps of "writing for the teacher." If you think of your reader as your instructor, two bad things may happen to you as a writer:

▶ You may fall into the trap of feeling that your purpose in writing the paper is to prove to the instructor that you have done your research properly. You will be tempted to drag in every source you have read, whether it applies to your argument or not, just to show your instructor that you have read this material. In other words, thinking that your purpose is to prove to your instructor that you did your research properly may encourage you to write a "memory dump" paper.

▶ You may fall into the trap of feeling as if you have no right to say anything about this subject because your reader (the instructor) knows far more about your subject than you do. This perception will hurt the paper you produce because you will be tempted to leave out some essential information because you will say to yourself, "My instructor already knows what X is." This perception will hurt the paper you produce because you will fail to explain ideas that need to be explained, simply because you assume your instructor already knows what you are talking about.

The best way to avoid the traps inherent in writing only for your instructor is not to think of your instructor as your audience (reader). Instead, plan to address your paper to other students, either the other students who are enrolled in your class or the students who are majoring in the field/department in which your course is offered. Assume that these students are interested in your general subject; surely they have demonstrated their interest by taking the course or majoring in this field. Because you have been going to class regularly and reading the required material, you know what your fellow students in the class already know. But remember: they have not done the research you have done, and they certainly do not know what your conclusions are. Therefore, you legitimately have to assume that you will have to show these readers what the parts of your idea look like, and you will have to explain clearly how the parts fit together. Addressing an audience of your fellow students, you will be like the experienced researcher whose purpose is to inform your audience about the work you've done and the conclusions you've reached. Because you want to persuade your fellow students to accept your view of your subject as a valid and legitimate view, you will present yourself as a serious, thoughtful, reasonable researcher. You will have a sense of confidence because you know that you have done a thorough job of researching and you have given your subject much thought, and you will not be intimidated because you know that you know more about your subject than your readers do.

In the world of experts, disciplines, and scholarship, there are differences in the specific purposes of papers that report on primary research projects, and those that are based on the work done by others. So I have divided the first part of this section into discussions of primary research reports and secondary research papers. You should now turn to the part of this section that applies to the type of research you have been engaging in.

B.   Primary Research Reports

A primary research report applies only to those research projects that have focused on studies or experiments in which you have gathered raw data directly from a source through a carefully designed series of tests or procedures, and in which you have analyzed your raw data by using objective, accepted procedures in the field. Primary research projects of the type I will discuss here are the studies or experiments normally done in the social and natural sciences. If your paper is based mostly on material you have read, you should turn to the section on secondary research papers (Section 5.C).

1.   General format

In a primary research report, the researcher is laying out his/her study or experiment for the reader in the order in which the study was conceived and carried out. A picture of the overall shape of the report follows. The report breaks down into three major parts (a, b, c, on the left of the diagram). Now I will talk about what belongs in each of these parts.

a. The first section (introduction, review of the literature, statement of the hypothesis)

In the diagram I have drawn the first section of the report is an inverted pyramid because I want you to see that, in this part of the report, you begin by introducing your reader to the general area of investigation (the general

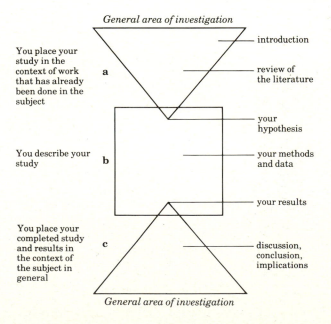

subject) and then gradually lead your reader to the specific hypothesis you tested. The purpose of this opening segment of the report is to put your study or experiment into the context of other work that has already been done in the field.

I assume that you have worked as other experienced researchers have worked. I assume that before you designed your specific study or experiment you investigated the theories that are current in the field and that you looked carefully at the studies and experiments that had been carried out by others. I assume that your specific study evolved out of your reactions to these previous studies and experiments, reactions like "Smith and Jones' hypothesis needs to be tested further with more subjects" or "Dr. X's theory needs to be tested by doing a study that would . . ." or "I wonder if procedure Y would give me more information about the way that DNA . . . ?" In other words, I assume that you did your study to fill a hole or gap in the knowledge that has already been accumulated about your subject.

In the first part of your report, then, you are doing two things:

▶ You are *informing* your reader about the theories that your study is based on and about published research projects that you have drawn on to develop your hypothesis and methodology.

▶ You are *explaining* to your reader where your study fits in the general picture of the theories that are current and the work that has been done.

An informal abstract of this section of your paper, the kind of abstract you would write for yourself, would go something like this:

> I need to tell my reader that my general area of investigation is learning styles. Then I need to say that there are 3 basic views of learning styles: view Y, view X, and view Z. I'll briefly describe X and Y and tell the reader that I'm not following these views. I'll then explain Z's theory in more detail, because, as I'll tell the reader, this is the theory I'm using. Briefly I'll show the reader what kinds of testing procedures have been used to test Z's theory, stressing Smith and Wesson's work. I'll point out that these studies haven't considered age as a variable. I will say that I think age is an important variable, and I will prove it by pointing to the work on age and learning in general done by Wilson, Johnson, and Smedley. Then I will say that age should also be considered when talking about learning styles, which will lead me right into my hypothesis that . . .

If you look at the research reports you have read as you were doing your library work, you will see that primary research reports are divided by headings in the text. Sometimes the section I have just described is headed "Introduction." Sometimes, particularly if this part of the report is long, the writer will use several headings (Introduction, Review of the Literature, Statement of Hypothesis) or she will subdivide the Introduction, using subheadings or headings that specifically describe the content of that section (Z's Theory of Learning Styles, Age and Learning).

b. The second section (a description of your study, including data and methodology)

The second general segment of the report is a description of the study you did. It includes a description of the material or subjects you used as your source for raw data, the procedures you used to acquire your data, the data themselves. The common headings for this section are "Methods," "Methods and Procedures," "Materials and Methods," "Experimental Section." Use the heading or headings that best describe the work you did. Check the published reports you read as you were doing your library research. You will notice that if this section is complicated or long, experienced researchers sometimes divide it with several headings or subheadings.

c. The third section (results, discussion, conclusions)

The final section of the body of the report is devoted to a presentation of the results you came up with when you analyzed your data and a discussion of the results/study. It begins with a straightforward report of your results/ findings and an explanation of the procedures you used to obtain those results. Once this is accomplished, the researcher is free to step back from the study/experiment she did and comment on the study as a whole or parts of it. This section allows you to critique your work and the results of your work (thus "Discussion") and to draw conclusions or to discuss the implications of your study for the field as a whole.

In preparing to write this section, then, what do you want to say about your results? What do you want to say about the whole study? If you feel that your procedures were flawed in any way, discuss that here. If you wished you had used other instruments or tests to generate more data, say so here. If you feel that you should have analyzed your data in other ways, say so here. You will want to compare your results with your original hypothesis. Do your results support the hypothesis? Were they inconclusive? Have your results suggested certain implications for the direction further research should take?

In other words, after you have described your results, you will be doing what you did in the beginning of your paper—you will be putting your specific study and the information you obtained from it back into the context of the general search for knowledge in this area of investigation. Thus, on the diagram, I have drawn this segment as a regular pyramid. You are moving from your specific study back to the general area of investigation. In the "Discussion" and "Conclusions" sections of this segment of your report, you will be telling your reader what you learned, in more general terms, by doing this study. If you look at the published studies you read as you were doing your library research, you will notice that some researchers label this part "Results and Discussion" and that others divide their reports into "Results" and "Discussion" sections.

d. The fourth section (appendixes and reference list)

If you need to include appendixes in your report (see B.2. of this section), you will place them after the text of your report. The report will end with your list of references (see Section 7 and Appendix C).

As you can see from my general description of the order in which you present your information, you are approximating the order in which you conceived and carried out your study. In this report, you are telling your reader what you did and explaining why you did what you did. Your information is complete enough so that your reader, if she wished to, could duplicate your study and compare her results with yours. The text is divided by headings so that the reader can quickly distinguish the parts, and the headings allow her to go straight to specific parts of the study if she is most interested in your methodology, or results.

2.   General guidelines for writing the report

Here are some "words of wisdom" that will help you produce a coherent, readable report.

▶   Since your report is divided into separate segments, you can begin to write the introduction and methodology sections even while you are analyzing your data and considering your conclusions/discussion.

▶   Because this paper is a formal, scientific report, you will want to use a style appropriate to such a report. Do *not* write in an informal, chatty way. You may want to avoid using the first person (*I* did this; this is *my* study); ask your instructor. Use technical language where it is appropriate, but remember your readers. Do your readers know what these terms refer to?

▶   Throughout your report, your goal is to be as clear and precise as possible. Even if your instructor helped you design your study and analyze your data, you may not assume that your readers know what you did in this study. Think of your readers as people who had no idea that you were working on any research project until they picked up this report.

▶   You must be precise and specific, but you do not want to overwhelm your reader with details to the point that your reader can't see the forest for the trees. Try these techniques:

   ▷   In each division of the text, begin with a summary statement of the material in that section, then go into more detail. Use this same "summarize-then-explain" pattern in each subdivision, and even each paragraph. For example, your "Methods" section might begin, "Thirty subjects participated in this study; all were male college students between the ages of 18 and 24. These subjects were given the Judson-Smith Personality Inventory Test, the Wilson-Jones Selected Interest Test, and were asked to fill out a questionnaire designed to elicit their career objectives."

▷   Whenever possible, use graphs and charts to report results or to summarize data. In your text, do not simply write out your data in prose. The prose parts of your text should be statements you make to draw your reader's attention to numbers you consider important or significant and to tell your reader why you consider these numbers important.

▷   Do not attempt to put all your raw data in the body of your paper. If you feel obliged to give data that cannot be represented in summary charts and graphs, put these data in appendixes at the end of your report. If and when you want to refer to these data, you can refer your reader to the proper appendix.

▷   If you were gathering data from people by using tests or instruments that your reader could not easily obtain (such as a questionnaire that you made up), you should include a copy of this test or instrument. However, put this material in appendixes at the end of the paper and refer your reader to the appropriate appendix when you talk about this material in your text.

▶   Whenever you refer to the work of other researchers and experts, you must document your sources. See Section 7 and the appropriate appendixes in this book.

▶   As I have suggested in part B.1. of this section, your text should be divided by headings. If you are not sure how to divide your text, either look at the studies you have read as you were doing your library research, or ask your instructor. Mainly, in cases like this, you should use your common sense. Your object is to isolate the important parts of your report so that your reader could go directly to specific portions of your study if he were interested only in, say, your results and conclusions.

▶   As I said in part A of this section, you should plan to write several drafts of your report. Start with the overall shape of the report, outlined in part B.1. of this section, determine general divisions within these parts, and work down to individual paragraphs. See part D of this section. You may also find some suggestions that you can use in writing the first segment of your report in my guidelines for writing a critical paper, part C.2 of this section.

C.   Secondary Research Papers

---

1.   Guidelines for a review or a review of the literature paper

In addition to describing one section of a primary research report, the term "review of the literature" also applies to an entire research paper, one that is based on material you have gathered from books and articles. In the natural sciences, this type of paper is often called simply a review. Don't confuse this type of review with an evaluation of a specific book, play, or film. The review that I am describing here is a review of the research that has been done in a specific field.

A review of the literature, or review, is a summary of the "state of the art" of a particular area of investigation. A researcher selects a particular subject (clinical therapies for depression, field dependent-independent learning theory, Legionnaire's disease, etc.); his objective is to point out to his readers the patterns and trends that have been developing in research done on this subject. Unless the writer has a particular reason for doing an historical study, she is usually interested in the most recent trends and patterns of research (what has happened in the last ten, or even five, years).

Reviews of the literature are a common form of paper in academic disciplines. As the knowledge explosion increases and experts become more specialized, these experts find it difficult to keep abreast of developments in areas outside their narrow field of interest. Reviews help them stay informed about subjects in their general field about which they have not had time to read in depth. An instructor may ask students in his/her classes to write reviews on topics outside his/her area of specialization as one means of remaining informed about developments in the field in general.

If your research project assignment was to write a review of the literature, then your obligation has been to find and read *everything available* on the topic. Since this has been your obligation, I would expect that you have narrowed the topic down if you have found that a great deal has been written on the general subject with which you started. The two most common ways to narrow down the topic are to narrow down the area of investigation (the function of vitamin E in the body rather than the function of all vitamins) or to restrict your research to a given period of time (what clinical therapies for depression have been used in the past five years?)

When you write a review or review of the literature paper, the most valuable evidence you have are the summaries of books and articles that you have written on the backs of your bibliography/reference cards (see Section 4.B.4).

The trickiest part of writing a review of the literature is deciding how to organize your paper. The one thing you *do not* want to do is simply to *list* the studies you have read. Let me remind you that your purpose in writing a review is to tell your reader about the main *trends* and *patterns* you see in the work that has been done on this subject. Thus, as you have researched, you should have been looking constantly for trends and patterns (and considering these in the Working Thesis section of your Researcher's Notebook). In determining the overall structure of your paper, you should use the basic trends and patterns you see as the focal point of the paper.

Here are some strategies you can use in determining what the basic trends and patterns are:

▶ What theory or theories seem to be the most popular? (which theories are referred to most often? which theories are the basis for most of the studies or experiments you looked at?) Has there been a shift in the popularity of theories?

▶ What basic assumptions do most of the researchers seem to be making about the subject?

▶ Can you categorize the research reports you've read according to the test procedures used in the studies/experiments?

▶ Can you categorize the research reports you've read according to the kinds of subjects or material tested or observed?

▶ Can you see any patterns in the results reported?

▶ Are there any patterns in the conclusions drawn by the researchers?

▶ What experts' names pop up most frequently? Are certain experts associated with certain types of research, certain theories, certain areas of investigation?

If it helps you, make actual charts by putting these questions in categories at the top of the page and the works you've read along the left-hand side, then fill in the blanks.

Here are some other strategies to use in writing your paper:

▶ When you have determined what you consider to be the two or three most important trends or patterns in the subject you've researched, organize your paper around them. Write out a thesis statement that summarizes these major trends or patterns. You may want to turn to part C.2 in this section when you have reached this point in writing your paper. The steps I outline in part C.2 may help you write your review. But one word of caution: in a review of the literature your purpose is *not* to focus on your personal ideas about the topic. Your thesis statement must be a statement of the conclusions you have reached about *the major trends and developments you see in the research that has been done on your subject.*

Another word of caution: in a review of the literature your obligation is only to indicate the *type* of work that is being done or has been done and the most *influential* theories. Of course you will illustrate and support your argument by referring to specific works, but this can be done with summary statements and *some* descriptions of actual studies. Do *not* give *detailed* descriptions of *every* study and book. Use detail where it is important to make your point. A review is not a memory dump paper.

▶ At the end of your review, you should devote a few paragraphs to your conclusions about the work that still needs to be done in the field. You won't be able to do this unless you have thought about the general picture you have seen emerging in the research to date.

▶ Obviously, your reader will expect you to refer to specific books and articles as you support and illustrate the points you are making (it would be very difficult indeed to write a review of the literature without a large number of these references, since your job was to survey the field). All works you refer to must be documented in your paper. So see Section 7 and the appropriate appendixes.

▶ Plan to write several drafts, working from the overall shape of your paper
   to specific parts. Let me say again that the steps I outline in part C.2 of
   this section may help you in writing your paper. Be sure to read part D of
   this section.

2.   Guidelines for critical papers

The most common type of research paper assigned to students in college
courses falls into the category of critical papers. In doing a research project
that is going to culminate in a critical paper, a researcher starts with his
assumption of what he will find when he gathers the evidence, he turns that
assumption into a working thesis, and he constantly tests that working thesis
as he studies and evaluates the evidence he finds. If you have been working
on this type of research project, your major objective has been to draw your
own conclusions, conclusions based on your critical assessment of what the
evidence adds up to.

   In a critical paper, the most important ingredient is the main conclusion
you have reached about your subject. The paper you write will focus on this
conclusion, and this conclusion will determine the shape—the organization—of your paper.

   So take out your Researcher's Notebook, and in the Working Thesis
section answer these questions:

▶ Was my original assumption/working thesis valid?
▶ Based on the evidence I have found, what conclusions have I drawn
   about my subject?
▶ What statements do I feel comfortable making about my subject? (You
   want inferences and judgments here, not factual statements.)

Freewrite on these questions.

   Don't worry if you decide that your original assumption/working thesis
was not correct; don't worry if you find that the conclusions you are drawing
cover only a part of the general area you began investigating. You should
know by now that the more you research, the more you realize how broad
and complex a subject is.

   As you are developing the conclusion, I'd better calm your fears about
those two matters that seem to drive students to write poor critical papers.
Do *not* try to find a conclusion that will cover everything you read just so you
can refer to all your research in your paper. Your bibliography will show your
instructor at a glance all the material you looked at; there is no need to refer
to all of this material in your paper. Most of all, the *quality* of the conclusions
you draw and the argument you present is the real test of a critical paper. The
more evidence you studied, the more time you spent thinking about your
subject, the higher will be the quality of the conclusion you draw.

a. Developing your conclusion: The thesis statement

Before you can do anything on your final paper, you must determine *the*
conclusion that you want to focus your paper on.

Can you summarize your conclusion in *one sentence*? When you are able to summarize your conclusion in one sentence, you will be ready to proceed with the other steps.

It may take a while to come up with the sentence that feels exactly right. Don't put it off. Here are a few strategies to follow:

▶ What do you feel confident in saying about your subject?
▶ You may come up with several statements. In these cases you will have to choose one. Which statement comes closest to expressing what you want to say about your subject?
▶ Don't just stare at a blank page, forming and dismissing statements in your head. Write down something, anything. If the first statement you write is "wrong," don't erase it or scratch it out. Move down on the sheet of paper and write another statement.
▶ If you write a statement that is not quite right, underline the parts of the statement that are wrong and rewrite those parts until they say what you want them to say.
▶ As you write and rewrite these statements, keep saying to yourself, "*Exactly* what do I want to say about X in this paper?"
▶ Be sure the statement you end up with covers only what you want to say in your paper and that it does cover what you want to say, precisely and completely.

Your conclusion should look like this:

> The creation of "independent" homelands in South Africa as part of South Africa's policy of separate development will have harmful effects for the African people of South Africa for two basic reasons: (1) These "independent" states have no economic bases that could allow them to support their new citizens; (2) Africans who will become citizens of these new countries will lose South African citizenship without gaining any of the benefits of internationally recognized sovereignty.

> In their efforts to learn more about human evolution, physical anthropologists and paleontologists focus their investigations on the development of three human characteristics—bipedalism, brain size, and tool use; their purpose is to attempt to determine when these characteristics developed, and under what conditions.

Once you have a statement that you are sure states clearly and precisely the conclusion you have reached, you are ready to begin sketching out your paper.

Don't let the specter of "how can I write ten pages on this?" spook you now. You now *know* that you have a great deal of knowledge of your subject. Never forget that it takes a great deal of space to make your ideas clear to other people. And the abstract you will write in the next step will immediately calm your fears, because you will immediately begin to fill in pages with your prose.

b. Writing an abstract of your paper: The first draft

The conclusion you have reached, expressed in the thesis statement you developed in the last step, is your whole paper in a nutshell. You know what the statement means to you, but nobody else but you knows all those "meanings." Therefore you must write a paper which will be a full explanation of how and why you arrived at this conclusion. That is, you will now be reconstructing, in all its detail, a picture of that idea/concept/machine I was talking about in the first part of this section. From now on, I will call this reconstruction of your idea your *argument.*

Many students try to begin writing a paper by writing a polished introduction. I tell students to write the introduction last, after the body of the paper is complete. How do you know what you are introducing until the body of the paper is complete? Actually, what these students are doing when they write these polished introductions is figuring out what they are going to say in the rest of the paper. There is, however, a less painful way of figuring out what you want to say, one that does not involve agonizing over individual sentences.

Since you need to see the overall shape of your paper, what you need to do now is to write a basic summary of your argument (since this summary of your argument is really an abstract of your argument, I am going to call this summary an *abstract*). Do *not* use your notecards at this stage of the process; do not even look at your notecards. As you've been doing while you've been writing in the Working Thesis section of your Researcher's Notebook, write your abstract by using only the ideas and information you have in your head. And don't try to write polished prose. You are still writing for yourself, attempting to discover what you mean by the idea you've summarized in your thesis statement.

In writing your abstract, you have two objectives:

▶ to express the *major* ideas or parts of your argument
▶ to express clearly the ways these ideas are related to each other

Here are examples of abstracts for the two thesis statements I gave in the last section:

ABSTRACT FOR THE PAPER ON THE AFRICAN "INDEPENDENT" HOMELANDS:

First I will briefly explain the meaning of South Africa's "separate development" policy and the way South Africa is trying to turn the homelands into independent nation-states for the separate African peoples of South Africa, forcing these peoples to take citizenship in these newly independent countries and stripping them of their South African citizenship. Then I will turn to the issue of the economies of these homelands. My main point here will be that these independent homelands cannot be economically independent. I will show that none of the industry in South Africa is located in the homelands (because of conscious policy on the part of the white government) and there are few resources here that could lead to the development of industry in the future. This implies that any solid economic base will necessarily be agricultural.

Then I will show the problems with an agricultural economy. I will talk about the amount of land available in the homelands, and its quality. On both counts my statistics show that the land is inadequate for even the present inhabitants of these homelands. My statistics on population distribution in South Africa will also show that the situation is even worse since only a small proportion of the people who will be made citizens of these homelands currently lives there. So, if these areas are to be truly independent, the currently inadequate agricultural resources of these areas will have to support even more people in the future than they do now. Since this is clearly impossible, I will conclude that these independent countries will have to continue to export laborers to white South Africa to find work.

Thus, these homelands will not be economically independent at all. These points about the economies of the homelands will lead to my next major point, that no countries outside of South Africa are likely to recognize these homelands as independent states, both because of their lack of economic independence from South Africa and because recognizing them as independent states would be seen as the equivalent of approving of South Africa's apartheid policies. This means that the new citizens of these countries will receive none of the benefits of internationally recognized sovereignty in their dealings with the rest of the world. Yet, as far as South Africa is concerned, the citizens of these homelands will be foreigners working in South Africa. Hence they will have no rights to a claim on South Africa's riches and no rights to participate in South Africa's government.

ABSTRACT FOR THE PAPER ON HUMAN EVOLUTION:

I will begin my paper by making the point that the history of evolution is recorded in fossils. I will have to show the reader that paleontologists and physical anthropologists look for certain characteristics of skeletons to decide if the fossil is of the ape family or is a hominid (the primate family of which *homo sapiens* is the only remaining species). Apes are distinguished from hominids by such physical features as the shape of the jaw, the kind and shape of teeth, the way the backbone connects with the skull, and the size and shape of the skull. In trying to determine if a fossil is an ape or a hominid, paleontologists and physical anthropologists also make note of the type of rock in which the fossil is embedded and how old the fossil is believed to be. I also need to note that the scientists' task is made harder by the fact that, usually, only fragments of skeletons are found.

Based upon this information, I will say then that most paleontologists and physical anthropologists agree that bipedalism was the first human characteristic to evolve. It is also generally agreed that bipedalism evolved about 4 million years ago in the grasslands and savannas of Africa. Using specific examples, I will show that it is known that fossils found in the African savannas are bipedal hominids because of specific skeletal features. Then I will say that the scientists infer that the environment encouraged the development of bipedalism. In wide open spaces, standing on one's rear legs allows a creature to spot predators from a distance (a survival technique). An added advantage of standing on one's rear legs is that it frees the hands—for such human activities as carrying and manipulating objects, a prerequisite for using tools. Then I will point out that these bipedal organisms in Africa 4 million years ago (*Australopithecus*) had small brains, and that no tools have been found with these fossils.

My next major point will be that fossils indicate that the next evolutionary step was increasing brain size (skulls found in Africa that date between 4 million and a half-million years ago). Then I will go into detail about the fossil record of hominid skulls and growing size (*homo habilis, homo erectus,* modern man). My big point here is that the advantages of larger brains and the conditions under which they evolved are controversial subjects among paleontologists and physical anthropologists. I need to be sure the reader sees that the various statements made by these scientists on these issues are strictly inferences; there is no solid evidence for these speculations and conclusions.

My last point has to do with the third human characteristic, tool use. I will say that, right now, most speculation among paleontologists and physical anthropologists is that the evolution of larger brains is tied to tool use. Most people, I will point out, assume that using tools gives an organism a measure of control over the environment and thus the development of tool use is an important step in human evolution. I will say that some scientists infer that the larger the brain, the greater the potential for tool development. Then I want to get into a really interesting issue; to me it seems that some paleontologists and physical anthropologists want to draw a causal relationship between increasing brain size and tool use (as brains got bigger, hominids had more potential to develop tools). But the point I want to make is: isn't there another, complicating factor? In this same period of increasing brain size, there is evidence of the development of culture (living in groups, cooperative food gathering, specialization of tasks—some members of a group hunt, others fix the food, etc.). Larger brains, in general, allow for more flexible behavior and adaptation. If culture is developing, behavior (like using tools) could be as easily influenced by the culture as by physical environmental factors (like standing on one's rear legs to spot predators). Is increasing tool use simply a factor of increasing brain size, or was the increasing development and use of tools an indirect result of increasing brain size—that is, was increasing tool use encouraged by a variety of cultural factors?

At this stage in the writing process your focus must remain on these *major* elements of the *entire* paper. Your first abstract may be only a half-page long. Do *not* allow yourself to start writing detailed parts of the paper. Your abstract will grow longer as you continue to test and explain the relationship of individual parts. As you work on the abstract, keep asking yourself, "How do I get from this idea to that idea?" "What idea do I need to explain to my readers first so that they will understand the other ideas?" Write out to yourself why you are putting certain ideas where you have them and explain to yourself how the ideas are related. For example, "I have to tell the reader that vitamin C is not retained in the body. That has to come first, or else the reader won't understand why we have to take vitamin C every day.

So I'll explain that idea. Then I'll say next that the issue is how much vitamin C a certain body needs every day. I'll explain that there are three variables that determine this need . . ." At this stage of the process it is imperative that you keep the entire argument in mind as you sketch in your ideas.

Working with the skeleton of your argument, as you are now, you will find that it is much easier to decide if you have the main ideas in the best places and, if you decide that the main ideas are not properly placed, it is a simple matter to rearrange them. If you are unable to explain to yourself why a particular idea is in the paper, it is very possible that this idea does not belong in this paper. Continue to check your abstract against your thesis statement. If you find, as you sketch out your abstract, that your main conclusion changes, then simply go back and change your thesis to match the new conclusion.

When you are satisfied that you have all the main points of your argument in their proper places, and when you have explained to yourself how the parts fit together (the argument "flows" smoothly from one point to the next), you have your first draft. Because my abstracts/first drafts attempt to hit only the major points of my argument, sketched in language essentially written just for me, my abstracts/first drafts are usually only a couple of pages long. But the length of your abstract/rough draft isn't as important as its content. At this stage of the process you are testing your own argument to see if you have an argument that is logical and coherent.

c. Writing an outline, if you feel you need one

When you have an abstract/first draft that *you* know

▶ includes the *major* ideas in your argument,
▶ places these major points in such a way that the argument builds from one point to the next (if . . . then; because . . . it follows),
▶ *explains* how each major point relates to and builds on the previous point,

you have the skeleton of your paper. The next steps of the writing process will involve putting flesh on this skeleton. Now you will spell out each of these major points for the reader, defining each clearly, supporting each with the necessary evidence, explaining clearly to the reader how you have related each of these points to form your central idea.

When you start writing individual sections and paragraphs of your paper, you will need a map of the entire paper. As you write, you must always know what this paragraph or section is intended to say in light of the central idea you are setting forth in this paper. Without a map of the whole paper to guide you, you may find yourself going off on tangents, developing ideas that are not integrally related to the argument you are building. Your abstract/first draft can function as such a map. However, if you find that your abstract/first draft does not work well as a map for you, or if your paper is going to be long because your argument is complex and full of intricate parts, you may find that you will want to make an outline.

Let me warn you, however, that the only appropriate outline for your paper is an outline that is your abstract/first draft written out in a different form. The only difference between your abstract and your outline should be that your abstract is prose in paragraphs and your outline is a series of statements written to indicate major categories and subdivisions. The content must be exactly the same. Below you will find the abstracts of the papers on the African "independent" homelands and on evolution translated into outlines.

Thesis: The creation of "independent" homelands in South Africa as part of South Africa's policy of separate development will have harmful effects on the African people of South Africa for two basic reasons: (1) These "independent" homelands have no economic bases that could allow them to support their new citizens; (2) Africans who will become citizens of these new countries will lose South African citizenship without gaining any of the benefits of internationally recognized sovereignty.

I. South Africa's policy of "separate development" is the old policy of apartheid in a new guise.
   A. As part of that policy, "homelands" will be given independence.
   B. People in South Africa who belong to the tribe associated with the homeland will be stripped of South African citizenship and given citizenship in the appropriate homeland.

II. The economies of the homelands cannot be viable independent economies, and so will continue to be dependent on the economy of white South Africa.
   A. There is almost no industry in the homelands because of conscious policy on the part of the South African government.
   B. Nor are there enough resources to make the future development of industry likely.
   C. The agricultural base of these areas is now inadequate and is likely to become even more inadequate.
      1. Only a small percentage of South Africa's land is in the homelands.
      2. Very little of that land is good agricultural land.
      3. Because of those two considerations it cannot even support its present populations adequately.
      4. Many Africans who will become citizens of these countries now live in the white areas of South Africa; the land clearly cannot support these additional numbers.
   D. Therefore, the economies of the homelands will have to continue to do what they do now to support themselves: export labor to white South Africa.

III. Outside countries will not recognize the independence of the homelands.
   A. One reason for the lack of recognition is the lack of economic independence.
   B. The other reason is that recognition of the independence of the homelands implies approval of the South African apartheid policies.
   C. So citizens of the homelands will get no benefits from internationally recognized independence and sovereignty for their countries.

IV. South Africa will be able to treat the citizens of the homelands as foreigners working in South Africa.
  A. These people will have no claim on the riches of South Africa.
  B. They will have no right of participation in the South African government.

Thesis: In their efforts to learn more about human evolution, physical anthropologists and paleontologists focus their investigations on the development of three human characteristics—bipedalism, brain size, and tool use; their purpose is to attempt to determine when these characteristics developed, and under what conditions.

 I. The history of evolution is recorded in fossils; therefore, paleontologists and physical anthropologists will distinguish the ape from the hominid (family of humans) by certain skeletal features.
  A. Apes and hominids are distinguished by certain physical features.
    1. One difference is the shape of the jaw.
    2. Another difference is the kind and shape of teeth.
    3. Another difference is the way the backbone connects with the skull.
    4. Another is the size and shape of the skull.
  B. Other observations paleontologists and physical anthropologists make in distinguishing the ape from the hominid are the type of rock in which a fossil is embedded and how old the fossil is believed to be.

 II. Using observations of physical characteristics, the type of rock in which a fossil is found and the age of the fossil, paleontologists and physical anthropologists generally agree that bipedalism evolved before large brain and tool use; it is generally agreed that bipedalism evolved in the expanding grasslands and savannas of Africa about 4 million years ago.
  A. It is known that the fossils found in the African savannas and grasslands represent bipedal hominids because of specific skeletal features.
  B. Paleontologists and physical anthropologists infer that the environment encouraged the development of bipedalism.
    1. In grasslands, standing on one's rear legs allows a creature to spot predators coming across these wide-open spaces.
    2. A consequence of standing on one's rear legs is that it frees the hands for carrying and manipulating objects (a prerequisite for tool use).
  C. Evidence shows that these bipedal organisms found in Africa 4 million years ago (*Australopithecus*) had small brains, and no tools were found with the fossils.

 III. After the development of bipedalism, there is rapid evolution toward increasing brain size, as clearly evidenced in fossil skulls found in Africa that date between 4 million and a half-million years ago, the period in which the first recognizable humans appeared.
  A. The evidence for the evolution of brain size is clear.
    1. *Australopithecus* fossils had a brain capacity of 400 cc.; by 3 million years ago, hominids (named *homo habilis* by Louis Leakey) had brain capacities of around 600 cc.

   2. By 2 million years ago an organism called *homo erectus* had a
      brain capacity of about 1,000 cc.
   3. Modern-day humans have a brain capacity of 1400 cc.
   B. The advantages of larger brains, however, and the conditions
      under which they evolved are controversial subjects among
      physical anthropologists and paleontologists; speculations and
      conclusions about these issues are strictly inferences at this time.
IV. Most current speculation among paleontologists and physical
    anthropologists about why larger brains developed is tied to tool use.
   A. It is axiomatic among these scientists (as it is in the culture as a
      whole) that tool use gives humans a measure of control over the
      environment and thus tool use is an important step in human
      evolution.
   B. It is inferred by some scientists that the larger the brain, the
      greater the potential for tool development.
   C. Some paleontologists and physical anthropologists want to draw a
      causal relationship between increasing brain size and tool use.
      However, it may not be that tool use alone encouraged the
      development of larger brains.
      1. During this period in human evolution, there is evidence of the
         development of culture—living in groups, cooperative food
         gathering, specialization of tasks among members of the group,
         etc. The development of culture is clearly related to brain size.
      2. Larger brain size allows for more flexible behavior and
         adaptation; within a culture, behavior (such as tool use) can
         easily be influenced by the culture itself as by physical
         environmental factors.
      3. Is increasing tool use a simple factor of increasing brain size
         alone, or was the increasing use and development of tools an
         indirect result of increasing brain size—that is, was increasing
         use and development of tools encouraged by a variety of
         cultural factors? Any answers to this question would now have
         to be inferences and speculations, but I believe that the
         variable of culture should be taken into account by paleontolo-
         gists and physical anthropologists as they continue their search
         for more knowledge about human evolution.

     When I help students write outlines, I insist that the students write
sentence outlines. Notice that each item in the examples I have just given is a
full grammatical statement, not a key word or phrase. When you write full
grammatical statements, you tell yourself clearly what you want to say about
this key term/idea at this point in your paper. The sentence outline, as an
outline should, reproduces your central argument and thus keeps the argument on track. Very often you will find that you can use these sentences in
your outline as the topic sentences for the relevant sections of your paper.

     As you write your paper, plan to work back and forth between your
current draft and your outline, your current draft and your abstract. Always
keep your thesis statement in front of you. Remain flexible. If, as you write,
you find a better way to express your argument, make any necessary changes
in your outline or abstract.

I realize that I am repeating myself, but I think it is necessary for me to come back to a central idea that I have pushed hard throughout this book. When you were researching, I stressed that it was imperative that you always have a sense of direction. I said that your conclusions might, and should, change if the evidence indicated such changes. The same principles apply to the paper-writing process. As you spell out your argument in your paper, it is very possible that you will discover that your idea has a different shape from the shape you originally thought it had. You must write a paper that accurately reflects the idea that you have in your head; if this idea changes its form as you write, then the paper must change. But the paper must be coherent, just as your idea must be coherent. When you change one part of your idea, that change affects other parts of the idea. Therefore, you must always have a map of the central idea/argument so that you always have a sense of direction. I stress, over and over again, the relationships among ideas because it is these relationships that make an argument an argument. Otherwise, in your head and on paper, you have a series of ideas that float about with no core of meaning.

d. Reviewing your evidence: Your notecards

Once you have developed your conclusions and your argument in your abstract and/or outline, it is safe to review your notecards and evidence. I say it is now "safe" because you have focused your paper on what *you* want to say rather than having your paper dictated by your evidence and sources. Once you have your thesis statement and the outline of your argument, your evidence can play only its proper role, which is to support *your* argument.

I will talk to you in some detail about how to decide what evidence to use and how to incorporate it into your text in the next part of this section and in Section 6. But first I want to talk about a mechanical issue, keeping the record straight.

As you write your paper, all your mental energy must be focused on presenting your ideas to your readers. But, because your explanation must include the evidence you've gathered from a variety of sources, you must keep a record *in your text* of the sources of the various pieces of evidence you use. In the final draft of your paper, you must be able to document, accurately, all of the material you have taken from others.

I will give you a couple of techniques you can use to keep track of the sources of each piece of information as you write. You may use the systems I offer, or develop your own system. Regardless of the system you use, it must meet these criteria:

▶ You must use a system that tells you, in the text of your paper, that the information you have just used is taken from one or more of your sources.
▶ You must use a system that tells you, in the text of the paper, what that specific source is.
▶ You must use a system that allows you to go directly from the text to the

appropriate notecard, so that you can double-check the information to make sure that what you have in your text is accurate.

▶ You should use a system that will allow you to document your sources in the final draft with a minimum of wasted time and energy.

If the number of notecards and bibliography/reference cards you are going to use in writing the paper is fairly small (say, thirty), the following system should work:

▶ Whenever you use information from one of your notecards, in the text of your paper, immediately after the sentence that contains the information, write the following information in parentheses:
  ▷ the author's full name
  ▷ a short version of the title
  ▷ the page number

Include all this information for each source you refer to.

Example

Several experts in the field of diplomatic history have pointed out that the United States tends to take a confrontive rather than a conciliatory stance in its dealings with other countries (John Williams, *Dip. History of US*, p. 497; *Looking at Diplomacy*, pp. 297–300; Elwin Carter, "US and Other Nations," p. 406). Confrontation certainly characterizes the way the United States handled the Cuban missile crisis. The US acted immediately, creating a blockade around Cuba to prevent the delivery of more missiles from the USSR and declaring that the firing of these missiles would be met with full military retaliation (Robert Corwin, *Cuban Crisis*, pp. 905–30) . . .

If you find that you will be using a great number of bibliography cards and notecards, a more elaborate system might be more efficient. A system I developed for myself involves coding bibliography and notecards, then using these codes in the text of the paper. Here's how I code my cards:

▶ Pull all of the *bibliography cards*. Put them in alphabetical order, according to the author's last name.

▶ Code these cards by using the alphabet. In the upper-right-hand corner, put an A on the first card, a B on the second, a C on the third, and so on. If you have more than twenty-six cards, start with double letters (AA on the twenty-seventh, BB on the twenty-eighth, CC on the twenty-ninth, and so on).

▶ Now separate the *notecards*, making a separate stack for the notes taken from the sources indicated by each bibliography card. For example, make a stack of all the notes you took from the source indicated on bibliography card A, another stack for the notes taken from the source indicated on bibliography card B, and so on.

▶ When all the notecards have been separated and stacked, code them with the bibliography card letter, and simply number them. Thus, the first card in stack A will be A1, the second will be A2, the third A3, and so on.

When you are writing, you will code your information with the letter and number of the card from which the information is taken. No matter how much rewriting you do, you will always be able to identify the source of the information because you will be able to get straight back to the original notecard. When your final draft is complete, you can write up your footnotes *and* double-check the notecard to be sure that the information or quotation you have used in your paper is absolutely correct. The system can save you time and frustration.

e. Incorporating evidence into the text: A preview

Once you have decided how you are going to keep track of your sources as you write your paper, you are ready to decide what evidence you are going to use.

▶ With your outline or abstract in front of you, review all of your notecards and the summaries you have written on the backs of your bibliography cards.

▶ Make a separate stack of these cards for each section and division of your paper.

▶ Read over each section of your abstract or outline to remind yourself of the major points you want to make in each section. Select the specific evidence you want to use in each section by using these criteria:
  ▷ what information/evidence helps you *explain* this point?
  ▷ what information/evidence helps you *substantiate* this point?
  ▷ what information/evidence helps you *illustrate* this point?

Your goal is to end up with separate stacks of cards that correspond to each section of your paper; these stacks should include *only* that information/evidence directly relevant to each section. It is very possible that, when you have finished sorting, you will have a stack of cards left over that you will not use in the paper. That's fine. Your goal is not to squeeze in everything, whether it fits or not.

In Section 6 of this book I talk in more detail about ways to incorporate your evidence into the text of your paper. Let me preview and summarize the main points here.

In most cases, you will be *summarizing* information, referring to the work of others in the context of your idea.

Examples

Most studies have shown that DMSO is effective in alleviating pain (E6, F7, H12, B4).

Smith and Hardison concluded that the adverse side effects of DMSO are insignificant (R2).

The dependence of the South on slaves as a form of cheap labor is evident in the statistics alone; in 1850, there were 50,000 slaves in Georgia (B9) and 70,000 in North Carolina (D14) working in the fields; only 5,000 white men were paid to do hard field work in these states in the same year (F12).

Quote the words of your source *only* when the point you want to make *is* the particular way the author sees or assesses an idea.

> ### Examples
>
> Most experts agree that slavery was an important factor in the South's secession (F12, J16), but Harvey Corker concludes that "slavery was *the* issue over which North and South went to war." (H7)
>
> As Mark Mellon, research director at MIT, sees it, genetic research is "in the Dark Ages." (B5)

For further advice about proper (and improper) ways to introduce your evidence into your text, see Section 6 of this book.

D.   Drafting and Revising

No matter what type of research paper you are writing—a primary research report, a review of the literature, or a critical paper—you should plan to write several drafts. As I pointed out in the opening part of this section, you can make the act of writing far easier for yourself if you focus on one mental activity at a time rather than trying to accomplish several different tasks at once.

▶ Your first objective is to make sure you see the basic shape of your argument, that you have included all the main points in your argument, that these main points are in their proper places, that you clearly know (and show) how these points are related to each other to form your central idea. Don't worry about spelling, punctuation, or grammar at this stage. Your only concern is to put enough on paper so that you tell yourself what shape your argument has.

▶ Once the general shape of the argument is clear to you, you must create a map of the paper that you will use as a guide as you write individual sections and parts (see C.2.c of this section).

▶ As you write specific sections, you have two objectives:

▷ You must have a system of keeping track of the sources of the specific information/evidence you are now incorporating into your text (see C.2.d of this section).

▷ Your *major* objective is to make your ideas clear to your readers.

You can save yourself a great deal of time and energy once you start your second draft if you

▷ write on only one side of the piece of paper
▷ write only on every other line of each sheet
▷ leave wide margins on each sheet

These simple devices will allow you to change parts of your draft without having to copy over parts of the text that don't need to be changed. By writing on every other line and leaving wide margins, you can add sentences or change sentences without having to recopy. If you write on only one side of each sheet of paper, you can cut your draft apart and paste paragraphs and sections together in different ways if you decide to introduce an idea in a different part of the paper.

As you write specific sections of your paper, never forget that you are presenting an argument, which means that you are relating certain ideas to other ideas to create a meaning. If you expect your readers to understand this argument, then you must explain clearly what you are talking about, and you must *show* your readers *exactly* how each idea is related to the others. Never assume that your readers know what you mean. Even if these readers are acquainted with your subject matter, they cannot know how you see this subject until you *tell* them how you see it. Such explanations apply to all parts of the argument.

Never introduce facts or information unless you have shown your readers what to do with these facts or this information. Each section, each paragraph of your paper should include a statement (the sooner, the better) that clearly states the point you are making here. As you complete one point and move on to the next, show your readers how the two points are related. Don't assume they know; spell it out.

At this stage of the writing process you should be writing in complete sentences, and you should be looking for the words and sentence structures that best express your ideas, but don't worry yet about spelling, punctuation, and grammatical points like subject/verb agreement. If a paragraph doesn't seem to be coming out right, refer back to your outline. Say to yourself, "What is the point I want to make here?" Or go back and reread the two or three pages that precede the paragraph. Remind yourself where you are going.

▶   As you finish individual sections, keep going back to the whole paper. Reread the entire draft over frequently, matching it against your outline or abstract. As you reread, you are checking to make sure that each section is fitting properly with the rest of the argument. As you note problems in the "flow" of the argument, do whatever revising is necessary. Write a note to yourself in the margin, expressing the problem.

As you revise, keep your draft as clean as possible. You must be able to read it easily at all points in the writing process. If certain pages become so messy that you can't read them easily, recopy these pages right away. If you can't follow what you are saying, you are losing control.

Be sure to number each page of the draft, and renumber the pages as necessary. How can you read your draft if you don't know which page comes next?

▶   When you have read over the entire draft from beginning to end and you are satisfied that your argument is spelled out so clearly that your readers will readily understand the idea you are setting forth in this paper, you have a final rough draft. Only three more steps are left.

► When you have a final rough draft, you must double-check the accuracy of the information you have taken from your sources, and you must document these sources. Using the coding system in the text, begin with your first reference to a source. Check what you have in the text against the information or quotation on the notecard. Then document the source (using notecard and bibliography card), using the proper documentation form. For more information on documentation and documentation systems, see Section 7.

► The next step is to proofread your final rough draft. Examine each sentence and paragraph carefully. Make sure all words are spelled correctly, make sure all sentences are punctuated properly (including quotation marks), make sure that you have used one basic tense for the paper, check pronoun references, and so on.

► Making the final clean draft of the paper should be a simple act of transcription. You should never make a substantive change in sentences or paragraphs at this stage. A substantive change in a sentence changes its meaning, which in turn calls for changes in other sentences in the paragraph, and you are, suddenly, back to revising. You should not be revising when you make your final clean draft.

E. May I Use the First Person in My Paper? And Other Issues Related to Style

One question that students often ask me when they are writing their research papers is, "May I use *I* in this paper?" I cannot always answer the question for them. Because conventions of style differ from discipline to discipline and from type of paper to type of paper, your instructor is the person who can tell you if the first person is appropriate in the specific paper you are preparing for him or her. So, your safest course is to address specific questions about style to your instructor. However, there are general guidelines that experienced writers use for determining the style and tone of papers (not only research papers but all types of expository writing). In the rest of this subsection I'll briefly discuss some of these guidelines; they could help you determine the most appropriate style for your paper.

At the beginning of this section I talked about the audience for whom you are writing your paper and the image of yourself that you want to project to this audience. Thinking about yourself as a speaker and thinking about the audience you are addressing put your paper in a communication context. If, when you write, you think about yourself as communicating with a group of readers, then one issue that arises is, "What is my relationship with the members of my audience?" Determining the relationship between themselves as speakers/writers and their audience/readers helps experienced writers decide the style and tone of the prose they are composing. Let us say, for example, that you are a senior psychology major who has done a research project on teenage drug abuse. If you stop to consider it, you would discuss your work differently if you were writing to a close friend, if you were talking to a class of junior high students, and if you were presenting your work at a conference of social workers, psychologists, and school officials. The differences in the way you present your work are determined by the differences in your relationship with each of these groups.

In writing to a close friend, you would probably be very casual. You might use slang and colloquial expressions. You probably wouldn't worry about your sentence structure and punctuation. Instead of presenting your ideas in a tight, logical fashion, you'd probably dash off ideas as they came into your mind. It would be natural to make connections between what you've learned in your study and instances of drug abuse that you've noticed among the people you know. You'd probably refer to events that you and your friend have shared. In other words, in this letter you'd use a casual or informal style; it is the most appropriate style for this communication context because you are "talking" to someone you know very well, someone with whom you share a certain intimacy.

However, in making a presentation on this same study on teenage drug abuse at a conference, your style and tone would change because you have a different relationship with this audience. In this group of psychologists, social workers, and school officials, there are probably many people you do not know. Even if some of the members of the audience are friends of yours, this is a "professional" communication situation and you are playing the role of "budding professional." You want the members of the audience to see you as a knowledgeable, reasonable, thoughtful researcher. Because the situation is more formal, you would use a more formal style.

The communication context of the research paper you are now writing is much closer to the presentation of the study on teenage drug abuse at a conference than to writing about the subject to a close friend. Thus your paper will be in a more formal style.

In writing your paper in a more formal style, here are some of the features of your prose that you will want to pay attention to.

▶   You will want to avoid slang, colloquialisms, and informal speech mannerisms like "well," "you know," "as I was saying," etc.

     This diction is usually inappropriate in a more formal communication situation because it implies a casual, more intimate relationship with your audience than actually exists. Even if you have decided to write your paper for your classmates, you are speaking to them in the more formal context of the classroom. You want them to take you and your work seriously. In formal situations, slang will work against your efforts to communicate, not only because some of your readers may not know what the slang words mean but also because slang tends to be very vague and thus imprecise.

▶   You will use the jargon or technical terminology associated with your subject because it is the most precise language to use; at the same time, in using this jargon you will always consider the amount of knowledge your audience has about this subject.

If you are positive that your readers know what a term means (and thus know the concept that it represents), you will use the term without explaining it. If you know your readers do not know the term (and thus the concept it represents), you must be prepared to educate your readers about this concept as you make your own point. And remember: explanations need not be exhaustive. You can tell your readers only what they need to know in order to understand the point you are making.

▶ In deciding whether or not to use the first person in your paper, Mary-Claire van Leunen in her *Handbook for Scholars* (New York: Alfred A. Knopf, 1978) offers a nice rule of thumb: "When you're a part of your story, bring yourself in directly, not in a submerged or twisted way. . . . When you have nothing to do with your story, leave yourself out" (pp. 39–40).

This simple guideline can also help you decide whether your own personal experiences belong in your paper. From the beginning, were you and your experiences meant to be a part of the subject you were researching? If they were, then references to yourself are an appropriate part of your paper and should be presented in the first person. If you and your personal experiences were not intended to be a part of the subject you were researching, then they probably do not belong in your paper.

Many of you may have been taught not to use the first person in any expository prose. This ban on the first person is all tied up with the development of the modern scientific method and an approach to knowledge that could be summed up this way: "The role of the scientist/researcher is to observe and record phenomena that have no connection with the scientist/researcher herself. Thus, in reporting what she has observed, the researcher/scientist will obviously not appear in the paper." If you are writing a critical paper, however, you are certainly a part of that paper since the inferences and judgments you have made—your ideas—are the major informing element of the paper. This fact does not automatically mean that each of your inferences or judgments needs to be prefaced with "I think" or "I feel" or "It is my opinion." Your readers will assume that inferential and judgmental statements are your inferences and judgments unless you indicate otherwise. It is for this reason that I urge you in Section 6 (see 6.B.2) to name in your sentences the authors of the ideas that you have taken from your sources.

If you feel comfortable that you know which ideas are yours and which belong to your sources, and if you realize that your readers will assume that an inference or judgment is yours unless you tell them otherwise, you should find that you really won't have to use the first person very often. You will probably notice that frequently, when you are not reiterating the opinions of other authors, you are saying that the facts speak for themselves; the most accurate way of expressing this idea is, "However, it is clear from the evidence that . . ." or "There is no substantial evidence for these positions." On those few occasions when you feel that you need to tell the reader directly that a certain idea is yours, you should feel free to do so in the first person. If your instructor has told you not to use the first person, you will have to refer to yourself in the third person: "This author has concluded . . ."; "It is the opinion of this author that . . ."

▶ Be very careful about the use of the first person plural (*we, us, our*).

Such pronouns are appropriate only when they are used to represent a specific group of which you are actually a member and only when you have made it clear to your reader which group you are referring to. If a music teacher is addressing other music teachers about common teaching experiences, he could appropriately write, "We music teachers often find that our students . . ." But don't use the editorial *we* as a roundabout way of saying *I*. And, if the group you are referring to is the human race, it is clearer to say *people* or *human beings* than *we*, at least in initial references to this group.

▶ Whether or not you use the second person (*you, your*) will again depend on your relationship with your readers and the purpose you have in writing your paper.

A *you* in a paper automatically means *me* to the reader; if the remark seems to me, the reader, to apply to me, all is well; but I resent it when you make a remark in your paper about *you* (me) that I don't think applies to me. Perhaps you've noticed that the second person is usually found in prose intended to instruct readers how to do something or to exhort them to think, feel, or behave in a particular way. If the purpose of your paper is to instruct (as it is the purpose of this book) or if it is to exhort your readers to change their ways, then the second person is appropriate. If your paper is not a "how-to" paper or a piece of persuasive writing, the second person isn't appropriate. Also, watch out for *you* as it is used in informal prose to represent *anybody/everybody* as in "When a dog growls, you assume it will bite." In more formal writing, it is better to use either *a person, people*, or *one*: "When embarrassed, a person (one) is likely to become hostile or defensive."

▶ Finally, formal style is usually characterized by paragraphs and sentences that are self-explanatory.

Because your readers cannot know how you have put your ideas and the evidence together, all of these relationships must be made absolutely explicit. This is the reason that writers, in formal communication contexts, usually use a topic sentence that gives their readers an overview of the point that is being introduced; this is the reason that writers are careful to use transitions; and this is the reason that sentences in formal writing tend to be longer and to fall into the category of complex sentences (sentences with one or more dependent clauses).

In talking to a friend it might be appropriate to say "I left the party early. I was sick" and to leave it to the listener to infer a cause-effect relationship. In formal writing, you don't want to take the chance that the reader might not see the cause-effect relationship, so you make it explicit: "I left the party because I was not feeling well."

Precision is the other reason that sentences tend to be longer in formal writing. You want to qualify your point so that the statement is exact: "In this case, Outer Slobovia felt that if it did not send troops to the Isle of Herron, it risked losing the support of its allies, Inner Slobovia and Alcimene."

As a writer addressing a group of people whom you do not know very well, your major objective is your readers' complete understanding of your exact point. Thus, above all, you want your prose to be clear and precise. You can judge the clarity of your prose by asking, "Will my readers comprehend my point after one reading of this sentence/paragraph?" You can judge the precision of your prose by asking, "Will my readers see exactly what I mean here?" If you are not sure how your readers would answer these questions, you may want to ask one of your readers to read your draft and to tell you what messages he/she is receiving from your prose. If you have decided to write your paper for the members of your class, it shouldn't be too hard to find such a reader.

Before I leave this issue of more formal style, there is a warning I must give you. Formality of style is not measured by the "look" or the "sound" of the words on the page. To put it another way, you are not making your paper more formal if you simply search around for the longest, classiest words you can find and then string them together in phrases that have a certain "ring" to them—"the proposition of annihilation tactics"; "integrated monitored hardware."

I realize that you are tempted to throw big words around in long, convoluted sentences because such sentences seem to look and sound like the sentences of the authors you've been reading. It is natural for you to assume that you need to impress your readers and that the best way to impress them is to sound impressive. I see papers every day that are collections of such impressive sounding sentences; unfortunately, very often they don't communicate any ideas to me. A few weeks ago when I was discussing a collection of such sentences with Tony Abena, the student who had written them, Tony had a flash of insight: "I'm writing to impress, not to express," he said. I am borrowing Tony's phrase because it says so well what many students are doing when they are trying to write in a formal style.

My usual response to the student who is working hard to impress me rather than to communicate with me is this. Words carry meanings for me. If a particular group of words doesn't make sense to me, I'm not impressed; I'm confused, frustrated, and angry. What impresses me is the idea that is expressed, the idea that is carried by the words. So, if you want to impress your readers, choose those words and phrases that best represent the idea you have in your mind. Those people who are worth impressing are too smart to be snowed by an avalanche of meaningless verbiage.

Section 6

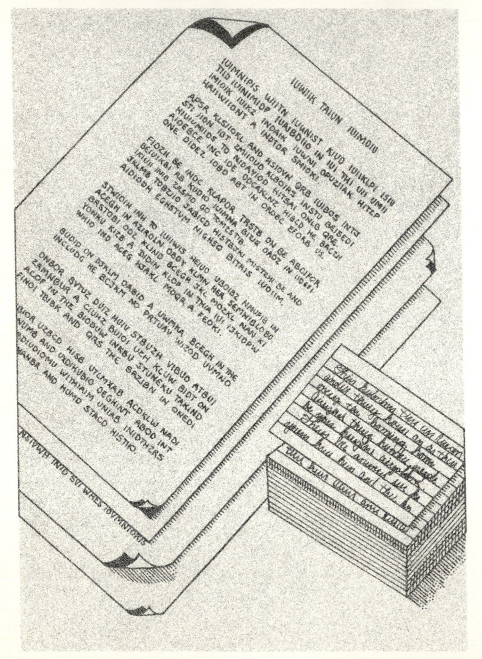

How to, and How not to, Incorporate Your Evidence into Your Paper

A. If You Don't Use and Acknowledge Your Sources Properly, You May End Up Plagiarizing

I don't like beginning this section with an unpleasant subject, but plagiarism is a serious offense and, after all the time and energy you have put into your research project up to this point, you certainly do not want your instructor to accuse you of having plagiarized parts of the paper you hand in. In my experience in working with students who are writing research papers, I have found that much plagiarism is unintentional. Papers, or parts of papers, are plagiarized not because the student intended to plagiarize but because the student either did not know how to use his sources properly or because the student did not know how to acknowledge his sources properly. To express it negatively, the purpose of this section is to save you from falling into unintentional plagiarism; to express it more positively, the purpose of this section is to show you how experienced writers follow the basic rule of using the ideas and works of others: giving credit where credit is due.

1. What plagiarism is

Quite simply, plagiarism is theft. Common thieves take cars, stereos, silverware, and other material goods that legally belong to others, then use this property as if it were rightfully theirs. Plagiarists steal the words, the ideas, and/or the work that rightfully belong to others. Plagiarists then present these words, ideas, and/or work as if this material were their own words, ideas, or work.

Just as there are laws against taking the material goods that belong to another, so there are laws against plagiarism. If you were to copy an article or the section of a book and publish this work under your own name, clearly implying that this work was yours, you could be taken to a court of law. But you do not have to publish plagiarized material to be in serious trouble. College instructors put plagiarism in the same category as cheating on exams, and punish offenders with stiff penalties.

Obviously, you'd be in serious trouble if you intentionally passed off the work, the ideas, or the words of another person as your own. You'd be in serious trouble if you put your name on a paper that was, in fact, copied from a published book or article. You'd be in serious trouble if part of your paper were words copied from a book or article that were not enclosed in quotation marks. You'd be in trouble if all or part of your paper was illegitimate paraphrase (see subsection B.3).

Occasionally students are guilty of premeditated or intentional plagiarism. Consciously they attempt to pass off the work of others as their own. But, as I've said, many cases of plagiarism are cases of unintentional plagiarism. I am sure that you don't want to be one of those students who plagiarize without realizing that they are plagiarizing.

2. Common sources of unintentional plagiarism

If plagiarism is the act of presenting the words, ideas, or work of others as if they were your own, then the proper use of the work of others is

always give credit where credit is due.

Or, to put it another way, in our papers we frankly tell our readers that we are making use of the material of another, and we give our readers all the information they need to find and read the original source. In academic circles the two basic ways we give credit where credit is due are these:

▶ We frankly acknowledge to our readers that certain ideas or work has been taken from other sources by saying so in the text of the paper and/ or by documenting the sources of these ideas in our papers. In Section 7 of this book and the appendixes that follow, I show you the three basic modes of documentation. Although these forms differ, each is an accepted system for giving credit where credit is due.

▶ We frankly acknowledge to our readers that the words we are using are the words of another person by putting these words in quotation marks *and* documenting that source by using one of the accepted modes of documentation. I talk more about the proper ways of quoting material in subsection B.4 of this section.

Often students neglect to follow these simple procedures for giving credit where credit is due. Here are some of the reasons I've discovered for unintentional plagiarism.

▶ One major source of unintentional plagiarism is carelessness in the research process.

In Section 4 I stressed the importance of using notecards or a comparable system for keeping track of your sources; one reason that I stressed careful notetaking is to avoid the risk of unintentional plagiarism.

You can, if you are sloppy, fail to make a record of the source of a piece of evidence (forgetting to record the author or the title of the work, or the page number on which this information was given). Or you can fail to keep a complete record of the necessary bibliographic information for the source. If, when you write your paper, you want to use this information, you are going to have trouble giving the credit you are expected to give.

In Section 4 I also stressed how important it is to put quotation marks around the exact words of an author on your notecards. If your notecard doesn't indicate that the words are the words of the author, you will assume that these words are yours and thus fail to give credit where credit is due. If you are not careful to paraphrase properly, you may have notecards that are illegitimate paraphrases (see subsection B.3).

Thus, carelessness in the research process can lead to inadvertent plagiarism.

▶ Another source of unintentional plagiarism is sloppiness while writing your paper.

You may fall into plagiarism if you fail to keep track of the sources of your evidence in your drafts as you write and revise your paper. You can easily avoid this source of unintentional plagiarism by developing a system of noting your sources as you write (see Section 5.C.2.d).

▶ A more general source of unintentional plagiarism is ignorance of the "giving-credit-where-credit-is-due" rule.

Many students unknowingly fall into plagiarism because they do not know that they are obliged to give credit where credit is due, or because they do not know the proper ways to give such credit.

▶ Perhaps the most common source of unintentional plagiarism is the "passive-sponge" approach to research.

If a student mindlessly gathers great quantities of information without digesting, thinking about, and assessing this information as she researches, it is very easy for her to fall into plagiarism because she can easily assume that everything she reads is, somehow, *the truth.* She will not see a need to document sources or to give credit to specific experts because she will assume that all of the evidence she has gathered falls into the category of received truth or common knowledge, common knowledge like table salt is sodium chloride or the American Civil War occurred between 1861 and 1865.

Or, a passive sponge may panic when he sits down to write his paper. Suddenly he may realize that all he has is material that belongs to others. Because he has not been developing his own ideas, he is trapped into following the ideas in his sources. He may conclude—probably accurately—that everything in his paper will have to be acknowledged as belonging to others. He may find himself using long passages from his sources, either quoting directly or falling into illegitimate paraphrase. Overwhelmed and oppressed by the idea of having to document everything in the paper because the paper actually belongs to his sources, he may rebel and document haphazardly.

Throughout this book I have attempted to save you from falling into the traps that lie in wait for passive sponges. Saving you from unintentional plagiarism is only one reason I have stressed taking control of your research project from the beginning of the process. But obviously one of the advantages of taking control of the research process from the beginning is that, when you reach the point of writing your papers, you have a clear sense of your own ideas and the debts you owe to others. Thus, if you have taken your notes carefully and systematically, if you have been careful to make out bibliography/reference cards, and especially if you have used your Researcher's Notebook as I have advised you to do, you have the necessary basic foundation for avoiding plagiarism.

However, you may still have questions about the best way of incorporating your evidence into your text and the best way of giving credit where credit is due. These are the issues I will discuss in the rest of this section. So, when you have a good, solid first rough draft of your paper, when you have developed a system for keeping track of your sources as you write and revise, and when you have reviewed your evidence and decided what you want to use, you should stop and read over all of the subsections of this section.

B.   Using and Acknowledging Your Sources . . . Properly

Obvious signs of plagiarism are not the only problems instructors find in the way that students use, or abuse, sources. Whenever I read a student paper that includes a large number of direct quotations, particularly a large number of *long* direct quotations, I worry that I am reading the paper of a student who has allowed herself to be used by her sources. Instead of writing a paper in which she is expressing her own point of view, supported by evidence from various sources, she is letting others write her paper for her. Whenever I read a paper in which the same source is footnoted in paragraph after paragraph, or page after page, I worry that I am reading another paper in which a student has allowed himself to be used by his sources. Instead of developing and formulating his own point of view, this student is content to repeat the argument of one of his sources.

Throughout the research process your goal has been to use your sources, rather than having your sources use you. Now, at this last stage of the research process, you do not want to fall victim to your sources. So I will test your patience by repeating, one last time, that in your paper you are articulating and presenting *your* perception of the subject you have been investigating. The phrase "your perception of the subject" should not be read as "a completely new, original, unique perception of the subject." If I were to read your paper, I would not expect your conclusions to be startlingly new, nor does your instructor. Your instructor and I both know that Einsteins and Newtons are rare birds indeed; I know that I am not capable of such dramatically different perceptions of the world, and I know that my perceptions of various subjects are highly influenced by the perceptions of others. Your instructor and I do not expect your paper to be original in this sense; what we do expect to see in your paper are very obvious and clear signs that *you* have made *your own decision* about the way the intellectual puzzle you have been working on should be put together. A passive-sponge paper sounds like a person who would say to you, "Mom has told me not to major in chemistry because . . ." A researcher-as-detective paper sounds like the person who says "I have decided to major in geology because, as my Dad says, geology is . . . Also, as Uncle Harry points out, a geology major would . . . Besides, several people who have majored in geology have found that . . ."

Confidence is the key, the confidence that you have drawn your own conclusion and that there is a solid basis for it. Just as it is natural for my hypothetical student to explain her decision to major in geology by calling on the arguments and facts offered by her Dad and her Uncle Harry and other majors, so in your paper you should find that you automatically refer to the sources upon which you have drawn to form your conclusion. You should find it natural to say, "After considering the theories of X, Y, and Z, I find that Z's argument is most convincing because . . ." or "I agree with Jane Doe's assessment of the problem." Because you have worked out your own picture of the puzzle, you won't be tempted to present Jane Doe's or Z's argument in great detail because you know that their arguments are *their* perceptions of the puzzle and, while you agree with their general perceptions, you have your own reasons for doing so. You will use Doe's work, or Z's, and that of your other sources as it suits your needs.

I urged you to do your first full draft without your notecards so that you would have the confidence that I've been talking about. Now that you have this confidence, let's talk about using those sources you've decided to use.

1.   Use what you need, where you need it—and document what you've used

In most cases, as you write your paper, you should find that the evidence you are using is either

> discrete pieces of information from your sources

or

> summaries of the conclusions, work, or opinions of one or more of the experts you've read.

Using sources does not imply quoting the sources directly, and, in fact, you should be very judicious in using direct quotations. Look upon direct quotations only as supporting evidence, never as a substitute for your own expression of the point you want to make. You should use the exact words of others *only* when the expert's words are the best or most direct illustration of that expert's point of view. In subsection B.4, I talk at length about how to quote your sources effectively and properly. But here let me illustrate what I mean when I say that in most cases you will be using discrete pieces of information or summarizing the work or conclusions of others.

USING DISCRETE PIECES OF INFORMATION

Example 1

Your paper

Breakdowns of expenditures on arms throughout the world between 1971 and 1980 show that the Third World countries are increasing their military expenditures while, in comparison, the amount being spent by the U.S. and the U.S.S.R. is decreasing. In 1971, Third World countries accounted for only 9 percent of worldwide military expenditures; by 1980, the proportion had increased to 16 percent of the total.[9]

Your notecard

world military expenditures

1971	1980
USA 32%	USA 24%
USSR 25%	USSR 24%
Third World 9%	Third World 16%

p. xix, Stockholm International Peace Research Inst., *SIPRI Yearbook, Armaments 1981*

Your documentation (humanities form)

9. Stockholm International Peace Research Institute, *SIPRI Yearbook of World Armaments and Disarmament, 1981* (London: Taylor and Frances Ltd., 1981), xix.

Example 2

Your paper

When considering the reign of the Ayatollah Khomeini in Iran, one must always keep in mind two central points about the Islamic religion. The first is that the essence of Islam is submission.[11] The other is that the Islamic religion pervades all aspects of the state. Whereas in Western countries one can distinguish between the laws of a particular religion and the secular laws of the state (like civil and criminal codes), in an Islamic state all the laws of the country are dictated by the religious laws.[12]

Your notecards

"*Islam* means submission, the believer's submission to Allah. The word expresses, first and foremost, a feeling of dependency on an unbounded omnipotence to which man must submit and resign his will. . . . Submission is the dominant principle inherent in all manifestations of Islam: in its ideas, forms, ethics, and worship."

pp. 3–4, Goldziher, *Islamic Theology & Law*

"But the conduct of life in conformity to the law includes more than ritual. For in Islam, religious law encompasses all legal branches: civil, criminal, and constitutional."

p. 54, Goldziher, *Islamic Theology & Law*

**Your documentation
(humanities form)**
11. Ignaz Goldziher, *Introduction
to Islamic Theology and Law,*
trans. Andras and Ruth Hamori,
Modern Classics in Near Eastern
Studies (Princeton, N.J.: Princeton University Press, 1981), 3–4.
12. Ibid., 54.

SUMMARIZING THE WORK OF OTHERS

Example 1

Your paper

Recent studies indicate that the
medical benefits of DMSO
outweigh potential side effects
(Jones 1981; Smith 1979; Wilson
and Johnson 1980).

**Your documentation
(author-date form)**

The reference to the articles by
Jones, Smith, and Wilson and
Johnson in the body of your paper is comparable to a footnote
citing these three articles. The
reference tells us that the studies
of these experts all point to the
conclusion you've stated. In the
Reference List at the end of your
paper, you will give complete bibliographic information about
these three sources.

Example 2

Your paper

In his recent study of Supreme
Court Justice Felix Frankfurter,
H. N. Hirsch joins other
historians and political scientists
who are exploring the
possibilities of psychobiography.[21]

**Your documentation
(humanities form)**

21. H. N. Hirsch, *The Enigma of
Felix Frankfurter* (New York:
Basic Books, Inc., 1981). See pp.
3–10.

Since your reference is to the entire book, your note need not
give any specific page numbers.
Here, however, you suggest that
your reader look at the first chapter (pp. 3–10) because on these
pages Hirsch discusses the how's
and why's of his use of psychological theories in this biography.

Example 3

Your paper

Irene Athey points out that research indicates a strong correla-
tion between a child's self-con-
cept and his/her reading
achievement.[17] These findings,
combined with other research on
the self-images of dyslexics,
would suggest that college-level
students who suffer from
dyslexia would have more
negative self-concepts than
would college students who have
always had average or
better-than-average reading skills.

Your notecard

"In general, the research literature suggests that good readers
tend to have more positive self
concepts than poor readers (*26,
40, 41, 43, 57, 78*). This finding
seems to hold for a variety of
measures of self concept, and for
all grade levels from one through
nine. More specifically, feelings of
adequacy and personal worth,
self-confidence and self-reliance
seem to emerge as important
factors in the relationship with
reading achievement. Conversely,
underachieving readers tend to
be characterized by immaturity,
impulsivity, and negative feelings
concerning themselves and their
world (*7, 8, 56, 69*)."

p. 110, Athey in Singer & Ruddell, *Theo. Models*

**Your documentation
(humanities form)**

17."Affective Factors in Reading,"
in *Theoretical Models and Processes of Reading,* ed. Harry
Singer and Robert Ruddell (New-
ark, Del.: International Reading
Association, 1970), 110.

Notice that in your paper you
must give credit to Athey for
summarizing the results of the
research.

To give you a clearer sense of the way that information from other
sources is digested and used by a researcher for her own purposes, I am now
going to show you a short excerpt from a research paper I wrote several
years ago, and excerpts from the sources I used in this paragraph of my
paper.

Take a little time to compare the original sources with my use of the
information. Pay close attention to the focal points, or points of view, of my
paragraph and the paragraphs from which I took ideas and information. My
point, summarized in the first sentence of the paragraph ("Once come to
Court . . ."), was developed from my reading of Zagorin, Cheyney, Stone, and
others. I built my idea from their ideas and the information they used. But

notice that each of us has a different point of view, a different argument that each of us is developing.

The Final Draft of My Paper

Thus, as the Queen called on her nobility to live up to their responsibilities and return to the land, economic realities and the centralization of power created a counter-force, pulling them toward London and the Court.

Once come to Court, however, the nobleman found the road to power and riches anything but a primrose path. The golden apples of "titles and places of honour, . . . rewards of land or money, grants of valuable fiscal privileges under the royal prerogative, such as monopolies and custom farms, miscellaneous rights in the crown's gift . . . and appointment to office" were tightly held by Elizabeth and her intimates.[14] To earn such an apple the courtier had to attract the Queen's eye and ear, and this meant working one's way up the ladder of preferment by winning patrons whose "letters of introduction" were paid for with promises and gold. The process was costly, in moral as well as monetary terms. The constant need to jockey for favorable positions, and the whimsies of the Queen herself, bred envy and hatred among her courtiers. Often the Court was split into dangerous and vicious factions; the infighting of the friends of the Earl of Essex and the Cecils darkened the last years of Elizabeth's reign.[15] Moreover, the Virgin Queen, who was always frugal with her favors, became excessively parsimonious in her later years.[16] In the 1590s a courtier often found the efforts of many years rewarded with only bitterness and a long list of debts.

[14] Perez Zagorin, *The Court and the Country: The Beginning of the English Revolution* (New York: Atheneum, 1970), 47–48.
[15] Zagorin, 47; Edward Cheyney, *A History of England from the Defeat of the Armada to the Death of Elizabeth*, 1 (London and New York: Longmans, Green and Co., 1914), 49–50.
[16] Lawrence Stone, *The Crisis of the Aristocracy 1558–1641*, abridged ed. (New York: Oxford University Press, 1967), 94; Cheyney 1:9. Stone ties James I's notorious granting of knighthoods in part to a "fierce pressure from below from a squirearchy too long starved of titles" (*Crisis of the Aristocracy*, 42).

Footnote 14

Original passage from Perez Zagorin, *The Court and the Country: The Beginning of the English Revolution* (New York: Atheneum, 1970), 47–48:

The Court's resources for gratifying the hope of preferment were of diverse kinds. They ranged from the bestowal of titles and places of honour, through rewards of land or money, grants of valuable fiscal privileges under the royal prerogative, such as monopolies and customs farms, miscellaneous rights in the crown's gift that could be a source of profit to their recipients, and appointment to office. The commonest aim, however, of the seeker after advancement was office, which might also afford access to other benefits obtainable in the Court. We shall therefore confine our attention to the nature and significance of office.[1]

In particular, we shall wish to consider how far officials constituted a *bloc* committed to the support of the King's power and whether they were a body socially distinct from men without Court affiliation.

Footnote 15

Original passage from Zagorin, 47:

> Beyond all these considerations, great rising and an eminent career in the Court were attended by envy, hatred, and faction. 'Happy the favourite,' wrote Fuller, 'that is raised without the ruin of another.'[2] The actors on the Stuart political scene long retained the memory of the rivalry between the Essex and Cecil factions and of Essex's fall and execution at the setting of Queen Elizabeth's reign. The reigns of James and Charles likewise witnessed the disgrace of such Court personages as the earls of Somerset and Suffolk, Bacon, and Bishop Williams, whose calamity pointed up the perils incident to high office. . . .

Original passage from Edward Cheyney, *A History of England from the Defeat of the Armada to the Death of Elizabeth*, 1 (London and New York: Longmans, Green and Co., 1914), 49–50:

> These relationships and instances of favoritism combined with influences of temperament and interest to group the men surrounding the queen into factions. These showed themselves sometimes in the council, but more frequently outside. The Cecils and Howards against the friends of Essex, the Norrises against the Knollys, Sir Walter Ralegh against his rivals, and many other factions and temporary intrigues divided the courtiers, fretted the queen, and weakened the government. The greater ministers for the most part rose above these quarrels, but they played a conspicuous part in the routine of court life and increased in bitterness in the later years of the queen's reign. Elizabeth's court was not characterized by high-mindedness or appreciation of the more delicate sentiments of life, and if actual violence and disorder were repressed, and if there was less open immorality than in some of the other courts of Europe, it was nevertheless filled with petty jealousies, conflicts and intrigues.

Footnote 16

Original passage from Lawrence Stone, *The Crisis of the Aristocracy 1558–1641*, abridged ed. (New York: Oxford University Press, 1967), 94:

> The instability of landed fortunes at this period was not the product of some strange freak of genetics which caused an abnormal proportion of stupid and dissolute children, or no children at all. To the inevitable changes wrought by the eccentricities of human reproductive capacity were added in the late sixteenth century exceptional temptations and compulsions to overspend on conspicuous consumption, royal service, or marriage portions, exceptional need for adaptability in estate manage-ment, novel opportunities and exceptional dangers in large-scale borrowing. Compensations were lacking during the reign of Elizabeth,

owing to exceptional stinginess in the distribution of royal favours and snobbish objections to marriage with heiresses of lower social status. To make matters worse, legal obstacles to breaking entails and selling land were exceptionally weak, and moral objections to the dismemberment of the family patrimony exceptionally feeble. A landed aristocracy has rarely had it so bad.

Original passage from Cheyney 1:9:

Elizabeth had few generous impulses. No one of the great men of her time, in literature, learning, civil, military or naval life was fully recognized or adequately rewarded by her. She was occasionally liberal to her favorites, but never lavish, except for her own personal adornment or gratification. While her mariners and soldiers starved, her unpaid servants suffered and patriots found themselves neglected or disowned, her signature was being affixed to warrants for £1,700 for a pearl chain for herself, or £1,200 "for a great diamond with a pendant," or "£761, 4s, 4d for fine linen for her Majesty's own person."[2]

Original passage from Stone, *Crisis of the Aristocracy*, 42:

Knighthood was the first dignity which the Crown openly allowed to be sold, not by the King himself but by deserving courtiers and servants. The causes of this development are clear enough. Fierce pressure from below from a squirearchy too long starved of titles, a financial stringency that precluded the distribution of direct cash gifts to servants and followers, a laudable desire to please both courtiers and clients, the fact that offices, monopolies, and favours were already being granted to courtiers for resale, all led the easy-going James to succumb to temptation and make knighthood a saleable commodity. Fluctuating according to the conflicting needs to reward followers, to keep up the price, and to preserve the dignity from falling into complete contempt, sales continued until Charles's decision after the death of Buckingham to put a stop to all such practices.

2. Experts openly acknowledge their sources in the body of their papers; so should you

If you look carefully at articles in popular magazines and newspapers, you will notice that the authors of these articles are constantly giving the sources of their information right in the body of their stories.

The office [Congressional Budget Office] . . . said in its annual economic report the economy will grow 4 percent in 1983 and 4.7 percent in 1984, and the budget deficit will be $194 billion this year. . . .
     The report estimates unemployment, which reached 10.8 percent in December, will be 10.6 percent this year and then slowly decline to 7.5 percent by 1988. The [1984] Reagan budget predicts unemployment of 10.9 percent this year, 10 percent in 1984 and 6.6 percent by 1988.
          Robert MacKay, "Congressional Budget Office says recession ending,"
          The (Portland) Oregonian, 4 Feb. 1983, Business Section, p. C 1.

> Thanks to new engines and wings, and the use of lighter composite materials, United [Airlines] says that the 767 is 30% to 54% more fuel efficient than the older planes it replaces. Boeing claims that airlines can save up to $2.5 million annually for every 767 they fly.
>
> Janice Castro, "Boeing Buckles Up for Takeoff," Time, 24 Jan. 1983, 60.

Journalists must indicate the sources of their information in the body of their stories because this is their only opportunity to document their sources. But if you look at the scholarly books and articles you've been reading, you will see that the experts also take every opportunity to name the source of their information in the body of their texts, as well as giving complete bibliographic information in notes or reference lists. They recognize a principle that journalists have long been aware of—naming the source of certain information not only acknowledges the source of the information but it also lends more credibility to the information.

Thus, as you work on the drafts of your paper, whenever possible you should name the source of the information you are using in the sentence you write. Particularly, you should give the names of the experts whose opinions you are summarizing or quoting.

Here are a few examples from published works that show how the experts acknowledge the sources of their evidence in the body of their texts.

> Professor E. H. Carr has recently reminded us that the historian does not exist who is unaffected by his upbringing and background.
>
> Lawrence Stone, The Crisis of the Aristocracy 1558–1641, abridged ed. (New York: Oxford University Press, 1967), 4.

> However, as recently discussed by Ulrich (1975), paleoclimate evidence concerning the long-term temperature variations on the earth suggests that the sun's luminosity has not changed from its present value by more than about 3% over the past million years, although the Dilke and Gough mechanism would induce at least a 10% change in the solar luminosity over that time scale.
>
> Robert W. Noyes, "New Developments in Solar Research," in Frontiers of Astrophysics, ed. Eugene H. Avrett (Cambridge, Mass.: Harvard University Press, 1976), 45.

> Within the United States, Clifford Shaw and Henry McKay are considered to have pioneered this approach (see Shaw 1929; Shaw and McKay 1931, 1942, 1969), providing the empirical and theoretical standards that have guided many subsequent large-scale studies.
>
> Robert J. Bursik, Jr., and Jim Webb, "Community Change and Patterns of Delinquency," American Journal of Sociology 88 (July 1982): 24.

> Fukui, who has studied this phenomenon back as far as 1890, has shown how there has been a steady decrease in the proportion of members of the House of Representatives with a background in local politics.
>
> Nobutaka Ike, Japanese Politics: Patron-Client Democracy, 2nd ed. (New York: Alfred A. Knopf, Borzoi Books, 1972), 86.

> Wagner[31] has recently published the far-infrared spectrum of liquid bromine, and Chantry et al.[32] have studied the long-wavelength absorption of various nonpolar liquids using interferometric techniques. This group of authors attribute the long-wavelength absorption to a

vibrational motion of the disordered lattice in the liquid, the so-called 'liquid lattice absorption.'

> Karl D. Möller and Walter G. Rothschild, *Far-Infrared Spectroscopy*, Wiley Series in Pure and Applied Optics (New York: John Wiley and Sons, Wiley-Interscience, 1971), 409.

The urban gangster was also a striking departure from the nineteenth-century criminal figures of the outlaw and the domestic murderer. His legend was, as Daniel Bell and Robert Warshow have noted, a complex mirror image of the American myth of success and social mobility.

> John G. Cawelti, *Adventure, Mystery, and Romance: Formula Stories as Art and Popular Culture* (Chicago and London: University of Chicago Press, 1976), 59.

For the field of reading, Robinson (*73*) has suggested that confusion might be reduced if models would be subgrouped into three categories: models representing 1) theories or procedures of teaching, 2) processes utilized or mobilized in reading, and 3) skills and abilities required for reading attainment.

> Harry Singer, "Theoretical Models of Reading: Implications for Teaching and Research," in *Theoretical Models and Processes of Reading*, ed. Harry Singer and Robert B. Ruddell (Newark, Delaware: International Reading Association, 1970), 147.

In Iran, Bharier's data for the 1960s show output growing faster in the larger establishments but employment growing faster in the small-scale sector. For Pakistan, Falcon and Stern[12] show the output of large industrial plants growing faster than total manufacturing output: 10.7 percent per year compared with 7.4 percent per year over the period 1954/55–1968/69.

> Lloyd G. Reynolds, *Image and Reality in Economic Development* (New Haven and London: Yale University Press, 1977), 316.

To live for the moment is the prevailing passion—to live for yourself, not for your predecessors or posterity. We are fast losing the sense of historical continuity, the sense of belonging to a succession of generations originating in the past and stretching into the future. It is the waning of the sense of historical time—in particular, the erosion of any strong concern for posterity—that distinguishes the spiritual crisis of the seventies from earlier outbreaks of millenarian religion, to which it bears a superficial resemblance. Many commentators have seized on this resemblance as a means of understanding the contemporary "cultural revolution," ignoring the features that distinguish it from the religions of the past. A few years ago, Leslie Fiedler proclaimed a "New Age of Faith." More recently, Tom Wolfe has interpreted the new narcissism as a "third great awakening," an outbreak of orgiastic, ecstatic religiosity. Jim Hougan, in a book that seems to present itself simultaneously as a critique and a celebration of contemporary decadence, compares the current mood to the millennialism of the waning Middle Ages. "The anxieties of the Middle Ages are not much different from those of the present," he writes. Then, as now, social upheaval gave rise to "millenarian sects."

> Christopher Lasch, *The Culture of Narcissism: American Life in an Age of Diminishing Expectations* (New York: W. W. Norton and Co., 1978), 5.

Look over each of these examples. Notice how, in each, the author I have quoted includes at least the last name of the expert whose work he is referring to and makes it clear in his statement that the ideas outlined belong to the person named. These published writers show you how you can acknowledge your sources directly in the body of your paper.

I have included the longer example from Christopher Lasch to show you how one expert, Lasch, uses other experts to make his own point. Lasch's point is stated in the third sentence: "It is the waning of the sense of historical time—in particular, the erosion of any strong concern for posterity—that distinguishes the spiritual crisis of the seventies from earlier outbreaks of millenarian religion, to which it bears a superficial resemblance." He points out that others (Fiedler, Wolfe, and Hougan) have seen a resemblance between the cultural revolution of the seventies and millenarian movements of the past, but continues with his own argument that the resemblance is superficial by arguing that Fiedler, Wolfe, and Hougan fail to see important differences between the previous millenarian movements and the cultural movement of the seventies. In the paragraph following the one I have quoted, Lasch shows what he considers the flaws in their thinking. But first he must establish that these three men do see the current spiritual crisis as a religious awakening. The purpose of this paragraph is to make Lasch's idea clear to his readers; he uses Fiedler, Wolfe, and Hougan to make his own argument.

3. Summarizing the work and ideas of another expert: How experienced writers do it

Because, in your paper, you are using the work of others, rather than having the work and ideas of others use you, in most cases you will need only a sentence or two to summarize the work and ideas of others. You will have selected what you need from these sources and you will put this material into a paragraph, like the one I quoted from Lasch in the last subsection, in which you are developing your own idea. Occasionally, however, you may decide that you need to give more information about the ideas or argument of a particular author.

If you find yourself giving a detailed, extended summary of an author's idea or argument, you must be very careful. In these situations you run the risk of letting your source take over your paper, which can all too easily lead you into a form of plagiarism that I will call illegitimate paraphrase. Let us say, for example, that you are reading a paper on the American Civil War and you come across this passage:

> Eighty-seven years earlier the Founding Fathers had brought forth a new nation on this continent, born in liberty and dedicated to the idea that all men are created equal. But this nation was now engaged in a great civil conflict, testing whether the United States or any country set up on the principles upon which the United States was founded could continue to endure. People on the Union side met on a famous battlefield of this civil

war. They were there to dedicate part of this battlefield as a final resting-place for those who gave their lives that the nation might live. They were there to dedicate themselves to a large task that still remained before them. From those who died they would take increased devotion to the cause for which these men died. They resolved that these dead should not have died in vain; that this nation, under God, should have a new birth of freedom; and that government of the people, by the people, for the people should not perish from the earth.

Your first reaction ought to be "Why, that's Lincoln's Gettysburg Address!" You recognize Lincoln's famous speech because this passage is the Gettysburg Address with only a few words and phrases changed here and there. If I ran across this passage in a paper I would consider this passage plagiarized. I would consider it plagiarized first of all because there is no mention of Lincoln or his speech. But even if the author of this passage had prefaced the passage by saying, "As Lincoln said at Gettysburg," I'd still consider the passage an illegitimate paraphrase because what are expressed in this passage are essentially Lincoln's ideas and words, not the writer's. The ideas are introduced in the same order in which Lincoln introduced his ideas, and the relationship among the ideas expressed here is exactly the relationship Lincoln expressed. The writer has done nothing but change a few words and phrases; the difference between Lincoln's Address and this paraphrase is that the passage is slightly less precise than Lincoln's actual Address, and much less eloquent.

In your efforts to understand the ideas of others you may find it helpful to take a passage from a work and do a paraphrase like the preceding one. Your purpose would be to change difficult language into words that are more meaningful to you in order to increase your comprehension of the author's ideas. But such direct paraphrases do not belong in the papers you write. You would go through the exercise of doing a paraphrase so that ultimately you could express your understanding of the author's idea, so that you could reach your own conclusions about what the author means. Having digested the basic ideas of another person, in your paper you will want to express, in your own words, your understanding of what this author is saying. In your paper you will put summaries, not paraphrases, and in these summaries you will clearly indicate to your readers that you are talking about the ideas of another person, and you will put in quotation marks those phrases and sentences that are taken directly from the source.

A legitimate summary of Lincoln's Address would look like this:

In his short but eloquent dedication of the cemetery at Gettysburg in 1863, Lincoln focuses his audience's attention on the Union's cause, the preservation of the United States as it was constituted eighty-seven years earlier. Time and again he returns to ideas formalized in the Declaration of Independence and the Constitution, reminding the audience that the United States was "dedicated to the proposition that all men are created equal" and that it is a "government of the people, by the people, for the people."

If, as you are writing your paper, you find yourself slipping into close paraphrase of one of your sources, it is time to step back from your paper and ask yourself why you are following your source in such detail. Is this author's argument / idea central to *your* argument? How? What is your point? What is the relationship between the author's point and your point? You should not continue with a detailed summary of an expert's argument until you know exactly why you are using this material and until you know what point you want to make about it.

If, after considering the issues I have just raised, you decide that a more extensive description of another person's idea is critical to your argument, follow these guidelines in doing your summary:

▶ Determine what *your* point is. Write out your point in a sentence (that sentence would probably make a good topic sentence for your paragraph). If you have decided that the author's analysis of the problem is the most convincing analysis, then I would expect your sentence to read: "Richard Jones's analysis of the problem of welfare fraud is the most convincing analysis because Jones stresses the role that desperation plays in the lives of people who are likely to commit such fraud."

▶ Acknowledge the source of the idea in your paragraph by naming the person to whom the idea belongs.

▶ Do not get caught in the trap of simply reiterating the author's argument. Pull out those points that are critical to the point you want to make. Use only those ideas that you want and need.

▶ Throughout your summary, explicitly indicate which ideas belong to your source ("according to Smith," "he notes," "Smith goes on to say"), so that your readers know what is yours and what belongs to your source.

▶ Put quotation marks around words and phrases that are taken directly from the source.

To illustrate ways to follow these guidelines, I am including some examples of ways that published writers give more extended summaries of the work of others. Study these examples carefully. Note how each writer follows the guidelines I have just laid out.

Example 1

Virgil Whitaker, in his biographical-analytical study, *Shakespeare's Use of Learning*, asserts this current religious view of Shakespeare's comic and tragic art with admirable boldness. Shakespeare as a man of the Renaissance, he assures us, had accepted the basic religious training of his youth and had never experienced "a genuine skepticism." It follows from such a premise that Shakespeare "did believe profoundly that God had made man in His own image and that, as all men had fallen once in Adam, so each man might fall again if he disobeyed the fundamental laws of God."[4] Whitaker, when he turns to aesthetics, is therefore led to argue, for example, that "Macbeth's sin is so awful simply because, like Shakespeare, he knows and believes in the foundations of human morality and in their ultimate basis in the mind and will of God."[5] This is no doubt to praise Shakespeare and Macbeth as sternly religious men, rather than as superlative playwright and brilliantly conceived character. Moreover, the implications seem to be that the sternness of the religion begot the strength of the play. And some such assumption of a highly self-conscious, febrile religious orthodoxy, both in Shakespeare and in his audience, seems to underlie the critical comments on Shakespeare by the whole contemporary school of Christian aesthetics.

> David Lloyd Stevenson, *The Achievement of Shakespeare's "Measure for Measure"* (Ithaca, N.Y.: Cornell University Press, 1966), 94–95.

The first and last sentences of Stevenson's paragraph indicate very clearly why he is summarizing the work of Whitaker. Stevenson wants us to see the Christian approach to Shakespeare in detail. Stevenson's point is that the critics who take this approach assume that Shakespeare, Shakespeare's characters, and Shakespeare's audience were very conscious of Christian teaching and that these Christian ideas were the essence of the meanings of the plays. So that we see clearly what he is talking about, and in order to support his argument, Stevenson summarizes the argument of one of these Christian critics, Whitaker, and quotes passages from Whitaker that illustrate this religious view.

Example 2

Shaw and McKay never claimed that they were the first to investigate the geographical distributions of juvenile delinquency. In their introduction to the 1942 volume, they cite not only the spatial work of European criminologists (especially in France and England; see Morris [1957] or Phillips [1972]) but also the American research of Breckenridge and Abbott (1912), Blackmar and Burgess (1917), and McKenzie (1923) that preceded their first major report in 1929. However, Shaw and McKay were not satisfied with the descriptive emphasis found in these studies and sought to interpret the spatial distributions within a general macroscopic theory of community processes. It was this important empirical/theoretical synthesis that gave the Shaw and McKay research its significance. Broadly stated, they proposed that the spatial distribution of delinquency in a city was a product of "larger economic and social processes characterizing the history and growth of the city and of the local communities which comprise it" (1942, p. 14).[2]

> Robert J. Bursik, Jr., and Jim Webb, "Community Change and Patterns of Delinquency," *American Journal of Sociology* 88 (July 1982): 25.

In this paragraph, Bursik and Webb's major point is that although Shaw and McKay were not "the first to investigate the geographical distributions of juvenile delinquency," Shaw and McKay's research is very important because they "sought to interpret the spatial distributions within a general macroscopic theory of community process." The body of the paragraph provides specific illustration and support for this major idea. Notice how Bursik and Webb constantly refer to their source (Shaw and McKay never claimed . . . they were . . . their introduction . . . they cite . . . their first major report . . . Shaw and McKay were not satisfied . . . the Shaw and McKay research . . . they proposed . . .).

Example 3

The idea of writing the earlier essay on the "Utility of Religion," its title and its specific theme, had first originated with his wife. Her proposal was clear in intention if incoherent in expression:

> Would not religion, the Utility of Religion, be one of the subjects you would have most to say on—there is to account for the existence nearly universal of some religion (superstition) by the instincts of fear, hope and mystery etc., and throwing over all doctrines and theories, called religion, and devices for power, to show how religion and poetry fill the same want . . . —how all this must be superseded by morality deriving its power from sympathies and benevolence and its reward from the approbation of those we respect.[4]

The essay, as Mill then wrote it, reflected most of these views. Religion, he wrote, was indefensible both on the grounds of truth and of utility, the appeal to the latter being a form of "moral bribery or subornation of the understanding."[5] There was, he concluded, nothing in Christianity that was not better supplied by the Religion of Humanity. At the same time, using her very words, he subtly altered their effect: religion, he suggested, had a more honorable origin than fear; the idea of religion as a device for power was only the "vulgarest part" of his subject; and religion, while comparable to poetry, was also distinct from it, for it addressed itself to reality in a way that poetry did not.

> Gertrude Himmelfarb, "The Other John Stuart Mill," in *Victorian Minds: A Study of Intellectuals in Crisis and of Ideologies in Transition* (New York: Harper & Row, Harper Torchbooks, 1970), 151–52.

Himmelfarb's focus in this paragraph is an early essay written by John Stuart Mill entitled "Utility of Religion." Using a proposal for the essay by Mill's wife as a convenient summary of the major ideas in the essay, Himmelfarb shows us major changes Mill made in the essay he wrote. In the paragraph that follows this one in "The Other John Stuart Mill," Himmelfarb goes on to compare "Utility of Religion" with an essay on religion that Mill wrote later in his life. Himmelfarb's overall concern is the way Mill's thinking changed and evolved.

Example 4

In June 1905, *Annalen der Physik* published an article by Einstein entitled "On a Heuristic Viewpoint Concerning the Production and Transformation of Light." Physicists usually refer to this as "Einstein's paper on the photoelectric effect," but that description does not do it justice. Einstein himself characterized it at the time as "very revolutionary," and he was right. This is the paper in which he proposed that light can, and in some situations must, be treated as a collection of independent particles of energy—light quanta—that behave like the particles of a gas. Einstein was well aware that a great weight of evidence had been amassed in the course of the previous century showing light to be a wave phenomenon. He knew, in particular, that Heinrich Hertz's experiments, carried out less than twenty years earlier, had confirmed

Maxwell's theoretical conclusion that light waves were electromagnetic in character. Despite all this evidence Einstein argued that the wave theory of light had its limits, and that many phenomena involving the emission and absorption of light "seemed to be more intelligible" if his idea of quanta were adopted. The photoelectric effect was one of several such phenomena which he analysed to show the power of his new hypothesis.

> Martin J. Klein, "Einstein and the Development of Quantum Physics," in *Einstein: A Centenary Volume*, ed. A. P. French (Cambridge, Mass.: Harvard University Press, 1979), 134.

Klein is clearly not reproducing Einstein's argument in detail. Rather, in the last five sentences he abstracts the main points in the argument, beginning with Einstein's hypothesis (light is a collection of particles of energy) and then giving, in their logical order, the major points that Einstein makes in his article. Notice that Klein constantly reminds us that this is Einstein's argument by using either "Einstein" or "he" in each of these five summary sentences. Notice also that Klein tells us first of all, in sentences two and three, why this article is important and thus worth summarizing.

4. Using direct quotations properly

If you go back and review the examples I have used in the last two subsections of this section, you will see that published authors do occasionally quote directly from their sources. You will notice, however, that they don't use direct quotations as a way of letting other people write their essays for them. Rather, they quote the words of another person when the idea they are developing involves the perspective or point of view of another person, a point of view that is best established or illustrated by this person's exact words. You will also notice that in most cases this point of view can be established or illustrated by quoting just a few words, or perhaps a sentence, and these few words are always integrated into a statement or sentence by the writer, a sentence that usually includes a direct acknowledgment of the source of the words quoted.

> "The anxieties of the Middle Ages are not much different from those of the present," he writes.
>
> Christopher Lasch, *The Culture of Narcissism*, 5.

> Religion, he wrote, was indefensible both on the grounds of truth and of utility, the appeal to the latter being a form of "moral bribery or subornation of the understanding."
>
> Gertrude Himmelfarb, *Victorian Minds*, 152.

> Broadly stated, they proposed that the spatial distribution of delinquency in a city was a product of "larger economic and social processes characterizing the history and growth of the city and of the local communities which comprise it."
>
> Bursik and Webb, "Community Change and Patterns of Delinquency," 25.

Einstein himself characterized it at the time as "very revolutionary," and he was right.

> Martin J. Klein, "Einstein and the Development of Quantum Physics,"
> in *Einstein: A Centenary Volume*, ed. A. P. French, 134.

From these examples, we can develop our first four guidelines for using quoted material.

1. Quote directly from the source *only* when the point you want to make involves calling the reader's attention to the point of view of the author you are discussing, and his/her point of view is *best* established or illustrated by using this person's exact words.
2. Quote only those words, phrases, or sentences necessary to make your point about the author's point of view. You should never use the words of another to express ideas that you should be expressing in your own words.
3. Quoted material should never stand alone in your paper. Always incorporate the words of others in your own sentences.

   ▶ *Avoid* using quotations this way:

   > The value of many diet drugs is highly questionable. "Starch blockers are a fraud,"[14] "Many hunger suppressants are dangerous because they raise the blood pressure."[15]

   ▶ Use this approach:

   > The value of many diet drugs is highly questionable. Based on a series of studies he has conducted, Dr. Benjamin Stokely flatly states that "starch blockers are a fraud."[14] Tests of other diet drugs reveal potentially dangerous side effects. A report by the Science Research Institute concludes that "many hunger suppressants are dangerous because they raise blood pressure."[15]

4. Punctuation before and after direct quotations is determined by the grammar of your sentence.

   > Dr. Carl Smith has stated that "there is no evidence that large doses of vitamin C have any beneficial effect."[17]

   > Dr. Carl Smith doubts the value of taking large amounts of vitamin C; "there is no evidence," he states, "that large doses of vitamin C have any beneficial effect."[17]

   > Dr. Carl Smith doubts the value of taking large amounts of vitamin C: "There is no evidence that large doses of vitamin C have any beneficial effect."[17]

The fifth guideline for using direct quotations properly pertains to the use of material that is quoted in the source you read. If you remember, in Section 4.C.1, I alerted you that you should make every effort to find the work in which the quotation originally appeared and, if you decide to use this material, to quote from the original source. If, however, you want to use quoted material whose original source you have not been able to locate, here are guidelines to follow.

5. When quoting material that is quoted in your source,
- ▶ be sure to name the source of the words you are quoting in the body of your paper;
- ▶ be sure to put the material in quotation marks. If you quote words of the author of the secondary source you are using as well as the words of the person he/she is quoting, put double quotation marks around the material from your source, and single quotation marks around the material quoted in this source. If you use only the words quoted in the source, you may use double quotation marks alone, but be sure that you acknowledge that this work is quoted in your documenting note (see below).

Example 1

The secondary source
"If our civilization is destroyed, as Macaulay predicted," wrote Henry Demarest Lloyd in an assessment of the robber barons, "it will not be by his barbarians from below. Our barbarians come from above. Our great money-makers have sprung in one generation into seats of power kings do not know. . . ."

> Richard Hofstadter, *The Age of Reform from Bryan to F.D.R.* (New York: Random House, Vintage Books, 1955), 141.

Your paper
Writing about the nineteenth-century robber barons in 1894, Henry Demarest Lloyd did not paint a very flattering portrait of men whom he called "barbarians." These men had ascended, Lloyd said, to "power kings do not know."[11]

Example 2

The secondary source
Collins (1970, 1975), on the other hand, has argued for an extreme environmental position, suggesting that handedness is transmitted from one generation to the next by means of cultural and environmental biases. In this, he echoes the earlier conclusion of Blau (1946) who, after careful review of the evidence, wrote as follows:

> Preferred laterality is not an inherited trait. There is absolutely no evidence to support the contention that dominance, either in handedness or any other form, is a congenital, predetermined human capacity. Despite the popularity it has enjoyed with many investigators and the attempts to prove it by various techniques and in relation to different organs of the body, the theory of heredity must be put down as erroneous [p. 180].

> > Michael C. Corballis, "Is Left-Handedness Genetically Determined?" in *Neuropsychology of Left-Handedness*, ed. Jeannine Herron, Perspectives in Neurolinguistics and Psycholinguistics (New York: Academic Press, 1980), 159.

Your paper

On the side of those who argue that handedness is strictly the product of environment or culture is Blau, who wrote in 1946: " 'Preferred laterality is not an inherited trait. . . . Despite the popularity it has enjoyed with many investigators and the attempts to prove it by various techniques and in relation to different organs of the body, the theory of heredity must be put down as erroneous.' "[10]

▶   When you document this quoted material, you must clearly acknowledge that the words you have quoted are taken from a secondary source. In your note give at least the author and title, as well as the date, of the original source (you can find this information in the documenting note of the secondary source); then give full bibliographic information about the secondary source you used. Your notes for the two examples given above would look like this:

Example 1

    [11] Henry D. Lloyd, *Wealth Against Commonwealth* (1894; ed. 1899), quoted by Richard Hofstadter, *The Age of Reform from Bryan to F.D.R.* (New York: Random House, Vintage Books, 1955), 141.

Example 2

    [10] A. Blau, *The Master Hand* (New York: American Orthopsychiatric Association, 1946), quoted by Michael C. Corballis, "Is Left-Handedness Genetically Determined?" in *Neuropsychology of Left-Handedness*, ed. Jeannine Herron, Perspectives in Neurolinguistics and Psycholinguistics (New York: Academic Press, 1980), 159.

The sixth guideline concerns the methods you can use to indicate to your readers that certain words in your paper are the words of another person. The most common method is to put these words in quotation marks. Longer quotations, however, can be marked as quoted by setting this material off from the text of your paper.

6.   Indicate that material is quoted by using quotation marks, unless the quotation you are using is a long quotation. The general definition of a "long" quotation is one that consists of 100 words or more, or a quotation that will run for four or five lines in your paper. This is the format for a long quotation, called a block quotation:

▶   Double-space before and after the quotation.

▶   Single-space the text of the quotation.

▶   Indent all lines of the quotation five spaces from your left-hand margin.

▶   Do *not* use quotation marks around block quotations. Setting the quotation off from your text is equal to putting this material in quotation marks.

Example

Much of the material that Smith used in his novel about Napoleon is based on historical fact. In a letter to his friend Sam Spade in 1924, Smith explained that

I am starting work on a novel on Napoleon that I've spent the last six years researching. Don't misunderstand. I do not intend to write an historical romance, those so-called novels that pretend to be historical by piling up all sorts of accurate detail about furniture and clothes and architecture. Such bits and pieces of history do not add up to any real sort of authenticity. My novel is going to be a novel that recreates Napoleon himself. When I am finished, I will have made Napoleon a living, breathing person that the reader will feel he has met and lived with for years and years. I can do it. I've read everything that has been written about the man, and everything he wrote.[8]

Smith did not have to worry about someone who actually knew the Emperor calling his portrait into question, since all those people have long ago turned into dust; but ignoring the issue of the authenticity of the portrait for a moment, there is no doubt that Smith has created a three-dimensional character.

7. Occasionally it will be necessary to alter quotations slightly to meet the needs of your prose. Such modifications are acceptable only if you do not misrepresent the meaning of the original words and only if you use the accepted means of indicating that quoted material is being modified.

▶ Indicate *omission* of a word or words by inserting ellipsis points (. . .) where a word or words are omitted.

Original
In the corporate structure as in government, the rhetoric of achievement, of single-minded devotion to the task at hand—the rhetoric of performance, efficiency, and productivity—no longer provides an accurate description of the struggle for personal survival.

> Christopher Lasch, *The Culture of Narcissism: American Life in an Age of Diminishing Expectations* (New York: W. W. Norton and Co., 1978), 61.

Omissions indicated by ellipses (. . .)
In the corporate structure as in government, the rhetoric of . . . single-minded devotion to the task at hand . . . no longer provides an accurate description of the struggle for personal survival.

▶ Indicate *additions* or changes of certain words by putting your changes in brackets [ ].

Original
Was the King regulating trade in the national interest, or to oblige his friends?

> Lawrence Stone, *The Crisis of the Aristocracy 1558–1641*, abridged ed. (New York: Oxford University Press, 1967), 202.

Modification indicated by brackets [ ]
Stone asks, "Was [King James] regulating trade in the national interest, or to oblige his friends?"

Original

Knipling believed the most significant implication of his theoretical results was that the two complementary techniques allowed a pest controller to overcome the law of diminishing returns.

> John H. Perkins, *Insects, Experts, and the Insecticide Crisis: The Quest for New Pest Management Strategies* (New York and London: Plenum Press, 1982), 118.

Modification indicated by brackets [ ]

Perkins writes: "Knipling believed the most significant implication of his theoretical results was that the two complementary techniques [of using insecticides and releasing sterile male insects] allowed a pest controller to overcome the law of diminishing returns."

Please note that brackets have squared-off corners and are therefore different from parentheses. If your typewriter doesn't have bracket keys, you will have to draw in the brackets neatly with a pen. Do not use parentheses for additions or changes of words in direct quotations. You always want a clear distinction between material you have modified or added and material that the author of the passage may have put in parentheses.

Modifications or additions to quotations should be limited to changes of pronouns to nouns, changes of verb tense, additions of the first name of a person mentioned or of the full name of an event or company, and other such changes for clarification and readability. If you find yourself adding a great deal of information in brackets in a quotation, you should probably write out the statement you want to make, and then put in quotation marks those words that are taken from your source. Other examples of modifications of quotations can be found in the beginning of subsection B.2 of this section and Section 4.B.6.

Note: Normally, when you are quoting only a phrase or a part of a sentence from a source, it is obvious that you are quoting only a part of the author's original sentence. It is, therefore, not necessary to put ellipsis points at the beginning and the end of these quotations.

Not necessary

As Frederick comments, *The Great Gatsby* is ". . . one of America's classics. . . ."

Accepted form

As Frederick comments, *The Great Gatsby* is "one of America's classics."

You may, however, want to use ellipses in a few cases where it may not be obvious from the context that you are using only a part of what is a larger whole. For example, I used ellipses at the end of the quotation by Henry Lloyd quoted by Hofstadter on page 133 to let you know that Hofstadter quoted more of Lloyd than I did.

8. Finally, there are a few things you should know about quoting from novels, short stories, poetry, and plays. In general, when quoting from a work of literature, you should use the same guidelines I have outlined in this subsection on quoting properly. Thus, you should quote from the actual text of a piece of literature only when the specific words of the text are essential to the point you are making. Otherwise, as in using other kinds of sources, you will find that the most effective way for you to make your point is to summarize, in your own words, the material in the text to which you are referring.

   If you decide that you must quote the exact words of the text in order to support the point you are making, be sure to introduce the quotation by giving your readers enough information to put the quotation into its proper context. If you are quoting the words of a character in a novel or a play, for example, be sure to tell us which character is speaking. Similarly, the words you quote often will be more meaningful if you tell us, briefly, what circumstances led that character to speak these words.

Example 1
As he draws toward the end of his story of the "great" Jay Gatsby, Nick Carraway passes judgment on Daisy and Tom Buchanan; "they were careless people," Nick decides; "they smashed up things and creatures and then retreated back into their money or their vast carelessness, or whatever it was that kept them together, and let other people clean up the mess they had made. . . ."[11]

   [11] F. Scott Fitzgerald, *The Great Gatsby* (New York: Charles Scribner's Sons, 1953), 120.

Example 2
In *To the Lighthouse*, Mrs. Ramsey is constantly giving of herself to her husband, her children, her neighbors. This self-giving is what brings other personalities into harmony and communion. At the dinner with which section I ends, Mrs. Ramsey surveys the group seated around the table: "They all sat separate. And the whole of the effort of merging and flowing and creating rested on her."[7]

   [7] Virginia Woolf, *To the Lighthouse* (New York: Harcourt, Brace and Company, 1927), 126.

Example 3
Richard's helpless self-pity is eloquently expressed as he prepares to give up his role as king, and his identity:

> What must the King do now? Must he submit?
> The King shall do it. Must he be depos'd?
> The King shall be contented. Must he lose
> The name of king? a' God's name let it go.
> *Richard II*, 3.3.142–45

As example 3 illustrates, several lines of poetry may be quoted by setting them off from the text in a block quotation. Shorter passages of poetry, however, should be put in quotation marks and integrated into the prose of your text. If the passage you quote runs from one verse line to another, you should indicate the end of the verse line with a slash mark and the beginning of the next verse line by capitalizing the first letter of the first word.

Example

The tragedy in the story of Michael is that his only son, heir to his land and to his life, is forced to apprentice himself to a kinsman, "a prosperous man,/ Thriving in trade" (Wordsworth, "Michael," ll.249–50).

Section 7

Documenting Your Sources

A. General Overview

If you have attended carefully to what I have been saying in the preceding sections of this book, you will realize that you have one important step left before you are ready to type your paper: you must find a method of documenting your sources. Documenting your sources involves letting your reader know, in the body of your paper, that certain information and ideas have been taken from specific sources, and giving your readers complete publication information about each of the sources you have used.

If you are like many students I have worked with, you face the process of documenting your sources with a mixture of dread and exasperation. Perhaps in the past you have written a research paper, struggling to get the footnotes and bibliography right, only to find that your instructor has scribbled red-inked corrections all over the notes and bibliography and he/she has taken off points because of these mistakes. Or perhaps your instructor has asked you to use the APA style or the MLA style in the paper you are now finishing, and you don't have the foggiest idea what the APA style or the MLA style is. Your attitude may be that you ought to be able to document your sources in your own way and that instructors who insist that you follow a specific form exactly are tiresome nitpickers.

In one sense, your attitude toward documentation is reasonable. Documenting sources correctly is not very exciting, or creative, work. It can be especially troublesome for novices who have not had much experience with a particular documentation system. On the other hand, documenting sources correctly is an important part of learning how to become a responsible detective-researcher, and you do not want to endanger your research project at this late stage of the process by becoming sloppy and careless. I cannot promise you that I will make this final step quick and painless for you, but I think that I can make it easier by helping you to understand what documentation systems are all about.

In this section I will give you a general overview of documentation systems, explaining the purpose that lies behind all documentation systems and helping you to select the system that is most appropriate for the paper you are now writing. In the appendixes that follow this section, I have laid out basic information about the two basic documentation modes, those used in the sciences and in the humanities. Before you turn to these appendixes, though, you should read over the rest of this section.

From your experience in doing research papers in the past, you may be aware that there are different documentation forms. The form that your psychology instructor wants you to use is not the form your literature teacher wants, and the form recommended by your chemistry professor may be different from these other two. Perhaps you have noticed, as you've checked the notes and references of different books and articles you've been reading for this research project, that there are differences in documentation form from one of your sources to the next. Such variations do exist, and they can seem bewildering. It would be natural for you to assume that there is no such thing as a correct form, and that people like me and your instructors pretend there is a correct form simply to increase the burdens and suffering of an overworked student like yourself. Because you have not spent time studying documentation systems, it is difficult for you to see that in this seeming chaos there is an order. It is true that there are variations within actual documentation systems, but behind these variations there lie two basic premises.

B.   The Basic Premises of Documentation Systems

Premise 1:   A writer must clearly signal his/her readers, in the body of a paper, where he/she is using material that is taken from someone else, and this writer must also give the readers full information about each source so that the readers, if they chose, could locate each source themselves.

Regardless of the specific form it takes, each documentation form is designed to allow you to give credit where credit is due. In addition to paying your debt to your sources by acknowledging them, you are also being a generous researcher. In giving your readers full information about each of your sources, you are sharing these sources of information with your readers. By allowing them to locate and read this material themselves, you are enlarging their knowledge of your subject. If you think about it, you yourself have profited from the generosity of other researchers when you have taken the titles of books and articles from their notes, bibliographies, and reference lists.

Premise 2:   The information about the writer's sources should be given in a form that is least obtrusive and that takes the least amount of space without sacrificing completeness or intelligibility.

As the costs of publishing books and journals have risen, space itself has become an increasingly valuable commodity. Publishers would rather devote as much space as possible to an author's ideas, keeping the amount of space necessary for documentation to a minimum. The result of this need to save space in documentation has been the development of systems of shorthand. Thus many citations in footnotes and bibliographies on the surface seem to be mysterious series of words and numbers:

Proc. Nat. Acad. Sc. 7:186.

But this shorthand system allows this author to say "you will find this article in volume 7 of *The Proceedings of the National Academy of Sciences* on page 186" in much less space than it took me to write it all out.

Obviously, shorthand systems won't work unless there are rules that govern the "code" and unless both readers and writers know these rules. You could, of course, develop your own system of shorthand, but that would involve working out a complete system and then providing your readers with the key. Why re-invent the wheel? Over the years workable systems have been developed by publishing agencies and professional academic organizations that nicely meet the needs expressed in the two basic premises of documentation. Following one of these established systems saves you the trouble of having to develop your own code, and it has the advantage of being familiar to your readers.

Thus, my advice to you is to resolve that, as a responsible researcher, each time you do a research paper you will have this as your goal:

To select a system of documentation that is appropriate for the subject matter and audience of your paper, and to follow this system exactly.

C.   Selecting the Appropriate Documentation System

Although there are variations within a system, in academic circles there are actually two basic modes of documentation that split along disciplinary lines—the humanities system and the scientific system. One way to decide which of the two systems is more appropriate for a specific paper is to consider the approach taken by experts in your area of investigation to their subject matter. The scientific approach is generally characterized by objective measurement; data are collected and assessed by use of machinery or instruments, mathematical formulas, statistical procedures. Thus in the natural and applied sciences experts use the scientific system of documentation. Experts who gather information and test hypotheses by means other than those using machinery or instruments, mathematical formulas, or statistical procedures usually use the humanities form of documentation. The humanities form is the one you will usually find in works on history, literature, art, music, religious studies, philosophy. So, to determine which system is more appropriate for your paper, you can ask yourself: How has the information I have used in my paper been gathered and analyzed? Have most of the experts I have read used the scientific approach, or not?

The audience for which your paper is intended is also a factor you should consider in making your decision. Documentation systems are more effective if they are familiar to the readers you are addressing. A very pragmatic way to determine which system is more appropriate for your paper is to ask your instructor which system he or she prefers. Probably the best way to ask the question is this: "Which style or style manual do you want me to follow?"

1. Style manuals

A style manual is a pamphlet or book that outlines the general style appropriate for manuscripts that will be published by a particular publishing firm or journal. Style manuals cover much more than documentation form. In them you can find answers for questions like: How wide should my margins be? Should I use headings in the body of my paper? What do I do if I want to use charts and graphs? Should I include a table of contents? Style manuals also cover matters of mechanics, like punctuation, capitalization, setting up quotations, abbreviations, and so on. These style manuals can be seen as the professional counterparts of the handbooks often used in English composition courses. Obviously, such manuals can be very helpful to you in answering all sorts of questions you might have about the final form your research paper should take. Style manuals fall roughly into three categories:

▶ Style manuals developed by publishers for authors who are writing books or articles for that publishing firm
▶ "General" style manuals
▶ Style manuals developed by professional organizations

The most "public" of the manuals in the first category are the style manuals of the *New York Times* and the *Washington Post*. Perhaps you've seen copies of them in bookstores. Although these manuals are now being sold to the general public, they were put together for journalists who write for these two newspapers.

As a student, you will probably be most interested in the other two types of manuals.

a. "General" style manuals

> *The Chicago Manual of Style*. 13th ed., rev. and expanded. Chicago: University of Chicago Press, 1982.
> Turabian, Kate. *A Manual for Writers of Term Papers, Theses, and Dissertations*. 4th ed. Chicago: University of Chicago Press, 1973.
> Turabian, Kate. *Student's Guide for Writing College Papers*. 3rd ed., rev. and expanded. Chicago: University of Chicago Press, 1976.

Although I have listed three titles here, the two books by Turabian are really scaled-down versions of *The Chicago Manual of Style*. All present what is generally called the Chicago style. Technically speaking, *The Chicago Manual* should be listed with those manuals developed by publishing firms for its authors because *The Chicago Manual* was created by the University of Chicago Press for use by writers preparing manuscripts for this publishing house. However, *The Chicago Manual* has become accepted as the authoritative manual for people who write scholarly books in academic disciplines, and beyond. It is a complete style manual, answering almost any question you could think of about proper manuscript form. It includes descriptions not only of the humanities system of documentation, but also of the scientific system.

Because *The Chicago Manual* is a complete style manual written for professional writers, it can be intimidating and perhaps bewildering for novices like you. Recognizing this fact, the University of Chicago Press publishes two books for students that present the Chicago style in a form more in keeping with students' needs. If your instructor has asked you to follow the Chicago style, or if she has recommended Turabian, she is asking you to follow the humanities system. I introduce you to the Chicago style in Appendixes A and B of this book. But I have obviously not been able to cover the Chicago style in any depth. You may want to invest in a copy of one of the two Turabian books if you know that you will be writing a number of research papers before you receive your B.A. or B.S. Both of these books are published in inexpensive paperbacks that are usually stocked by college bookstores.

Of the two books by Turabian, the one more suitable for students who have had little experience with research papers is the *Student's Guide*. Although it gives a few specifics about the scientific system of documentation, it focuses on the humanities system. I particulariy like the *Student's Guide* because it includes over fifty pages of basic reference works in many subjects and disciplines, a very convenient resource for students who don't know where to start looking for information in a particular subject. *A Manual for Writers*, on the other hand, is written for more advanced students; in this book you will find more detailed information about using charts, graphs, appendixes, about how to document legal documents, and about other issues that arise when you are doing more sophisticated research papers.

b. Style manuals of professional organizations

In addition to the general style manuals I just discussed, you will also find that there are style manuals developed and published by professional academic organizations. Here is a list of a few such manuals:

> American Chemical Society. *Handbook for Authors.* Washington, D.C.: American Chemical Society, 1978. (available in paperback)
> *American Institute of Physics Style Manual.* 3rd ed. McGraw-Hill, 1978. Reprinted in the *Bulletin of the American Physical Society* 24 (December 1979).
> American Psychological Association (APA). *Publication Manual.* 3rd ed. Washington, D.C.: APA, 1983.
> *Council of Biology Educators Style Manual.* 4th ed. 1978.
> Joseph Gibaldi and Walter S. Achtert. *MLA Handbook for Writers of Research Papers.* 2nd ed. New York: The Modern Language Association of America, 1984.

The styles laid out in these manuals are usually variations of the two basic documentation systems found in *The Chicago Manual.* The two manuals listed here that you will probably hear the most about are those published by the American Psychological Association (APA) and the Modern Language Association (MLA).

The MLA style and the Chicago style constitute the two most popular variations of the humanities system. The APA style is perhaps the most widely known variation of the scientific system as it is used in the social sciences. The APA style can also be called the author-date form; this author-date form is the form recommended by *The Chicago Manual* for all papers in the natural sciences and for papers in the social sciences that take a scientific approach to the subject matter.

2.   Summary: Choosing the appropriate documentation system

I hope by now that it is clear to you that when we talk about documentation systems in academic papers, we are talking essentially about two systems—the scientific system and the humanities system. Although the two systems have differences, they are not differences in philosophy. Both are shorthand methods of alerting readers of a paper that material from other sources is being used, and both give full bibliographic information about these sources.

     The appendixes at the end of this book are general introductions to these two documentation systems. In Appendixes A and B you will find the basics of the two most popular forms of the humanities system, the Chicago style and the MLA style. As I explain at the beginning of Appendix A, the Chicago style uses the traditional system of note numbers (1) in the body of the paper, notes either at the bottom of the page (footnotes) or at the end of the paper (endnotes), and a bibliography; the new MLA style is similar to the scientific system in that it omits notes and uses instead parenthetical citations in the text (Smith 56), which refer readers to a list of works cited at the end of the paper. Because these two styles are rather different, you may want to ask your instructor which she prefers before you select a style for a paper you are writing in the humanities. In Appendixes C, D, and E you will find the basics of the scientific system. In Appendix C you will learn how to set up a reference list; I give the form for individual entries as recommended by *The Chicago Manual* and the APA *Publication Manual.* In Appendix D you can find the basics of the author-date method (Smith 1980), and in Appendix E you will learn about the numbered reference list form (*3*). If you have been asked to follow the APA style, use Appendixes C and D.

     Please be aware that these appendixes are only introductions to these systems and forms. I cannot answer all the questions you might have about the proper way to document every type of source. You should be prepared to locate copies of the various style manuals I have used in these appendixes.

     I believe that if you have read this section carefully, and if you read over the introductions to each of the appendixes, you will find the actual style manuals much less intimidating. They are not that difficult to use once you know what kinds of questions you have; each has a convenient table of contents and an index that will allow you to find just the information you need.

D.   Following the Form Exactly

Once you have selected the documentation system that is most appropriate for your subject matter and audience, you must follow the specific form exactly. If you choose the humanities system, for example, you must consistently use either the Chicago form or the MLA form in a particular paper; never mix the forms. The reason should be obvious. Since each documentation form is a form of shorthand, the placement of information, and such details as punctuation, underlining, and so on, all carry meanings. If you do not follow the form exactly, you run the risk of leaving out important information or of confusing your reader by signalling "this number is a volume number" when you meant to say "this number is a page number." The first time you use a system of documentation it will feel awkward to you and you will have to exercise a little patience to get it right. But after you have used the same system several times, you'll find that it becomes easier and easier as the form becomes familiar to you. By the time you are a senior, you should know the standard form in your major so well that you will have to consult a style manual only for special types of citations.

I hope that I have convinced you that there are reasons, beyond avoiding the ire of your instructor, for learning and using exactly the accepted forms of documentation. In the long run it is much easier to learn a standard form than it is to unlearn habits of sloppiness and carelessness.

Let me end by saying that documentation systems, like most other things in this world, grow and change to meet new needs and changing circumstances. Documentation forms are always being updated. So, when you use a style manual, make a special effort to find out what the most recent edition of that manual is, and try to use this most recent edition. You may find that some of the forms I give in the appendixes have changed since this book was published.

Appendix A

The Humanities System: The Bibliography or the MLA List of Works Cited

---

A. General Information

The humanities form is the form most often used in fields in the humanities—art, history, literature, philosophy, music, and so on—and in books intended for a broad audience. If your instructor has asked you to use the Chicago style or the MLA style in your paper or has urged you to look at Turabian, the humanities form is the style he or she wants you to use.

There are, however, major differences in the way in which you give credit in the Chicago style and in the MLA style. In this appendix and in Appendix B, I explain the principles of these two systems. I also give you specific information about the exact form to use in citing your sources. Before you dive into specific parts of this appendix or the next, however, please read the descriptions of these two systems that I give here. You must choose one or the other (do not mix the two in one paper) and follow the forms exactly. If you aren't sure which style is appropriate for the paper you are now writing, ask your instructor.

The Chicago style

The general system used in the Chicago style is probably the one you are most familiar with. In the body of the paper, the author uses a raised number ([4]) at the end of a sentence to refer the readers to a note that will contain the necessary bibliographic information about the source he or she used. The notes may appear at the bottom of the page (footnotes) or on a separate sheet at the end of the paper (endnotes). In addition to notes, the author usually includes a bibliography. A bibliography is an alphabetized list of the works this author used in the course of researching his or her paper. If your instructor has asked you to use Turabian or to use notes or footnotes, this is the style you should follow.

In the Chicago style, the form for notes differs from the form you must use for bibliography entries. In this appendix, I will discuss only the form for a bibliography. When you are putting together your notes for your paper, you should read and follow the form given in Appendix B.

The MLA Style

The major difference—and it *is* a major difference—between the Chicago style and the MLA style is that the latter eliminates the intermediate stage of notes. Instead of a bibliography, you create a list of works cited, where you give readers full information about the sources you have used in the paper. In the body of your paper you tell your readers which of these sources you are referring to simply by using the author's name. Thus, the reader can go straight from the body of the paper to the appropriate entry on the list, which is attached to the end of the paper. Here's an example.

Body of Your Paper
```
Many short stories published today leave the reader

bewildered because they have no clear beginnings and no

obvious endings (Jones 139).  But Alvin Peabody's story

"Searching" is an exception.  When Jed confronts his

brother, there is a very clear resolution of the plot

(69-70).
```

List of Works Cited
```
Jones, Arthur W. The Short Story Today. New York:
      Nameless, 1999.

Peabody, Alvin.  "Searching."  An Anthology of Recent
      Fiction.  Ed. John Q. Smith.  New York: Titanic,
      1995.  60-71.
```

Very simple—in principle. But as in any documentation system, there are specific conventions you must follow. If you decide the MLA system is the right one for your paper, I suggest you turn now to Appendix B and read section B.1. Once you understand the system, you can come back to part B of this appendix to learn about how to set up your list of works cited.

B.   Putting Together a Bibliography or a List of Works Cited

The content of bibliographies and lists of works cited are different. For this reason, I've divided this subsection to make it easier for you to use. But there are some similarities in the way you order your works on both bibliographies and lists, and I'll give you that information here.

Bibliographies and lists are both set up by starting each entry with the *last* name of the first author mentioned in the work you are listing. Here are some further hints about ordering your list.

▶ In alphabetizing your sources, use only the letters in an author's last name; ignore his or her first name and/or initials. If your list includes works by Stephen Green and Aaron Greenberg, the work by Green would come first.

▶ If you have several authors with the same last name, alphabetize according to the authors' first names, and then the middle initials.

> Johnson, Carl X.
> Johnson, Frances H.
> Johnson, Frederick J.
> Johnson, Frederick S.

▶ If your list includes more than one work by the same author or authors (John Jones),

  ▷ list all the works that Jones wrote by himself first. Order the entries according to the titles of the works (ignoring *the* and *a* as first words);

> Jones, John. *The Continental Congress* . . .
> ———. "The Political Contexts of . . ."

  ▷ then list any collections that Jones edited;

> Jones, John, ed. *Papers of the Continental Congress* . . .

  ▷ if Jones has written any works with other authors (or edited any works with others), these co-authored works would then be listed. Alphabetize according to the last names of the second co-author, and so on.

> Jones, John, and Herman Gotz. *America during the Revolution* . . .
> Jones, John, Aaron Greenberg, and Alfred Lutz, eds. *The Papers of Thomas Jefferson* . . .
> Jones, John, Aaron Greenberg, and Louisa Smith. *American Lives* . . .
> Jones, John, and James Jackson. *When We Were Young* . . .

NOTE: You may substitute a line for the author's name *only* when the author or authors are *exactly* the same. Otherwise, spell out every author's name.

▶ Books with a corporate author (an agency, committee, institute, etc.) are alphabetized according to the first main word (ignoring *the* and *a*) in the name of the group (see section C.2.c).

▶ If a work has no author, you will place it in your bibliography or list according to the first main word in the title.

1. Bibliographies

The content of a bibliography varies according to the purpose of the author. As a student preparing a bibliography for a paper for a college course, you should look upon your bibliography as a direct indication of the scope, depth, and thoroughness of the research you have done. Thus your bibliography should include *all* the sources that you cite in your notes plus those sources that you read or consulted in doing your research, even though you may not refer to them in your notes. You should not include works that you did not read or use in some way.

You may have noticed that in some books bibliographies are divided into different sections (like Primary and Secondary Works, or Books and Periodicals). You should not subdivide your bibliography unless it is very long (let us say over six pages) or unless you have a very good reason for separate sections. If you decide it would be wise to subdivide your bibliography, you should consult *The Chicago Manual of Style*.

I will assume that you have decided there is no reason to subdivide your bibliography. You should then begin to compile your bibliography by putting in order the bibliography cards of all the sources you read or consulted in investigating your subject. Be sure to look at your notes to make certain that you haven't left out any work that you cite in your notes.

In the following sections of this appendix I give you the proper form for the most common types of sources. Check the headings in the rest of this appendix, find the one that best matches your source, and follow the form *exactly*. Be sure to follow the form given under the Chicago heading and watch little details like capitalization, punctuation, and underlining very carefully. If you cannot find an example of the source you are recording in your bibliography, see section F. If you would like to see a sample bibliography, turn to section G.

2. Lists of works cited

As the heading "Works Cited" states, this list includes *only* those works that you refer to *directly* in the body of your paper. If you want to let your instructor know that you read other material, you may add these works, but you will have to label your list "Works Consulted." Both types of lists follow the form I outline in the rest of this appendix.

In compiling your list of works cited, keep in mind the basic principles of the MLA style:

▶ The citation in your text should be as short as possible.
▶ The name of the author you give in your text must be the name of the person whose ideas or words you are using.
▶ The entry on your list must begin with this person's name. (Otherwise, how are we to know which entry to look at?)
▶ You must have an entry for each author you cite.

You will have no problem if you are citing a book written by the author or if you are citing an article in a journal, magazine, or newspaper. If you refer to John Doe's book *Poetry* twelve times in your paper, just be sure you have *one* entry that begins "Doe, John. *Poetry.* . . ."

However, if you are using a work that you read in an anthology or a collection of essays, your task is a bit more complicated. If, for example, you are quoting from a poem by William Blake and a poem by John Keats, both of which you found in the same anthology, you will create *two* entries on your list, one that begins "Blake, William" and one that begins "Keats, John." Similarly, let us say that you are writing about Shakespeare's *Richard II* and you refer in your paper both to the play itself and to the introduction to the play written by Kenneth Muir in the Signet Classic edition. Even though the play and the introduction are in the same book, you will have two separate entries on your list, one that begins "Shakespeare, William" and one that begins "Muir, Kenneth." If you have any works in your paper that fit this description, be sure to read section C.2.g in this appendix carefully.

You must also be careful if you are using a work that is made up of several volumes. If you are using only one volume of that set in your paper, you may list just that volume (see section C.2.h. in this appendix). However, if you cite references to several volumes, list the whole set, and be sure to include the volume number *before* the page number in your citations (see Appendix B, section B.1.d).

Once you have jotted down the names of each author and work you cite in your paper, make a stack of the notecards and/or bibliography cards that contain the bibliographic information about these sources. Put them in alphabetical order according to the last name of the author you cite in the body of your paper. Now you are ready to put together your list. In the following sections of this appendix, I give you the proper form for the most common types of sources. Check the headings, find the one that describes your source, and follow the form *exactly.* Be sure to follow the form given under the MLA heading and watch little details like capitalization, punctuation, and underlining very carefully. If you don't find a heading that matches your source, see section F. I have also included a sample list of works cited in section G of this appendix.

NOTE: The examples given in the following sections of this appendix are single-spaced. However, when you put your own list together, be sure to double-space your entries. See the sample list in section G.

C.   Proper Form for Books

1.   Placement of information

A book entry is divided into four parts; each part is separated from the others with a period. The first line of an entry is flush with the left-hand margin; other lines in the entry are indented five spaces.

```
         author                              title
           |                                   |
|Jung, Carl G.|Four Archetypes: Mother, Rebirth,

  Spirit, Trickster.|

  ┌┤Translated by R. F. C. Hull. Bollingen Series,
  │
  │  no. 20.|Princeton, N.J.: Princeton
  │
  │  University Press, 1969.┌┐
```

particulars of   facts of
publication   publication

Author   The key to your bibliography or list of works cited is the name of the person or group responsible for the text. Begin with the last name of the first author listed on the title page of the work, and whenever possible, give each author's full first name and middle initial. If the party responsible is a corporate group, the name of the group will be used as the "author" (see section C.2.c). If the book is a collection of essays, the editor of the collection will be considered its author (see section C.2.f).

If you are using the Chicago style and you are referring to an article or essay included in a collection of essays, you have two options: (1) you can cite the article or essay, in which case you will enter this work in your bibliography under the name of the author of the article (see section C.2.g); or (2) you may cite only the collection itself, in which case you will enter this work under the name of the editor of the collection. If you have used several essays in a collection, it would probably be better to list only the collection itself in your bibliography.

If you are using the MLA style, remember that whenever you are using works published in an anthology or collection of essays, you must have a separate entry for each work, beginning with the name of the author of the specific work (see section C.2.g).

Title   Give the full title of the book, including any subtitles. The main words in all titles are always capitalized (see Appendix F.A). Titles of books are underlined. Notice that the title of essays, articles, and other works that were originally published in a larger collection are placed in quotation marks; periods or commas are placed *inside* the quotation marks. If you are referring to a work in a collection or anthology, you must give the full titles of *both* the work itself and the anthology or collection.

Particulars of publication   You must always include other information about the work because such information will help the readers locate the specific book you used. If you are using the Chicago style, give such information in this order after the title of the book:

> name of editor and/or translator
> titles of series, if any, and volume or number
> volume number or total number of volumes if book is a part of a set
> edition (if not the original)

If you are using the MLA style, give such information in this order after the title of the book:

> name of editor and/or translator
> edition used, if not the original
> number of volumes
> title of series, with volume or number

Please note that volume numbers and other numbers used in documentation should always be arabic numerals (33) rather than roman numerals (XXXIII).

Facts of publication   Publication information is given in this form:

> New York: Nosuch Press, 1983.

Always give the *city* of publication. The name of the *publisher* follows. The *date* is the date of publication. Check the title page; if no date is given, turn over the page and use the date with the latest copyright (the most recent date next to the ©). If you are using the Chicago style, you may add the state or country after the city of publication if the city is not well known (Englewood Cliffs, N.J.). If you are using the MLA style, you should be aware that the *MLA Handbook* recommends abbreviating the name of the publisher. Obviously I can't list their recommended abbreviations; if you wish to follow the form exactly, you will have to consult that handbook. However, I don't think your instructor would object if you spelled out the name of the publisher. Also note that if you are using a paperback that seems to have two publishers—Vintage Books, A Division of Random House—MLA asks you to give both names. List the paperback imprint name first, then the name of the parent publishing house: Vintage-Random. Finally, if you are listing a selection within an edited work, you will end your entry with the inclusive page numbers of the selection (see C.2.g).

2. Proper form for specific types of books

In the pages that follow I give you examples of the proper form for different kinds of books. Since each example focuses on one aspect of the citation, in some cases you may need to check a couple of headings to see how to write a specific entry in your list.

a. Book—one author

Chicago and MLA
```
Zagorin, Perez.   The Court and the Country: The Begin-
     ning of the English Revolution.   New York: Athe-
     neum, 1970.
```

b. Book—more than one author

Chicago and MLA

Evans, Rowland, and Robert D. Novak. <u>Nixon in the
    White House: The Frustration of Power</u>. New York:
    Random House, 1971.

Easton, Susan, Joan M. Mills, and Diane K. Winokur.
    <u>Equal to the Task: How Workingwomen Are Managing
    in Corporate America</u>. New York: Seaview Books,
    1982.

Note that the name of the first author is inverted (Easton, Susan) but the names of other authors appear in their normal form. Be sure to put commas after the last name *and* first name of the first author.

c. Book with corporate author

If responsibility for the contents of the book is taken by an agency, corporation, or institute, use the name of this group as the author. Alphabetize according to the first word in the name (disregarding *the* and *a*). Spell out the full name of the group. Give the name of the parent body before listing subdivisions of the organization (in the following example, Brooklyn College is responsible for the Institute of Puerto Rican Studies). If your bibliography is going to include a large number of works with group authors, and the names of the organizations are themselves long, consult *The Chicago Manual* for systems you can use to make your citations and the bibliography easier to use.

Chicago and MLA

Royal Institute of Philosophy. <u>Understanding Wittgen-
    stein</u>. Royal Institute of Philosophy Lectures,
    Vol. 7 (1972–1973). New York: St. Martin's Press,
    1974.

Museum of Graphic Art. <u>American Printmaking: The First
    150 Years</u>. New York: Museum of Graphic Art, 1969.

Brooklyn College. Institute of Puerto Rican Studies.
    <u>The Puerto Rican People: A Selected Bibliography
    for Use in Social Work Education</u>. New York: Coun-
    cil on Social Work Education, 1973.

d. Book—edition other than the original

Chicago and MLA

Lawrence, William W. <u>Shakespeare's Problem Comedies</u>.
    2nd ed. New York: Ungar Publishing Co., 1960.

Stone, Lawrence. <u>The Crisis of the Aristocracy 1558–
    1614</u>. Abridged ed. New York: Oxford University
    Press, 1967

e. Book with author and editor and/or translator

Chicago

```
Vygotsky, Lev S.  Thought and Language.  Edited and
     translated by Eugenia Hanfmann and Gertrude Vakar.
     Cambridge, Mass.: The MIT Press, 1962.
```

MLA

```
Vygotsky, Lev S.  Thought and Language.  Ed. and trans.
     Eugenia Hanfmann and Gertrude Vakar.  Cambridge:
     The MIT Press, 1962.
```

If editor and translator are different, list translator first, then editor.

f. Book with editor rather than author—a collection of works

Chicago and MLA

```
Chambers, William N., and Walter D. Burnham, eds.  The
     American Party Systems: Stages of Political Devel-
     opment.  2nd ed.  New York: Oxford University
     Press, 1975.
```

```
Wilbur, George B., and Warner Muensterberger, eds.
     Psychoanalysis and Culture: Essays in Honor of
     Geza Roheim.  New York: International Universities
     Press, 1951.
```

```
Witherspoon, Alexander M., and Frank J. Warnke, eds.
     Seventeenth-Century Prose and Poetry.  2nd ed.
     New York: Harcourt, Brace and World, 1963.
```

g. Work in a collection or anthology

The guidelines and forms for Chicago and MLA differ here. Be sure to follow the forms for the style you are using.

CHICAGO

If you are using only one work or essay from a collection, you may list only that work; I give you the proper form below. If you are using several works or essays from the same collection, it is probably easier to list only the collection, using the form in C.2.f.

```
Dekker, Thomas.  The Shoemakers' Holiday.  In English
     Drama, 1580-1642, edited by C. F. Tucker Brooke
     and N. B. Paradise, 263-293.  Boston: D. C. Heath,
     1933.
```

```
Halsey, Louis.  "The Choral Music."  In Robert Schu-
     mann: The Man and His Music, edited by Alan
     Walker, 350-389.  London: Barrie and Jenkins,
     1972.
```

```
Hays, Samuel P. "Political Parties and the Community-
    Society Continuum."  In The American Party Sys-
    tems: Stages of Political Development, edited by
    William N. Chambers and Walter D. Burnham, 152-
    181.  2nd ed. New York: Oxford University Press,
    1975.
```

The numbers that are given immediately after the names of the editors are the pages on which the essay or play appears. *The Shoemakers' Holiday* is underlined because this is a play which, when it first appeared, was published as a separate, entire work.

MLA

Since the citations in the body of your paper should be short, and since the author's name you use in the body of your paper must be the name of the person whose words you are referring to or quoting, you will list *separately* those poems, plays, short stories, articles, and essays that you have found in anthologies or edited collections. This guideline also applies to the prefaces, introductions, and afterwords you find in books or anthologies; an entry for a preface or introduction will begin with the name of the person who wrote it. Following are the appropriate forms for such entries. Before you look for the example that best fits the work you are using, please read over the following general guidelines.

▶ Your entry must *always* begin with the name of the person whose words or ideas you are using, followed by the full title of the poem, play, short story, selection, or essay.

▶ Titles of poems, plays, and other works that were originally published as books will be underlined (see the Dekker example that follows); poems, plays, essays, and other works that were originally published in a collection or journal will be put in quotation marks. Note that titles like Introduction, Afterword, and Preface are simply capitalized (see the Marcus example).

▶ You will give complete bibliographic information for your source, including the title of the anthology or collection, its editor(s), translator, edition, volumes, and so on (see C.1). If my examples do not completely match the source you are listing, check other categories in the C.2 section.

▶ The numbers at the end of your entry are the *inclusive* page numbers of the complete work you are listing: that is, the pages on which we will find the *whole* play, poem, essay.

▶ If you are using an essay or article that was first printed somewhere else, MLA asks you to include full information about the original source first; you can usually find this information at the bottom of the first page of the essay you read (see the Schwartz example).

► The abbreviation "ed." stands for "edited by," so never write "eds." in these situations.

► If you are using several works from the same collection or anthology, you can shorten your entries by using cross-references. I explain this technique after the following examples.

Crane, Hart. "To Brooklyn Bridge." <u>A Little Treasury of Modern Poetry, English and American</u>. Ed. Oscar Williams. Rev. ed. New York: Scribner's, 1952. 393–94.

Dekker, Thomas. <u>The Shoemakers' Holiday</u>. <u>English Drama, 1580–1642</u>. Ed. C. F. Tucker Brooke and N. B. Paradise. Boston: Heath, 1933. 263–93.

Halsey, Louis. "The Choral Music." <u>Robert Schumann: The Man and His Music</u>. Ed. Alan Walker. London: Barrie and Jenkins, 1972. 350–89.

Marcus, Steven. Afterword. <u>The Pickwick Papers</u>. By Charles Dickens. New York: Signet–NAL, 1964. 864–86.

Schwartz, Delmore. "Poetry and Belief in Thomas Hardy." <u>Southern Review</u> 6 (1940). Rpt. in <u>Hardy: A Collection of Critical Essays</u>. Ed. Albert J. Guerard. Twentieth Century Views. Englewood Cliffs: Prentice, 1963. 123–34.

MLA CROSS-REFERENCES

If you are using several works from the same collection or anthology, the MLA style allows you to shorten your list in the following manner. Create an entry for each separate work, including the author's name, the full title of the work, the name of the editor(s) of the anthology or collection, and the inclusive page numbers of this specific work. Then create a separate entry for the collection or anthology itself, starting with the name of the editor(s) (see C.2.f for this form). Obviously, if you have two works by the person who edited the collection, you will also have to add a short title of the collection in the entries for the specific works.

Donne, John. "IV. Meditation." Witherspoon and Warnke 61–62.

Johnson, Ben. "A Hymn on the Nativity of My Saviour." Witherspoon and Warnke 765.

Witherspoon, Alexander M., and Frank J. Warnke, eds. <u>Seventeenth–Century Prose and Poetry</u>. 2nd ed. New York: Harcourt, 1963.

h. Book in a multivolume set

Chicago and MLA

AN ENTRY FOR THE COMPLETE SET

Morison, Samuel E. <u>The History of United States Naval
    Operations in World War II</u>. 15 vols. Boston:
    Little, Brown and Co., 1947–62.

Bronson, Bertrand H., ed. <u>The Traditional Tunes of the
    Child Ballads with Their Texts, according to the
    Extant Records of Great Britain and America</u>.
    4 vols. Princeton, N.J.: Princeton University
    Press, 1959–72.

Note that these volumes were published over a number of years. Be sure to
indicate the dates of publication of the first and last volumes.

AN ENTRY FOR ONE VOLUME

Chicago

Morison, Samuel E. <u>The Rising Sun in the Pacific,
    1931–April 1942</u>. Vol. 3 of <u>The History of United
    States Naval Operations in World War II</u>. Boston:
    Little, Brown and Co., 1948.

This type of entry is appropriate since the individual volume has its own title
but is part of a larger series. Here I indicate only the date of this specific
volume.

MLA

If you are using only one volume of a multivolume set, you may list only that
volume. Note, however, that you will have to include the number of volumes
in the entire set. The first example shows you how to enter one volume of a
set with the same title. The second example shows you what to do if the titles
for each volume are different.

Bronson, Bertrand H., ed. <u>The Traditional Tunes of the
    Child Ballads with Their Texts, according to the
    Extant Records of Great Britain and America</u>. 4
    vols. Princeton: Princeton UP, 1959–72. Vol. 3.

Morison, Samuel E. <u>The Rising Sun in the Pacific,
    1931–April 1942</u>. Vol. 3 of <u>The History of United
    States Naval Operations in World War II</u>. 15 vols.
    Boston: Little, 1948.

If you are using only one selection from one volume of a multivolume set,
start with the author and/or title of the work you used; then at the end of the
entry, give the volume and inclusive page numbers of that selection.

"Robin Hood Rescuing Three Squires" (Child No. 140).
<u>The Traditional Tunes of the Child Ballads with
Their Texts, according to the Extant Records of
Great Britain and America</u>. Ed. Bertrand H.
Bronson. 4 vols. Princeton: Princeton UP,
1959–72. 3: 53–57.

i. Book in a series

Occasionally when you look at the title page of a book, you will notice that this book is part of a series; the series title may refer to subject matter (Documentary Monographs in Modern Art) or to the publisher (Smithsonian Miscellaneous Collection) or to both (Yale Judaica Series). Include information about the series in your reference. Give the name of the series (capitalize the main words but do not underline) and the volume or number of this work, if a volume or number is given.

Chicago and MLA

Bindoff, S. T. <u>Tudor England</u>. Pelican History of England, vol. 5. Harmondsworth, Middlesex, England:
Penguin Books, 1950.

McCoy, Garnett, ed. <u>David Smith</u>. Documentary Monographs in Modern Art. New York and Washington:
Praeger Publishers, 1973.

Moses ben Maimon. <u>The Code of Maimonides. Book 3: The
Book of Seasons</u>. Translated by Solomon Gandz and
Hyman Klein. Yale Judaica Series. New Haven:
Yale University Press, 1961.

j. Reprint of an older work

Once in a while you will use a book that is a reprint of a text that was originally published many years ago. A reprint of a work is different from an edition of a work. In an edition, some part or parts of the text have been changed; a reprint is a reproduction of the actual text the author originally wrote. If you give only the publication date of the reprint you are using, you give your reader the impression that this text is more recent than it actually is. This is the proper form for a reprinted book.

Chicago

Hegel, Georg W. F. <u>Lectures on the Philosophy of Religion, Together with a Work on the Proofs of the
Existence of God</u>. Translated from the 2nd German
ed. by E. B. Speirs and J. Burdon Sanderson;
edited by E. B. Speirs. London: K. Paul, Trench,
Truber, 1895; New York: Humanities Press, 1968.

When you have full information about the facts of publication of the original text, you give this information first (London . . . 1895); then give publication facts of the reprinted version. If you do not have publication facts about the original, follow this form:

> Author, title, date of original publication.
> Then write the word "reprint" (capitalize the first letter and put a period after it).
> Finish the citation with the facts of publication of the reprint.

> Woolf, Virginia. <u>The Second Common Reader</u>. New York: Harcourt, Brace and World, 1932; Harvest Books, 1960.

MLA

> Hegel, Georg W. F. <u>Lectures on the Philosophy of Religion, Together with a Work on the Proofs of the Existence of God</u>. Trans. from the 2nd German ed. by E. B. Speirs and J. Burdon Sanderson. Ed. E. B. Speirs. 1895. New York: Humanities Press, 1968.

> Woolf, Virginia. <u>The Second Common Reader</u>. 1932. New York: Harvest—Harcourt, 1960.

D. Proper Form for Encyclopedias, Dictionaries, and Similar Reference Works

---

Chicago

SIGNED ARTICLES

> <u>The Dictionary of National Biography</u>. 1931–40 ed., s.v. "Rackham, Arthur." By Herbert B. Grimsditch.

> <u>The Encyclopedia of Philosophy</u>. 1967 ed., s.v. "Hobbes, Thomas." By R. S. Peters.

UNSIGNED ARTICLES

> <u>The Focal Encyclopedia of Photography</u>. Rev. ed. (1965), s.v. "Daguerreotype."

> <u>Van Nostrand's Scientific Encyclopedia</u>. 6th ed. (1983), s.v. "Cyanogen."

The abbreviation s.v. stands for *sub verbo* (under the word). Since most encyclopedias and dictionaries are set up alphabetically according to key terms, the key word that headed the article will allow your readers to find the appropriate entry. In your bibliography, these works will be listed according to the name of the encyclopedia or dictionary (the first information in the entry).

> **MLA**
>
> SIGNED ARTICLES
>
> Grimsditch, Herbert B. "Rackham, Arthur." <u>Dictionary of National Biography</u>. 1931–40 ed.
>
> Peters, R. S. "Hobbes, Thomas." <u>The Encyclopedia of Philosophy</u>. 1967 ed.
>
> UNSIGNED ARTICLES
>
> "Cyanogen." <u>Van Nostrand's Scientific Encyclopedia</u>. 6th ed. 1983.
>
> "Daguerreotype." <u>The Focal Encyclopedia of Photography</u>. Rev. ed. 1965.

The signed articles will be listed according to the last names of the authors of the articles; the unsigned articles will be alphabetized according to the words used for the entry in the encyclopedia or dictionary.

E.   Proper Form for Periodicals

1. Scholarly Journals

a. General form

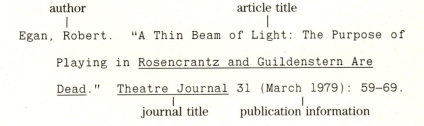

> author   article title
>
> Egan, Robert. "A Thin Beam of Light: The Purpose of
>
> Playing in <u>Rosencrantz and Guildenstern Are</u>
>
> <u>Dead</u>." <u>Theatre Journal</u> 31 (March 1979): 59–69.
>
>   journal title   publication information

Author Give the last name of the author first; if there is more than one author, give second and third authors' names in the normal order. See section C.2.b.

Article title Put the title of the article in quotation marks; place a period at the end, inside the quotation marks. Underline any words that are in italic type. Capitalize all main words in the title (see Appendix F.A).

Journal title   Although the titles of journals are sometimes abbreviated in notes and bibliographies, you should spell out the full title and underline it. Notice that there is no punctuation after the title.

Publication information   The number before the parentheses is the volume number; always use arabic numerals (31) rather than roman numerals (XXXI). The final numbers are the inclusive pages on which the article appears. Since most scholarly journals are paginated consecutively throughout the year, the volume number and the page numbers provide the readers with enough information to locate the article. The date of the volume is given to let the reader know how old, or recent, this article is; the month/season is not technically necessary, but it is useful information for the readers and you should include it. Some magazines and journals do not paginate consecutively throughout the year, but begin each issue with page 1. If you cite such a journal or magazine, you will have to give the issue number as well as the volume number (see E.1.b). Magazines, those periodicals written for a general audience, are usually cited by giving only the date of publication (see E.2).

Watch the punctuation carefully. A colon separates the date from the page numbers. Otherwise, notice that there is no punctuation. Put a period after the page numbers to indicate the end of the citation.

Chicago and MLA
```
Barish, Jonas A.   "The Double Plot in Volpone."   Mod-
    ern Philology 51 (1953): 83-92.

Grose, Lois M.   "The Able Student in a City School
    System."   English Journal 55 (October 1966): 891-
    94.

Jones, Jacqueline.   " 'My Mother Was Much of a Woman':
    Black Women, Work, and the Family under Slavery."
    Feminist Studies 8 (Summer 1982): 235-70.
```

b. Journal that paginates each issue separately

Because the *Journal of Popular Culture* begins each issue with page 1, you will have to give the issue number as well as the volume number.

Chicago
```
Wilson, Christopher B.   "The Era of the Reporter Re-
    considered: The Case of Lincoln Steffens."   Jour-
    nal of Popular Culture 15, no. 2 (Fall 1981): 52-
    60.
```

MLA
```
Wilson, Christopher B.   "The Era of the Reporter Re-
    considered: The Case of Lincoln Steffens."   Jour-
    nal of Popular Culture 15.2 (Fall 1981): 52-60.
```

2. Magazines

References to periodicals that are published weekly or monthly and that are intended for a general reading audience are usually cited by omitting the volume number and using the date of publication instead.

Chicago

"Alex and the Awards." The New Yorker, 21 June 1982,
      32–35.

Sragow, Michael. "Ghostwriters: Unraveling the Enigma
      of Movie Authorship." Film Commentary, April
      1983, 9–18.

Myers, Mary L. "Reproducing Raphael." Artnews,
      April 1983, 79–83.

MLA

"Alex and the Awards." The New Yorker 21 June 1982:
      32–35.

Myers, Mary L. "Reproducing Raphael." Artnews Apr.
      1983: 79–83.

Sragow, Michael. "Ghostwriters: Unraveling the Enigma
      of Movie Authorship." Film Commentary Apr. 1983:
      9–18.

Note that when a specific date is given, it is given in the European fashion (21 June 1982). If no author is given, use the title to introduce the entry, and alphabetize according to the first main word in the title, disregarding *the* and *a*.

3. Newspaper articles

Chicago

Bonner, Raymond. "A Guatemalan General's Rise to
      Power." New York Times 21 July 1982, A3.

"Madman Attacks Alligator." The Smithville (Florida)
      Observer, 14 August 1991, sec. 4, p. 5.

MLA

Bonner, Raymond. "A Guatemalan General's Rise to
      Power." New York Times 21 July 1982: A3.

"Madman Attacks Alligator." Smithville Observer
      [Smithfield, Florida] 14 August 1991, late ed.,
      sec. 4: 5+.

In using either of these forms, remember that you must give your readers enough information so that they can easily locate your article. Watch page numbers in a newspaper. Some newspapers are divided into sections, and each section begins with page 1. Thus, you must give your reader both the section designation and the page numbers. It would be wise to include the edition if the newspaper you are using appears in various editions.

F.   Forms for Other Types of Sources

Space in this book is limited, but, unfortunately, types of sources are not. For the proper form for other types of sources, I recommend that you consult *The Chicago Manual* or the *MLA Handbook.** The Chicago Manual* includes sections on unpublished material (including personal interviews), public documents (documents of local and federal governments), and nonbook materials (like records and films). The *MLA Handbook* has forms for films, interviews, public documents, theatrical performances, musical compositions, radio and television programs, and records, to name a few. If you are using the Chicago style but don't find a form in *The Chicago Manual* for the source you are using, check the form in the *MLA Handbook*. The forms for books and periodicals that I have provided will give you a sense of the general Chicago style; you can, by using your common sense, create a form that will be appropriate.

G.   The Final Bibliography or List of Works Cited, with Samples

Your final bibliography or list of works cited must be typed on a separate sheet (or sheets) of paper. Use the proper manuscript margins.

Chicago

If you are following the Chicago style, head this sheet "Bibliography." The heading should be centered, two inches from the top of the page; leave four lines of space between the heading and your first entry. Each entry should begin with the author's last name at the left-hand margin. All other lines of an individual entry should be indented five spaces. Single-space individual entries. Double-space between entries.

MLA

If you are following the MLA style, number this page consecutively with the other pages in your paper. If you are including a page headed "Notes," that

---

* In these appendixes, the Chicago style I have used is based on *The Chicago Manual of Style*, 13th ed., rev. and expanded (Chicago: University of Chicago Press, 1982). The MLA style I have used is that found in Joseph Gibaldi and Walter S. Achtert, *MLA Handbook for Writers of Research Papers*, 2nd ed. (New York: The Modern Language Association of America, 1984).

page should be numbered and placed between the last page of the body of your paper and this list. Head the list "Works Cited"; center the heading one inch from the top of the paper. Double-space; then start your first entry. The first line of all entries should be flush with the left margin. Additional lines within an entry should be indented five spaces. Double-space all entries and double-space between entries.

Works Cited

"Alex and the Awards." The New Yorker 21 June 1982: 32–35.

Barish, Jonah A. "The Double Plot in Volpone." Modern Philology 51 (1953): 83–92.

"Daguerreotype." The Focal Encyclopedia of Photography. Rev. ed. 1965.

Donne, John. "IV. Meditation." Witherspoon and Warnke 61–62.

Jonson, Ben. "A Hymn on the Nativity of My Saviour." Witherspoon and Warnke 765.

Muir, Kenneth. Introduction. The Tragedy of King Richard the Second. By William Shakespeare. Ed. Kenneth Muir. New York: Signet–NAL, 1963. xxiii–xxxvii.

Museum of Graphic Art. American Printmaking: The First 150 Years. New York: Museum of Graphic Art, 1969.

"Robin Hood Rescuing Three Squires" (Child No. 140). The Traditional Tunes of the Child Ballads with Their Texts, according to the Extant Records of Great Britain and America. Ed. Bertrand H. Bronson. 4 vols. Princeton: Princeton UP, 1959–72. 3: 53–57.

Shakespeare, William. The Tragedy of King Richard the Second. Ed. Kenneth Muir. New York: Signet–NAL, 1963.

Witherspoon, Alexander M., and Frank J. Warnke, eds.
    Seventeenth-Century Prose and Poetry. 2nd ed. New
    York: Harcourt, 1963.

Woolf, Virginia. _The Second Common Reader_. 1932. New
    York: Harvest-Harcourt, 1960.

Bibliography

"Alex and the Awards." The New Yorker, 21 June
    1982, 32–35.

Barish, Jonas A. "The Double Plot in Volpone." Mod-
    ern Philology 51 (1953): 83–92.

Bronson, Bertrand H., ed. The Traditional Tunes of the
    Child Ballads with Their Texts, according to the
    Extant Records of Great Britain and America.
    4 vols. Princeton, N.J.: Princeton University
    Press, 1959–72.

The Focal Encyclopedia of Photography. Rev. ed.
    (1965), s.v. "Daguerreotype."

Kluckhohn, Clyde, and William Morgan. "Some Notes on
    Navaho Dreams." In Psychoanalysis and Culture:
    Essays in Honor of Geza Roheim, edited by George
    B. Wilbur and Warner Muensterberger, 120–31. New
    York: International Universities Press, 1951.

Morison, Samuel E. The Rising Sun in the Pacific,
    1931–April 1942. Vol. 3 of The History of United
    States Naval Operations in World War II. Boston:
    Little, Brown and Co., 1948.

Moses ben Maimon. The Code of Maimonides. Book 3: The
    Book of Seasons. Translated by Solomon Gandz and
    Hyman Klein. Yale Judaica Series. New Haven:
    Yale University Press, 1961.

Museum of Graphic Art. American Printmaking: The First
    150 Years. New York: Museum of Graphic Art, 1969.

Sragow, Michael. "Ghostwriters: Unraveling the Enigma
    of Movie Authorship." Film Commentary, April
    1983, 9–18.

Witherspoon, Alexander M., and Frank J. Warnke, eds.
    Seventeenth-Century Prose and Poetry. 2nd ed. New
    York: Harcourt, Brace and World, 1963.

Woolf, Virginia. The Second Common Reader. New York:
    Harcourt, Brace and World, 1932; Harvest Books,
    1960.

Appendix B

The Humanities System: Notes or MLA Parenthetical Citations

A. General Information

In section A of Appendix A I describe both the Chicago style and the MLA style. If you haven't read that section, you should do so now so that you can decide if the humanities system is appropriate for the paper you are writing, and so that you can choose which of these two styles, Chicago or MLA, you want to follow.

If you decide the Chicago style is the one you want to use, follow the advice I give for notes in the rest of this appendix. And don't forget that you will have to put together a bibliography for your paper (see Appendix A). If you decide the MLA style is the one you want, I'd suggest reading section B.1 in this appendix first to familiarize yourself with the basics of the form. Then you'll have to turn to Appendix A for information about the list of works cited, which you must attach to the end of your paper.

B. Citing Sources in the Body of Your Paper

1. The MLA style—parenthetical citations

a. The basic principles

If you understand the basic principles of the MLA form, you should have little trouble using this style of documentation.

> PRINCIPLE 1   You need to give credit where credit is due. In the MLA style you tell your readers that you are using a source by giving the name of the author whose work you are using right in the body of your paper.

This form of poetry was very popular in the eighteenth
century (Jones 15).

Sneed wrote that "in our day we rarely saw automobiles"
(29).

PRINCIPLE 2   You need to give your readers full bibliographic information about each source you use in your paper. In the MLA style, this
information is given in your list of works cited, attached to the end of
your paper. Each work or source you cite in your paper is listed here,
in alphabetical order according to the last name of the author you
have given in your text. Each entry in this list gives your readers all
the information they need to find the source.

Jones, Richard M. An Introduction to Eighteenth-
    Century Poetry. 3rd ed. New York: Norton, 1999.

Sneed, Alfred P. "In the Good Ole Days." Memories.
    Ed. James W. Hunt. San Francisco: NoName, 1998.
    20-41.

PRINCIPLE 3   You need to tell your readers exactly where in each
source you found this information. Thus, in the body of your paper
you also give the appropriate page number(s) in parentheses.

Thus, when your readers see "This form of poetry was very popular in the
eighteenth century (Jones 15)," they know that you took this idea from a
work written by a person named Jones. They know that they can turn to your
list of works cited at the end of the paper, and there they will find *one* entry
that begins "Jones." In this entry they know that you will give them all the
information they need to find this work. The number (15) after Jones's name
tells them that they will find this idea on page 15 of Jones's work.

It's very simple. But as simple as the basics are, like all other forms of
documentation the MLA style has its forms and conventions that you are
expected to know and follow. In the remainder of section B.1 I explain the
basic form of parenthetical citations, I talk about where you place these
citations, and I give you variations of the basic form. Obviously, in this system
you must have a list of works cited since it is the only place your readers will
find such necessary information as title, edition, publication facts, and the
like. I'd suggest you read this whole section on parenthetical citations first.
Then go through the draft of your paper, jotting down the names of the
authors you quote or refer to. At that point you can turn back to Appendix A,
where I explain how to set up your list of works cited. In Appendix A you will
also find the proper form for the various sources you will be putting in your
list. If you have any questions that I have not answered here, you will have to
consult the *MLA Handbook;* see Appendix A.F.

b. The basic form

You cite a source in the body of your paper by giving the author's last name and the page number(s) in parentheses, normally at the end of your sentence.

> The poet Wilson was a recluse with odd ideas (Stark
>
> 24-30).

If you have used the author's name as part of your sentence, as I encouraged you to do in Section 6, you need to add only the page number(s).

> Sheila Stark points out that the poet Wilson was a
>
> recluse with odd ideas (24-30).

Similarly, if the context makes it clear whose ideas or words you are using, it isn't necessary to repeat the author's name.

> These musical instruments came into vogue about the time
>
> of King Henry VI (Harvey 134). The viola da gamba, for
>
> example, was being played in court in 1453 (140).

If you are referring to the entire work, the author's name is enough; no page number, obviously, is necessary.

> Shakespeare's <u>Richard II</u> is full of images of the sun.

If a work was written or edited by more than one author, you must give the last names of all the authors, just as they appear in the list of works cited. If your source has more than three authors, give the last name of the first followed by "et al." (Smith et al. 94).

> Felltham was a fanatic about the royalist cause
>
> (Witherspoon and Warnke 317).

c. Where to place your citations and how to keep your paper readable

As you can see, these parenthetical citations have the potential of becoming obtrusive and thus interferring with your readers' ability to pay attention to what you are saying. For this reason, keep these guidelines in mind when you place your citations in your text.

▶ Within the rules of the MLA form, keep your parenthetical citations as short as possible. One simple solution to this problem is to use the names of authors and their works in your sentence proper, as I advised you to do in Section 6. If you use the author's name directly in your sentence, you need to add only the page number(s) in parentheses.

▶ The citation must be placed so that it is clear what ideas have been taken from a source; at the same time, you do not want to impede the "flow" of your sentence. Whenever possible, place your parenthetical citation at the end of the sentence. Note that the period comes after the parentheses. If you are finishing a quotation, place the parentheses after the quotation mark and before the period. If it is not possible to put the citation at the end of the sentence, try to place it next to a natural "rest" point in the sentence.

```
As she wrote in her journal in May, "inspiration

ravishes me" (56).



This policy, although strongly opposed by Carlson

(Hindman 14-16), eventually was adopted by the court.
```

▶ If you are using the block style of quoting, place your citation two spaces after the conclusion of the quotation.

```
Describing the battle as he witnessed it from his

bedroom window, Kendall wrote to a friend:

          It was fierce and bloody.  Bullets flew.  Blood

          was everywhere.  The noise was deafening.

          Bodies lay on the sidewalk.  (34)
```

d. Variations of the basic form

▶ If your list of works cited contains more than one work by the same author, be sure to give a short title of the work each time you mention this author.

```
In his novel Kingdom Come, Withers often uses the

phrase "cold death" (68, 97, 110).



This form of poetry was most popular at court (Hall,

"Poems" 48).
```

▶ If you are citing works from several volumes of a multivolume set, you will need to include the number of the volume (in arabic numbers) before the page number. See Appendix A.C.2.h.

Freud discussed this notion in <u>Interpretation of Dreams</u>

(4: 136–38).

▶ If you are using the words or ideas of a person you read in a source other than the original, you will have to give your readers the names of both the author of these words or ideas *and* the author of the source where you found them. Use the phrase "qtd. in" (quoted in) to cite such references.

In 1850 a man who signed himself only "Angry" wrote a

fierce letter on the subject to the editor of the <u>Times</u>

(qtd. in Wallace 67).

▶ If you are citing a source that has no author, use a short title of the work as your reference. Be sure to use the first two or three main words of the title since your readers will have to be able to find this title quickly in your list of works cited. If you are referring to a source that is only one page long and this page number is given in the entry on your list, you need not repeat the page number in your text.

Such were the times that men earned less than a dime a

day ("Breadlines" 45).

▶ If you are quoting from or referring to a poem, play, short story, or novel, it is helpful to your readers if you include in your citation division markers used in the work itself (like chapter numbers, book numbers, line numbers, etc.). In your parenthetical citation, give the page number first; then use a semicolon to separate it from the division reference. Abbreviate chapter, book, and section, but spell out the word "line" since lower case l's can be confused with the number 1. If you are citing a classic poem or play, you can omit page numbers completely and just give the conventional division markers used in the work itself. If an act or book number precedes a line number, you don't have to spell out "line"; convention tells us this is a line number.

It is not until the middle of the novel that we meet the

heroine (200; ch. 6).

```
When Keats writes "what soft incense hangs upon the

boughs" (line 52), we can almost smell this dark garden.


Satan's return to hell was greeted by "a dismal

universal hiss" (Bk. X. 508).


The psychological aspects of Richard II become most

obvious in the moving soliloquy of the deposed and

imprisoned king (V.v.1-45).
```

▶ If you found the same information in more than one work, give all sources, separating the citations with semicolons. If you decide such citations might be obtrusive in the body of your paper, consider putting this information in a note (see the following).

```
(Smith 645; Clark and Hillsdale, "Keats" 47).
```

▶ Notes. At those times when the citation you feel you must give becomes long and/or cumbersome, or when you want to say something further about a topic you raise, place a note number in your paper, raised a half-space above the line ([1]), and then include the note itself at the bottom of the page or on a separate sheet at the end of your paper headed "Notes." For further information (and warnings!) about such notes, see section J in this appendix. Note that if you write content notes in the MLA style, the citations must be given in the form I've been outlining here.

2. The Chicago style—notes

After you have finished the final draft of your paper and before you make your typed or final clean copy, it is time to set up your notes. I encourage you to follow these steps to guarantee that your notes are completely accurate.

1. Put your bibliography cards in alphabetical order; or if you have written your final bibliography, you can use the bibliography itself.
2. Starting with the first page of your paper, locate the first reference you make to a source. Follow steps 3 through 6 for each note.
3. Find the notecard from which you took the information or quotation that you have used in your text. Check what you have written against your notecard to be sure the information or quotation in your paper is accurate; obviously, if anything in your paper is inaccurate, you must correct it.

4. Put the appropriate note number at the end of the sentence that contains the information/quotation you have used. I usually put a circle around the note number, or write it in a different color ink, so that I do not miss it when I am typing the final copy of the paper.
5. Locate the bibliographic information about the source on your bibliography card or in your finished bibliography.
6. On a separate sheet of paper headed "Notes," write the appropriate note number. Then write the note in the proper form (see sections D through K of this appendix). You will need your notecard for the correct page number or numbers, and you will need the bibliography card or bibliography entry for the rest of the information about the source.

Further information about notes:

▶ All notes are numbered consecutively throughout the paper, starting with number 1 for your first note and ending with the number that reflects the total number of notes in your paper.
▶ The note number is raised above the line (no punctuation) and should be placed, whenever possible, at the end of a sentence.

```
According to Richard Allen, the poem is based on a

traditional Navaho myth.⁶
```

```
Although James Johnson has argued that this battle was

"the most decisive of the war," other historians

disagree with Johnson's assessment.¹⁰
```

▶ There are different forms for the first reference you make to a source and subsequent references to the same source. Please read section C.
▶ It is not always necessary to repeat information in a note *if* the *full* bibliographical information is given in the body of your paper. Thus, if you have given the author's *full* name in your text, it is permissible to begin your note with the title of the work. Similarly, if you have given *both* the author's *full* name and the *complete* title of the work in the body of your paper, you may begin your note with the next piece of information required by the correct note form for that work. However, it is never incorrect to repeat the author's name and title in the note.
▶ Most notes will be used to acknowledge sources that you have used in your paper. However, you may also use notes to comment on a point you have made or to explain a point. See section J.
▶ If material that you use in one or more paragraphs of your paper is taken from the same source, your note should indicate the scope of your use of

this material. The note number for this note should be placed early in the section in which you use this material, ideally after a sentence in which you refer directly to the source.

```
10. Information in the following paragraphs on the Bat-
tle of the Bulge has been taken from John W. Sweet,
World War II . . .
```

If you quote from this source, each quotation will have to have a separate note. If you are using one work extensively in your paper, read section I.4.

▶ I discuss format for notes in section L, where you will also find a sample endnote page.

C.   First Notes and Subsequent Notes

The first time you cite a source in your notes, you must give full information about the source; this note would be a first note. However, if you refer to that source again later in your paper, you can use a shortened form to acknowledge the source; notes that refer to a source after the first full citation are called subsequent notes.

First note on Hays
```
1. Samuel P. Hays, "Political Parties and the Commu-
nity-Society Continuum," in The American Party Systems:
Stages of Political Development, ed. William N. Cham-
bers and Walter D. Burnham, 2nd ed. (New York: Oxford
University Press, 1975), 154.
```

First note on Jennings
```
2. William I. Jennings, Appeal to the People, vol. 1 of
Party Politics (Cambridge: Cambridge University Press,
1960), 14.
```

Subsequent note on Hays
```
3. Hays, "Political Parties and the Community-Society
Continuum," 156.
```

Subsequent note on Jennings
```
4. Jennings, Appeal to the People, 42.
```

Subsequent note on Hays
```
5. Hays, "Political Parties and the Community-Society
Continuum," 180.
```

In sections D through G, I give you more information about the proper form for first notes. You will find more information for the proper form for subsequent notes in section I.

D.   Proper Form for First Notes—Books

1.   General form

```
note number   author                          title
     |           |                              |
   | 14. | Carl G. Jung, |Four Archetypes: Mother,

          Rebirth, Spirit, Trickster.|

       ⌐| trans. R. F. C. Hull, Bollingen Series,

        | no. 20 |(Princeton, N.J.: Princeton

        | University Press, 1969),| 20.
                            |            |
other publication    facts of publication    page number(s)
information
```

Notice that author, title, and other publication information are separated by commas.

Author   Begin your note with the name or names of the author(s) of the material you are referring to in your paper. Names are given in their normal order.

Title   Be sure to give the full title of the article, poem, play, or selection if you are using a work in a collection; such titles should be put in quotation marks. Give the full title of the book as it appears in your bibliography; titles of books are underlined. Be sure to capitalize the main words in all titles (see Appendix F.A).

Other publication information   Information about editors, translators, series, and editions must be given. *The Chicago Manual* recommends placement of other publication information in the following order:

> editor and/or translator (when the original author is given)
> series and the number/volume of this work in the series
> edition (if not the original)
> number of volumes in the set if the work is a multivolume work

Facts of publication   Facts of publication, following the same form as that in the bibliography, are placed in parentheses. Never put a comma before a parenthesis.

Page or pages   The last numbers in the note indicate the page or pages on which the information you have used appears. If the work you are using is part of a multivolume set, the volume number will also be given here (see D.2.f).

2. Proper form for specific types of books

a. Book—one author

> 16. Perez Zagorin, <u>The Court and the Country: The Beginning of the English Revolution</u> (New York: Atheneum, 1970), 100.

b. Book—more than one author

> 4. Rowland Evans and Robert D. Novak, <u>Nixon in the White House: The Frustration of Power</u> (New York: Random House, 1971), 54.

> 5. Susan Easton, Joan M. Mills, and Diane K. Winokur, <u>Equal to the Task: How Workingwomen Are Managing in Corporate America</u> (New York: Seaview Books, 1982), 17.

c. Book with corporate author

> 15. Museum of Graphic Art, <u>American Printmaking: The First 150 Years</u> (New York: Museum of Graphic Art, 1969), 23.

When you are referring to a book with a corporate author, be sure to begin your note with the same words you used in the "author" position in your bibliography entry, so that your readers can easily find the correct entry in the bibliography.

d. Book—edition other than the original

> 8. William W. Lawrence, <u>Shakespeare's Problem Comedies</u>, 2nd ed. (New York: Ungar Publishing Co., 1960), 42.

e. Book with author and editor and/or translator

> 10. Lev S. Vygotsky, <u>Thought and Language</u>, ed. and trans. Eugenia Hanfmann and Gertrude Vakar (Cambridge, Mass.: The MIT Press, 1962), 85.

f. Book in multivolume set

Reference to a work in which all volumes have the same title

> 13. G. W. F. Hegel, <u>Aesthetics: Lectures on Fine Art</u>, trans. T. M. Knox (Oxford: Clarendon Press, 1975), 2:100.

The first number after the publication facts (2) refers to the volume; the second number (100) refers to the page.

Reference to a work in which each volume has a different title

17. William I. Jennings, The Growth of Parties, vol. 2 of Party Politics (Cambridge: Cambridge University Press, 1961), 90.

Notice that in this note you give the title of the volume you are using first and then the volume number and title of the complete series.

g. Book in a series

18. Moses ben Maimon, The Code of Maimonides. Book 3: The Book of Seasons, trans. Solomon Gandz and Hyman Klein, Yale Judaica Series (New Haven: Yale University Press, 1961), 101—03.

7. S. T. Bindoff, Tudor England, Pelican History of England, vol. 5 (Harmondsworth, Middlesex, England: Penguin Books, 1950), 70.

10. Letter to Edgar Levy, 1 September 1945, in David Smith, ed. Garnett McCoy, Documentary Monographs in Modern Art (New York and Washington: Praeger Publishers, 1973), 196.

Information about series should be given in the same order in which it is given in your bibliography entry. For more information, see Appendix A, section C.2.i.

h. Work in a collection

When citing a work in a collection, your note must begin with the name of the person who wrote the words to which you are referring and the title of the selection by this person.

14. E. B. White, "The Years of Wonder," in Essays of E. B. White (New York: Harper & Row, 1977), 172.

5. Clyde Kluckhohn and William Morgan, "Some Notes on Navaho Dreams," in Psychoanalysis and Culture: Essays in Honor of Geza Roheim, ed. George B. Wilbur and Warner Muensterberger (New York: International Universities Press, 1951), 120—31.

7. "Robin Hood Rescuing Three Squires" (Child No. 140), in The Traditional Tunes of the Child Ballads with Their Texts, ed. Bertrand H. Bronson (Princeton, N.J.: Princeton University Press, 1966), 3:53—57.

The last reference begins with the title of the selection because the actual author of these ballads is not known.

If you are referring to material in a collection that was written by the editor or editors of that collection (such as introductions), you may begin your note with the names of the editors, or you may begin with the title of the selection.

> 9. "John Donne: Introduction," in <u>Seventeenth-Century Prose and Poetry</u>, ed. Alexander M. Witherspoon and Frank J. Warnke, 2nd ed. (New York: Harcourt, Brace and World, 1963), 58.

> or

> 9. Alexander M. Witherspoon and Frank J. Warnke, eds., "John Donne: Introduction," in <u>Seventeenth-Century Prose and Poetry</u>, 2nd ed. (New York: Harcourt, Brace and World, 1963), 58.

Notice that if you begin with the editors' names, it is not necessary to repeat them after the title of the collection.

i. Reprint of an older work

For further information on reprints of older works, see Appendix A, section C.2.j.

> 10. Georg W. F. Hegel, <u>Lectures on the Philosophy of Religion, Together with a Work on the Proofs of the Existence of God</u>, trans. from the 2nd German ed. by E. B. Speirs and J. Burdon Sanderson; ed. E. B. Speirs (London: K. Paul, Trench, Truber, 1895; New York: Humanities Press, 1968), 85.

> 6. Virginia Woolf, "Donne after Three Centuries," in <u>The Second Common Reader</u> (New York: Harcourt, Brace and World, 1932; Harvest Books, 1960), 17-31.

E. Proper Form for First Notes—Encyclopedias, Dictionaries, and Similar Reference Works

---

UNSIGNED ARTICLES

> 10. <u>The Focal Encyclopedia of Photography</u>, rev. ed. (1965), s.v. "Daguerreotype."

> 11. <u>Van Nostrand's Scientific Encyclopedia</u>, 6th ed. (1983), s.v. "Cyanogen."

SIGNED ARTICLES

7. <u>The Encyclopedia of Philosophy</u>, 1967 ed., s.v. "Hobbes, Thomas," by R. S. Peters.

18. <u>The Dictionary of National Biography</u>, 1931–40 ed., s.v. "Rackham, Arthur," by Herbert B. Grimsditch.

If you have questions about these forms, see Appendix A, section D.

F.   Proper Form for First Notes—Periodicals

1.   Scholarly journals

a. General form

note number   author   title

15.   Jacqueline Jones,   " 'My Mother Was Much of a Woman': Black Women, Work, and the Family under Slavery,"

<u>Feminist Studies</u>   8 (Summer 1982): 236–37.

journal title   publication information

Note that the author, title, and journal title are separated by commas.

Author   Give the name or names of the author(s) in their normal order.

Title   Give the full title of the article, including subtitles. All main words should be capitalized (see Appendix F.A) and the entire title placed in quotation marks (place the comma inside the quotation marks). The single quotation marks here indicate that the first part of the title was placed in quotation marks in the original article.

Journal title   Although you may see the titles of journals abbreviated, you should spell out the full title.

Publication information   The first number given (8) is the volume number. The information in parentheses is the season and year of the issue. The final numbers are the pages to which you are referring.

13. Lois M. Grose, "The Able Student in a City School System," <u>English Journal</u> 55 (October 1966): 891–94.

5. Robert Egan, "A Thin Beam of Light: The Purpose of Playing in <u>Rosencrantz and Guildenstern Are Dead</u>," <u>Theatre Journal</u> 31 (March 1979): 63.

b. Journal that paginates each issue separately

> 6. Christopher B. Wilson, "The Era of the Reporter
> Reconsidered: The Case of Lincoln Steffens," Journal
> of Popular Culture 15, no. 2 (Fall 1981): 59.

2. Magazines

For more information about the distinction between scholarly journals and
magazines, see Appendix A, section E.2.

> 8. Michael Sragow, "Ghostwriters: Unraveling the Enigma
> of Movie Authorship," Film Commentary, April 1983, 10.

> 11. "Alex and the Awards," The New Yorker, 21 June
> 1982, 34.

3. Newspaper articles

> 14. Raymond Bonner, "A Guatemalan General's Rise to
> Power," New York Times, 21 July 1982, A3.

> 16. "Madman Attacks Alligator," The Smithville (Flor-
> ida) Observer, 14 August 1991, sec. 4, p. 5.

For more information about newspaper articles, see Appendix A, section E.3.

G. First Notes for Other Types of Sources

In addition to forms for the more usual kinds of books and articles in periodicals, there are also proper forms for citations of other types of sources—
documents of federal and local governments, interviews, films, recordings,
television programs, and the like. Unfortunately, there is not enough space in
this book to give you specific information about the proper forms for these
various kinds of sources. If you have used these types of materials in your
paper, consult Turabian or *The Chicago Manual* for the correct form. For
more information on documenting other types of sources in your paper, see
Appendix A, section F.

H. Notes for Quotations Taken from a Secondary Source

In Section 4, subsection C.1, I alerted you to the fact that you should not get
into the habit of quoting material that is quoted in one of the sources you
have used. I urged you to locate, whenever possible, the original work and to
quote from the original work.

In those cases when you have tried to locate the original source of a quotation but have not been able to, your note must clearly reflect that you have used a secondary source. In your note, you should first give your reader as much information as you are able about the original source; if you have full bibliographic information, give it in the normal order for that type of work. Then, in your note you will write "quoted by" and give full bibliographic information about the source you used. The page number you give will be the page number on which the quotation appears in the source you used.

> 15. Henry D. Lloyd, <u>Wealth against Commonwealth</u> (1894; ed. 1899), quoted by Richard Hofstadter, <u>The Age of Reform from Bryan to F.D.R.</u> (New York: Random House, Vintage Books, 1955), 141.

You can find more information about using material from a secondary source in Section 4.C.1 and Section 6.B.4.

I.   Proper Form for Subsequent Notes

A subsequent note, I will remind you, is a note that refers to a work that you have already cited in an earlier note (the first note). After you have given full bibliographic information in your first note, you may use a shortened form if you refer to this work again (subsequent notes).

1.   The shortened form

In a subsequent note, you will give the author's last name, a shortened title of the work, and the page number.

> 16. Jones, "'My Mother Was Much of a Woman,'" 240.

> 17. Moses ben Maimon, <u>The Code of Maimonides</u>, 116.

> 18. Morison, <u>The Rising Sun in the Pacific</u>, 56.

2.   Some advice on using the shortened form

▶ In shortening the title of a work, *The Chicago Manual* recommends that
  ▷ you do not change the order of the words from the order in which they appear in the original title (*The History of England* should not be changed to *English History*).
  ▷ if the main title of the work contains five words or fewer, you should use the entire main title (*The Court and the Country: The Beginning of the English Revolution* should be shortened to *The Court and the Country*).

▷   you should use those words from the main title that best identify the
subject of the work (*The Traditional Tunes of the Child Ballads
with Their Texts, according to the Extant Records of Great Britain
and America* should be shortened to *Child Ballads*).

▶   When you are referring to a work that is part of a multivolume set with
the same title, you must give the appropriate volume number.

        15. Hegel, <u>Aesthetics</u> 2:118.

▶   In using the shortened form, you must never forget that your first obligation is to allow your readers to locate easily the work to which you are
referring. Develop your shortened form entry so that your readers can
easily find the correct entry in your bibliography. Thus your note must
contain at least the name of the author by which you have listed a work in
your bibliography. This caution is particularly important to remember if
you are using a number of selections from a collection and your bibliography entry is an entry only for the edited collection. In these situations,
your note will have to contain full information about the selection or
article you are using and the name(s) of the editor(s) of the collection,
plus a short title of the collection.

        BIBLIOGRAPHY ENTRY
        Wilbur, George B., and Warner Muensterberger, eds. <u>Psy-
            choanalysis and Culture: Essays in Honor of Geza
            Roheim</u>. New York: International Universities
            Press, 1951.

        NOTE
        18. Clyde Kluckhohn and William Morgan, "Some Notes on
        Navaho Dreams," in Wilbur and Muensterberger, <u>Psycho-
        analysis and Culture</u>, 129.

3.   Ibid.

Ibid. is the Latin abbreviation for a term that means "in the same place." Thus
ibid. can be used only when a note refers to the source given in the note that
immediately precedes it. If, for example, you had three references in a row to
Mary L. Myers' article on Raphael, you could use ibid.

        15. Mary L. Myers, "Reproducing Raphael," <u>Artnews</u>,
        April 1983, 80.

        16. Ibid.

        17. Ibid., 82.

Note 17 is a reference to the same article, but this note refers to a different
page. You must also be aware that you cannot use ibid. if the note to which
you are referring contains citations for more than one work. If you have two

or three works listed, how does the reader know to which of the two or three you are referring?

Ibid. is the last of a number of Latin abbreviations that used to be used in subsequent notes. Op cit. (*opere citato*, "in the work cited") and loc. cit. (*loco citato*, "in the place cited") traditionally were used instead of a short title of the work. When a reader today encounters a note like "70. Williams, op. cit., p. 14," he or she must read through all of the previous footnotes, thumbing back through page after page, until he or she finds that earlier note in which the author gives the full bibliographical information for Williams' work. And sometimes the reader finds that the author of this book has re-ferred to two different works by Williams. To which work does footnote number 70 refer? Because op. cit. and loc. cit. can be cumbersome, if not downright confusing, for readers, *The Chicago Manual* and other style man-uals discourage their use. Because ibid., like op. cit. and loc. cit., refers the reader to previous notes, it too can be cumbersome, especially if your notes are on the bottom of each page of your text. If, for example, note 15 were on page 12, and note 17 were on page 14, you would have to turn back to page 12 to get any concrete information about this source.

Ibid. is becoming as old-fashioned as loc. cit. and op. cit. I would advise you to use ibid. only if you are putting all your notes on an endnote page; and the wisest choice of all would probably be to use the shortened form for *all* subsequent notes.

4. Extensive references to one source

If you have written a paper in which you use one work extensively—if, for example, you have written a paper on Karl Marx in which you refer frequently to his book *Capital*—you will have many notes that cite this work. An alter-native is to put these citations in the body of your paper. Here's the proce-dure for citing a work in the text.

▶ The first time you refer to this work, you must give a normal first note. After you document the source, it would be wise to inform your reader that further citations in your paper will be given in the body of the paper.

```
1. Sigmund Freud, Interpretation of Dreams (1900), in
The Standard Edition of the Complete Psychological
Works of Sigmund Freud, trans. from the German under
the general editorship of James Strachey (London: Ho-
garth Press and the Institute of Psychoanalysis, 1953),
4:136-38. All references to Freud's works in this paper
are references to this edition of the Complete Works;
citations will hereafter be given in the text.

2. Karl Marx, Capital: A Critique of Political Economy,
trans. from the 3rd German ed. by Samuel Moore and
Edward Aveling, ed. Frederick Engels, rev. according to
```

```
the 4th German ed. by Ernest Untermann (New York: Random
House, The Modern Library, 1906), 106. All references
to Capital are references to this edition; citations
will hereafter be given in the text.
```

▶ Each time you refer to this work in the body of your paper, you will put your citation in parentheses at the end of the relevant sentence. The reader must be given the same information that would be given in the normal shortened form. If part of this information (like the name of the author and the title of a specific selection) is given in your sentence or is obvious from the context, this information need not be repeated. If the work is part of a multivolume set, don't forget that you must include the volume number.

```
According to Marx, capital is "essentially the command

over unpaid labour" (Capital, 585).

Freud covers this subject in the first sections of In-

terpretation of Dreams (Complete Works 4:134-62).
```

Be judicious about putting any citations in the text itself. I would advise you to put subsequent notes in your text only for one or two works to which you refer extensively in your paper. In using this system, never forget that the purpose of documentation is to allow your readers to locate the specific information to which you are referring. If you are sloppy with subsequent notes in your text, you will not be giving your readers the information they need.

J.   Explanatory Notes

In the Chicago style you may use notes for purposes other than simple documentation of sources. Notes may also be used to refer readers to more detailed discussions of a particular topic, or they may be used to explain or elaborate upon a particular point.

```
11. For further detailed information about the Smith
raid, see Johnson, Indian Wars, 75-83.

19. Throughout the play the word "cold" is used in
reference to chastity, inactivity, and death. So, for
example, in speaking of the postponement of the sen-
tencing of the Duchess's youngest son, Spurio says . . .
```

It is perfectly acceptable to use explanatory notes, but you must use your common sense. Material that your reader must have to understand a point that you are making should never be hidden in a note; this information belongs in the body of your paper. And don't forget that note numbers are distracting; they encourage your readers to leave your argument and look at your footnote or endnote. Your readers are going to become very irritated if you use the note system to introduce information or ideas that are outside the bounds of the paper you are writing. So . . . use explanatory notes where you feel they are really needed. Do not use explanatory notes to show off all the knowledge you have about a topic.

K.   Citing More Than One Source in the Same Note

Occasionally you will want to tell your reader that the same information or ideas can be found in several different sources. In these situations, use one note number and list the various sources in one note. The various citations will be separated with semicolons. Use the first note form if this is your first reference to a specific work; use the shortened form if you have already cited this work in an earlier note.

> 14. Charles B. Long, <u>The Civil War</u> (New York: Never Press, 1997), 116–17; Curtis, "Lee and Grant," 108; James G. Gilligam, <u>A History of the War Between the States</u> (San Francisco: Nosuch Publishers, 1984), 2:35–70.

L.   Format for Notes, with Sample Endnote Page

Your notes may be placed at the bottom of the pages of your text (*footnotes*) or on a separate sheet at the end of your paper (*endnotes*).

1.   Footnotes

Unless your instructor requires that your notes appear at the bottom of the page, I would advise you to use endnotes. Putting notes at the bottom of the page can become a typing nightmare. If, however, you have no choice, this is the proper format for footnotes.

The note numbers on a particular page of your text tell you which notes must appear at the bottom of that page. The difficulty comes in figuring out which note numbers will appear on a specific page of the final typed copy and allowing sufficient space for the notes. The text and notes must all remain within the required margins for each page of text (one-and-one-quarter inches on the left, and one inch on the other three sides).

After the final line of the body of your paper on a particular page, single-space and type a line about an inch and a half long. Then double-space and begin your first note. Single-space individual notes; double-space between notes.

---

15. Jones, <u>If I Were a King</u>, 16.

16. Charles W. Long, <u>The French Monarchy</u> (New York: Instant Publishers, Inc., 1987), 5:167–85.

17. Harold Law, "Louis XIV," <u>European History</u> 35 (Spring 1990): 19.

2. Endnotes

Endnotes simply mean that all your notes for the paper are collected in one place, on a separate sheet or sheets of paper that you will put at the end of the text of your paper, between the last page of the paper and the bibliography. Margins on endnote pages are the standard margins. Head the sheet "Notes." Center the heading two inches from the top of the page and leave four lines of space between the heading and the first note. Single-space individual notes, and double-space between notes.

3. Sample endnote page

Notes

1. Lev S. Vygotsky, <u>Thought and Language</u>, ed. and trans. Eugenia Hanfmann and Gertrude Vakar (Cambridge, Mass.: The MIT Press, 1962), 85.

2. "Robin Hood Rescuing Three Squires" (Child No. 140), in <u>The Traditional Tunes of the Child Ballads with Their Texts</u>, ed. Bertrand H. Bronson (Princeton, N.J.: Princeton University Press, 1966), 3:53—57.

3. William I. Jennings, <u>The Growth of Parties</u>, vol. 2 of <u>Party Politics</u> (Cambridge: Cambridge University Press, 1961), 90.

4. "Robin Hood Rescuing Three Squires" (Child No. 140), in Bronson, <u>Child Ballads</u> 3:56.

5. Jennings, <u>The Growth of Parties</u>, 110.

6. <u>The Dictionary of National Biography</u>, 1931—40 ed., s.v. "Rackham, Arthur," by Herbert B. Grimsditch.

7. John Donne, "IV. Meditation," in <u>Seventeenth—Century Prose and Poetry</u>, ed. Alexander M. Witherspoon and Frank J. Warnke, 2nd ed. (New York: Harcourt, Brace and World, 1963), 61.

8. Vygotsky, <u>Thought and Language</u>, 156.

9. Christopher B. Wilson, "The Era of the Reporter Reconsidered: The Case of Lincoln Steffens," <u>Journal of Popular Culture</u> 15, no. 2 (Fall 1981): 59.

10. Donne, "IV. Meditation," in Witherspoon and Warnke, <u>Seventeenth—Century Prose and Poetry</u>, 61.

11. Wilson, "The Era of the Reporter Reconsidered," 52.

12. Jennings, <u>The Growth of Parties</u>, 120—125.

13. Jennings, <u>The Growth of Parties</u>, 167.

Appendix C

The Scientific System: The Reference List

A. General Information

In books and articles written in the sciences (the natural, social, and applied sciences) the author-date form and the numbered reference list form are two commonly accepted means of letting your readers know that you are using information or ideas taken from the works of others. I describe the author-date form in Appendix D and the numbered reference list form in Appendix E. If you are using either of these documentation systems in the paper you are now writing, you will need to include a reference list with your paper. The reference list is a central element in both of these systems of documentation because it is the only place where you give your readers full bibliographic information about specific sources.

B. Putting a Reference List Together

If you look at reference lists given at the end of articles or books you have been reading as you have done your research, you will notice that these lists may have headings like "References" or "Works Cited" or "Literature Cited." As these headings imply, these lists contain only those sources the writer has referred to in the body of his/her paper.

Therefore, your first step in putting together your reference list is to go through your paper and pull out the reference cards you have made for each of the sources you have referred to in your paper.

The next step is to put these cards in the order in which they will appear in your final list. The basic system used to order works on a reference list is to alphabetize the entries by using the last name of the first author given for every book and article. Order all sources you cite according to the last name of the first author given; ordinarily you should not separate books and periodicals or make any types of subdivisions. If you are using the author-date system of documentation in your text, remember that the names you cite in the body of your paper must lead your readers to the correct entry in your reference list. Thus, if, in the body of your paper, you cite an article that appears in a collection of articles, the entry that you make in your reference list must begin with the name of the author of the article, not the editor of the collection.

Here are a few more guidelines that will help you order your reference list properly.

▶ In placing authors' names in alphabetical order, use only the letters in the person's last name. Thus, if your list includes a work by S. H. Roberts and A. R. Robertson, the work by Roberts will come first.

▶ If your list includes single-author works by people with the same last name, alphabetize using the authors' first initial (and second initial, where necessary).

> Smith, B. C.
> Smith, C. F.
> Smith, H. A.
> Smith, H. B.

▶ If you have a series of works by the same person (let's say B. C. Smith),
  ▷ list all works written by B. C. Smith alone first,
  ▷ then list works that B. C. Smith has co-authored with others, alpha-betizing these co-authored works according to the last names of the second author.

> Smith, B. C. . . .
> Smith, B. C., R. J. Green, and S. Spade . . .
> Smith, B. C., and A. W. Weinberg . . .

  ▷ if you have a series of works by the same author(s), list the works chronologically according to the date of publication, starting with the oldest work and ending with the most recent.

> Smith, B. C., and A. W. Weinberg. 1967 . . .
> ———. 1972 . . .
> ———. 1978 . . .

If Smith and Weinberg have published more than one work in the same year, arrange the works alphabetically according to the first word of the title (disregarding *the* and *a*) and differentiate these works by putting a lowercase *a* after the date of the first work, a lowercase *b* after the date of the second work, and so on.

> Smith, B. C., and A. W. Weinberg. 1977a. The effects of pollution on the fish population . . .
> ———. 1977b. *Pollutants in the Great Lakes.*

If you have looked carefully at entries in the reference lists of the sources that you have been reading, you may have noticed that the forms used in different lists varied, both in placement of information and in me-chanical details like capitalization, punctuation, etc. Publishing houses and publishers do use variations of the forms I will be giving you in this appendix. In this appendix i am following the form recommended by *The Chicago*

Manual of Style in the 13th revised and expanded edition (University of Chicago Press, 1982). Where it differs from the Chicago form, I will also give you the APA style. If your instructor has asked you to use the APA style, she is referring to the style recommended by the American Psychological Association in its *Publication Manual* (3rd ed., Washington, D.C.: American Psychological Association, 1983).

Both forms are authoritative; you will be safe if you use either. In using this appendix, or any style manual, you must remember two things. Following the form exactly is of paramount importance. Pay very close attention, in the examples I give, to punctuation, capitalization, underlining, and other details. Consistency is also very important. Once you select a particular style, stay with it. Do not, for example, mix the APA and the Chicago in the same paper.

C.   Proper Form for Books in a Reference List

1.   Placement of information

author
date
title
other publication information:
    editors, translators
    title of series
    volume of series
    volume number, or number of volumes in the set
    edition (if not the original)
facts of publication:
    city
    publisher

Author   The author of a book is the person or persons responsible for what appears within the covers of that book. In many cases the person is an actual author, the person or persons who wrote the text. In other cases, the book is a collection of essays and the person responsible is an editor; in a few cases, the responsible party is a group—an agency, an institute, a corporation. In section C.2 of this appendix, I will show you how to write entries for books with actual authors, and books where the "author" is an editor or a group.

If you are using the author-date system of documentation, I'll remind you again that your readers' only key to the reference list is the author's name, so be sure to enter a work in your reference list under the name of the person or group that you intend to cite in the body of your paper. In reference lists, the preferred form is to give only the initial or initials of the author(s) rather than spelling out first name(s).

Date   The date of publication refers to the date on the title page, or the most recent copyright date of the work you use. If there is no date on the title page, check the back of the title page; use the most recent date that has a © before it. Ignore printing dates.

Note: One major difference between the Chicago and the APA styles is that, in APA references, the date is placed in parentheses.

Title   Give the full title of the book, including any subtitle. Underline the entire title. Notice that the only words capitalized in the title are (1) the first word of the title, (2) the first word of the subtitle (after the colon), (3) proper names that would always be capitalized. If the entry in your reference list is a reference to an article published in a book, the name of the author of the article and the title of the article will appear first. Titles of articles follow the capitalization rule I just gave; however, titles of articles are *not* underlined nor are they put in quotation marks.

Other publication information   Since you are responsible for giving your readers as much information as they will need to locate your source easily, you will need to include such information if it applies to the book you are putting in your list. I cover various examples of books with editors, translators, etc. in section C.2.

Facts of publication   Give the city in which the book was published. If the city is not a well-known city, also give the state (or country). Put a colon after the city (and state) and then give the name of the publisher.

New York: Nosuch Press.

2.   Forms for specific types of books

In the pages that follow I give you examples of the proper form for different kinds of books. Since each example focuses on one aspect of the reference form, in some cases you may need to check a couple of headings to see how to write up a specific entry in your list.

a. Book—one author

Chicago

Lasch, C. 1978. <u>The culture of narcissism: American life in an age of diminishing expectations</u>.
. New York: W. W. Norton and Co.

APA   The date is put in parentheses.

Lasch, C. (1978) <u>The culture of. . .</u>

b. Book—two or more authors

Chicago

Grawoig, D. E., and C. L. Hubbard. 1982. <u>Strategic
financial planning with simulation</u>. New York
and Princeton: Petrocelli Books.

> Easton, S., J. M. Mills, and D. K. Winokur. (1982).
> <u>Equal to the task: How workingwomen are managing
> in corporate America</u>. New York: Seaview Books.

Notice that the name of the first author is inverted; be sure to put a comma after the last name and after the person's initial(s). Names of other authors are given in their normal order.

APA

> Grawoig, D. E., & Hubbard, C. L. (1982). <u>Strategic
> financial planning with simulation</u>. New York:
> Petrocelli Books.

> Easton, S., Mills, J. M., & Winokur, D. K. (1982).
> <u>Equal to the task: How workingwomen are managing
> in corporate America</u>. New York: Seaview Books.

In the APA style the last name of *each* author is given first. You will have to put a comma after each last name and after each set of initials except the final one(s). Use an ampersand (&) rather than the word *and* in these citations.

c. Book with corporate author

If responsibility for the contents of the book is taken by an agency, corporation, or institute, use the name of this group as the author. Alphabetize according to the first word in the name (disregarding *the* and *a*). Spell out the full name of the group. Give the name of the parent body before listing subdivisions of the organization. For example, University of Maryland College of Business Administration. Center for Computer Use. Or, Smalltown Public Works Department. Streets and Roads Division. Pothole Section. If your reference list is going to include a large number of works with group authors and the names of the agencies are themselves long, consult *The Chicago Manual* for systems that will make your citations and the reference list easier to use.

Chicago

> Brookings Institution. 1972. <u>Reshaping the interna-
> tional economic order: A tripartite report by
> twelve economists from North America, the European
> community, and Japan</u>. Washington, D.C.: The
> Brookings Institution.

> Environmental Studies Board. Study on Problems of Pest
> Control. Forest Study Team. 1975. <u>Forest pest
> control</u>. Washington, D.C.: National Academy of
> Sciences.

> U.S. Congress. Office of Technology Assessment (OTA).
> 1982. <u>World population and fertility planning
> technologies: The next twenty years</u>. Washington,
> D.C.: U.S. Government Printing Office.

APA   Put the date in parentheses. If the author of a work is also the publisher (as in the first example above), write "Author" in the publisher position.

> Brookings Institution.   (1972).   Reshaping . . .   Washington, D.C.: Author.

If your source is a technical report, consult the APA manual; it gives detailed information on various types of technical and research reports.

d. Book—edition other than the original

Chicago

> Cohen, J. B., E. D. Zinbarg, and A. Zeikel. 1982. Investment analysis and portfolio management. 4th ed. Homewood, Ill.: Richard D. Irwin, Inc.

APA

> Cohen, J. B., Zinbarg, E. D., & Zeikel, A. (1982). Investment analysis and portfolio management (4th ed.). Homewood, IL: Richard D. Irwin.

e. Book with author and editor and/or translator

Chicago

> Freud, S. [1928] 1961.   The future of illusion. Trans. and ed. James Strachey. New York: W. W. Norton and Co.

The first date given, in brackets, indicates the year in which the work was originally published. If you are using the author-date form, in your paper the citation would be (Freud [1928] 1961).

APA

> Freud, S.   (1961).   The future of illusion (J. Strachey, Ed. and Trans.).   New York: Norton.   (Original work published 1928)

If you are using the author-date form, in your paper the citation would be (Freud, 1928/1961).

f. Book with editor rather than author—a collection of works

Very often in the sciences books are collections of articles written by a number of different people and collected together by an editor. These books will use the editor (indicated by ed., or eds. for more than one) as the author. In the examples that follow, I have included examples of references to specific articles in edited collections as well as examples of entries for the whole edited collection.

Chicago

> Mahowald, M. B., ed.   1978.   Philosophy of woman: Classical to current concepts.   Indianapolis: Hackett Publishing Co.

Spiro, R. J., B. C. Bruce, and W. F. Brewer, eds. 1980.
Theoretical issues in reading comprehension.
Hillsdale, N.J.: L. Erlbaum Associates, Publishers.

APA
Mahowald, M. B. (Ed.). (1978). Philosophy of woman:
Classical to current concepts. Indianapolis:
Hackett Pub. Co.

Spiro, R. J., Bruce, B. C., & Brewer, W. F. (Eds.).
(1980). Theoretical issues in reading comprehension. Hillsdale, NJ: Erlbaum.

g. Work in a collection

Chicago
Miller, N., and K. W. Gentry. 1980. Sociometric indi-
ces of children's peer interaction in the school
setting. In Friendship and social relations in
children, ed. H. C. Foot, A. J. Chapman, and J. R.
Smith, 145–77. New York: John Wiley and Sons.

The numbers following the names of the editors are the inclusive page numbers of the article cited; you do not need to include these page numbers.

APA
Miller, N., & Gentry, K. W. (1980). Sociometric indi-
ces of children's peer interaction in the school
setting. In H. C. Foot, A. J. Chapman, & J. R.
Smith (Eds.), Friendship and social relations in
children (pp. 145–77). New York: John Wiley &
Sons.

The numbers following the title are the inclusive page numbers of the article
cited.

h. Book in a multivolume set

Chicago
REFERENCE TO THE ENTIRE SET OF VOLUMES

Lindzey, G., and E. Aronson, eds. 1969. The handbook
of social psychology. 5 vols. 2nd ed. Reading,
Mass.: Addison–Wesley Publishing Co.

REFERENCE TO AN ARTICLE IN ONE VOLUME

Moore, W. E. 1969. Social structure and behavior. In
Group psychology and phenomena of interaction,
283–322. Vol. 4 of The handbook of social psychology, ed. G. Lindzey and E. Aronson. 2nd ed.
Reading, Mass.: Addison–Wesley Publishing Co.

The numbers following the title indicate the page numbers on which this article appears; you do not have to include these page numbers. If the title of all volumes in a set is the same, give the title of the work, the editors' names, followed by a comma. Then give volume number and page numbers.

In <u>The history of physics</u>, ed. I. Newton and A. Einstein, 176: 283–322.

(or)

In <u>The history of physics</u>, ed. I. Newton and A. Einstein, vol. 176.

APA

REFERENCE TO THE ENTIRE SET OF VOLUMES

Lindzey, G., & Aronson, E. (Eds.). (1969). <u>The handbook of social psychology</u> (2nd ed., 5 vols.). Reading, MA: Addison–Wesley.

REFERENCE TO AN ARTICLE IN ONE VOLUME

Moore, W. E. (1969). Social structure and behavior. In G. Lindzey & E. Aronson (Eds.), <u>The handbook of social psychology: Vol. 4. Group psychology and phenomena of interaction</u> (pp. 283–322). (2nd ed.). Reading, MA: Addison–Wesley.

i. Book in a series

Occasionally when you look at the title page of a book, you will notice that this book is part of a series; the series title may refer to subject matter (Studies in Social Economics) or to the publisher (Smithsonian Miscellaneous Collections) or to both (Wiley Series in Applied Statistics). Include information about the series in your reference. *The Chicago Manual of Style* recommends that you give information about the series in the following order:

> name of the series, including the agency responsible for its publication if this information is not spelled out in the publication facts (capitalize main words; do not underline)
> volume and/or issue number of this book (if such information is given)
> publication facts (if the publisher's name is included in the name of the series, it need not be repeated)

Chicago

Hatt, R. T. 1959. <u>The mammals of Iraq</u>. University of Michigan Museum of Zoology Miscellaneous Publications, no. 106. Ann Arbor.

Schapera, I. 1970. <u>Tribal innovators: Tswana chiefs and social change, 1795–1940</u>. Monographs on Social Anthropology, no. 43. New York: Humanities Press.

Allendoerfer, C. B., ed. 1961. <u>Symposium on differential geometry</u>. Proceedings of Symposia in Pure Mathematics, vol. 3. Providence: American Mathematical Society.

Sherald, J. L. 1982. <u>Dutch elm disease and its management</u>. U.S. Department of Interior, National Parks Services Ecological Services Bulletin, no. 6. Washington, D.C.: U.S. Government Printing Office.

Harris, L. S., ed. 1979. <u>Problems of drug dependence, 1979</u>. National Institute on Drug Abuse (NIDA) Research Monograph 27. Washington, D.C.: U.S. Government Printing Office.

Piaget, J., J.-B. Grize, A. Szeminska, and V. Bang. [1968] 1977. <u>Epistemology and psychology of functions</u>. Trans. F. X. Castellanos and V. D. Anderson. Studies in Genetic Epistemology, vol. 23. Boston: D. Reidel Publishing Co.

The first date given, in brackets, is the original year in which the work was published. If you are using the author-date form, the citation in your paper would be (Piaget, Grize, Szeminska, and Bang [1968] 1977) or, if this is the only work in your reference list by Piaget, it would be (Piaget et al. [1968] 1977). See Appendix D, section B.4.

APA

In the APA system, information about the series is included in parentheses.

Hatt, R. T. (1959). <u>The mammals of Iraq</u> (University of Michigan Museum of Zoology Miscellaneous Publications No. 106). Ann Arbor: University of Michigan.

Piaget, J., Grize, J.-B., Szeminska, A., & Bang, V. (1977). <u>Epistemology and psychology of functions</u> (F. X. Castellanos & V. D. Anderson, Trans. Studies in Genetic Epistemology, Vol. 23). Boston: D. Reidel. (Original work published in 1968)

Citation of this reference in the body of your paper would be (Piaget, Grize, Szeminska, & Bang, 1968/1977) or (Piaget et al., 1968/1977). See Appendix D, section B.4.

D.   Proper Form for Periodicals in a Reference List

As you will remember from Section 3, periodicals are publications that carry the same title and are issued on a regular basis (daily, weekly, monthly, quarterly, annually). When you are citing an article in a periodical, the title of the periodical is considered the title of the work. Generally it is easy to distinguish between books and periodicals, but monographs and proceedings of meetings may sometimes seem to fall between the cracks. If you do not know whether to treat a monograph or the proceedings of a meeting as a periodical or as a book in a series, I suggest that you use this guideline. If the work you are using is shelved in the library with other monographs in the series, and you have to use the title of the monograph series plus the volume and/or issue number to find the work you want, this monograph is considered a periodical and you should use the scholarly journal form (D.1) in your reference list. If the work you are using is catalogued in the library under the author and title alone, and it is not shelved with other monographs in the series, treat it like a book in a series (see C.2.i.). If you are using the APA style, consult the *Publication Manual.* There you will find detailed information about forms for monographs and proceedings.

   Note: Spell out the full title of the journal or magazine you are citing unless you are using the shortened form of the reference list (see section F).

1.   Scholarly journals

a. General form

Chicago
```
Fitzgibbons, D., L. Goldberger, and M. Eagle.   1965.
     Field dependency and memory for incidental mate-
     rial.   Perceptual and Motor Skills 21:743-49.
```

In this entry, 21 is the number of the volume of the journal in which this article appears, and 743–49 are the inclusive pages of the article. You may, if you think it would help the reader, add the month or quarter in which this issue of the journal appeared. Here's the form:

```
Perceptual and Motor Skills 21 (December): 743-49.
```

```
Anthony, R. G., and N. S. Smith.   1977.   Ecological re-
     lationships between mule deer and white-tailed
     deer in southeastern Arizona.   Ecological Mono-
     graphs 47 (Summer): 255-77.
```

APA
```
Fitzgibbons, D., Goldberger, L., & Eagle, M.   (1965).
     Field dependency and memory for incidental mate-
     rial.   Perceptual and Motor Skills, 21, 743-49.
```

In this entry, 21 is the number of the volume; notice that it is underlined; 743–49 are the pages on which the article appears.

```
Anthony, R. G., & Smith, N. S.  (1977).  Ecological re-
    lationships between mule deer and white-tailed
    deer in southeastern Arizona.  Ecological Mono-
    graphs, 47, 255-77.
```

b. Journal that paginates each issue separately

Most scholarly journals are paginated consecutively throughout the year, so a volume number and page numbers are all the reader needs to find an article. However, if you are referring to an article in a journal that begins each issue with page 1, you will have to give your reader further information. The usual procedure is to give the volume number and issue number.

Chicago
```
Weymann, R. J.  1978.  Stellar winds.  Scientific Am-
    erican 239 (2): 44-53.
```

```
Dittman, P., D. Glasby, and C. Benenati.  1981.  Logic
    analyzers simplify system integration tasks.  Com-
    puter Design 20 (3): 119-29.
```

In these entries, the numbers in parentheses are the issue numbers.

APA
```
Weymann, R. J.  (1978).  Stellar winds.  Scientific
    American, 239 (2), 44-53.
```

```
Dittman, P., Glasby, D., & Benenati, C.  (1981).  Logic
    analyzers simplify system integration tasks.  Com-
    puter Design, 20 (3), 119-29.
```

The underlined number is the volume number; the number in parentheses is the issue number.

Occasionally, you will need to give your readers even more information to help them find exactly the right work.

Chicago
```
Lazar, I., and R. Darlington.  1982.  Lasting effects
    of early education.  Monographs of the Society
    for Research in Child Development 47 (2-3).
    Serial No. 195.
```

APA
```
Lazar, I., & Darlington, R.  (1982).  Lasting effects
    of early education.  Monographs of the Society
    for Research in Child Development, 47 (2-3,
    Serial No. 195).
```

No page numbers are given in these entries because the entire issue is devoted to this report. The first numbers in parentheses are the issue numbers.

2. Magazines

General interest periodicals, which are usually published weekly or monthly, are cited by giving the date of publication rather than volume number.

Chicago
```
Anderson, K.   1983.   An eye for an eye: Death Row (pop.
     1,137) may soon lose a lot more residents to the
     executioner.   Time, 24 January, 28–39.
```

```
Mazlich, B.   1972.   Psychohistory and Richard M. Nixon.
     Psychology Today, July.
```

Page numbers for the Mazlich article are omitted because this article does not appear on consecutive pages; instead it begins in one part of the magazine and continues on pages in the back. Page numbers in citations indicate inclusive page numbers.

APA
```
Anderson, K.   (1983, January 24).   An eye for an eye:
     Death Row (pop. 1,137) may soon lose a lot more
     residents to the executioner.   Time, pp. 28–39.
```

```
Mazlich, B.   (1972, July).   Psychohistory and Richard
     M. Nixon.   Psychology Today, pp. 77–80; 90.
```

If an article does not have an author, begin your entry with the title. Alphabetize by using the first main word, disregarding *the* and *a*.

3. Newspaper articles

Chicago

The Chicago Manual recommends not listing individual newspaper articles in your reference list. However, the author-date and the numbered reference list forms demand full citation of all sources used. Therefore, if you have used newspaper articles in your paper, I recommend that you put them in your reference list, following the Chicago form for magazine articles (see D.2). For further advice, read over my comments below in the section on the APA form for newspaper articles.

APA
```
Shaffer, R. A.   (1983, April 29).   Digital audio
     already altering recording industry's practices.
     The Wall Street Journal, p. 27.
```

```
Panel slates NRC review.   (1983, May 29).   The Sunday
     (Portland) Oregonian (Sunrise ed.), sec. A, p. 14.
```

If either of these articles had appeared on more than one page, I would have given all pages (see APA form, D.2). Notice that I have included the city in which the newspaper is published, the edition, and the section designation. All of this information will help my readers locate the article easily.

Articles that have no author would be listed alphabetically in the reference list under the first main word in the title (disregarding *the* and *a*). In the author-date system, the citation in the text would begin with a shortened form of this title; in the case of the article above, the whole title would be used because it is itself short ("Panel slates NRC review," 1983).

E.   Forms for Other Types of Sources

I do not have space to cover the appropriate forms for materials that you might have used in your research, materials like films or television programs, unpublished materials such as papers given at a conference or dissertations, or information you received from telephone conversations or interviews. However, if you intend to use information or ideas you obtained from such sources, you do need to acknowledge these sources in your paper.

I can give you some general advice regarding documenting such sources.

▶ Remember the general rule of thumb about giving your readers all the information they would need to locate the source themselves. When you are making reference cards for such sources, follow the general outlines of the basic forms I have given in sections C and D; this is the kind of information you will have to provide. Be sure to take down all information about the source; it is better to have more information than you need rather than to find you are missing an important piece of evidence.

▶ If you find that you will be using information from these sources in the paper you write, and none of the forms I have given in sections C and D fit your source, plan to consult *The Chicago Manual of Style* or the *Publication Manual of the American Psychological Association* (APA). Both of these style manuals give detailed information on appropriate forms for public documents (materials published by local and federal governments), nonbook materials (sound and video recordings), and unpublished materials.

Since you may be using information from interviews and other personal contacts you have made with your sources and since I can give you the form for such personal communications briefly, here is the way to reference personal communications.

Chicago

REFERENCE LIST ENTRY

Schwartz, Harold.   Interview with author, Smalltown,
     Nebraska, 17 May 1984.

Robertson, Joan.   Telephone conversation with author,
     25 January 1984.

```
Schwartz (interview 1984) indicated that . . .
```

```
The agency is not financially solvent (Robertson, pers.
com. 1984).
```

APA Information from letters, memos, telephone conversations and other materials addressed only to you should not be listed in your reference list. However, information from such personal contacts must be cited in the body of your paper, using the following form:

```
Harold Schwartz (personal communication, May 17, 1984)
indicated that the agency . . .
```

```
. . . (Harold Schwartz, personal communication, May 17,
1984).
```

F.   Shortened Form of the Reference List

Primarily to save space, some scholarly journals, usually in the natural sciences, use a shortened form of the reference list. Sometimes the reference list is omitted and footnotes are used for documentation. These notes are usually given in the shortened form. The main characteristics of the shortened form are that the title of the article in a journal is omitted, and the title of the journal is abbreviated. Since this shortened form is designed for experts in a field speaking to other experts, I am advising you not to use the shortened form unless you are writing your paper for an upper-division course in a discipline that normally uses the shortened form *and* your instructor has asked you to use this form. If you find out that you are expected to use this shortened form, be sure to use the accepted abbreviations for journal titles. You can learn more about the shortened form by consulting *The Chicago Manual of Style* and by examining carefully the form used in scholarly journals in the field in which you have been doing your investigation.

G.   The Final Reference List, Including a Sample Reference List

Your final reference list will be written or typed on a separate sheet or sheets of paper which will be placed immediately after the body of your paper. You may head your list "References" or "Works Cited" or "Literature Cited," but notice that the last two headings imply published material and should not be used if your list includes unpublished material. Center the heading two inches from the top of the page, and leave at least two lines of space between the heading and the first entry. Single-space individual entries. The first line of the entry should be flush with the left-hand margin; other lines in an individual entry are indented five spaces. Double-space between individual entries.

If you are using the numbered reference list form, you will put an arabic numeral (1, 2, 3) in front of each entry, followed by a period. If you are using the author-date form, do *not* number the reference list.

The sample reference list that follows uses the Chicago form. If you are following the APA style, note that the actual form of individual entries will be different.

References

Freud, S.   [1928] 1961.   The future of illusion.   Trans.
    and ed. James Strachey.   New York: W. W. Norton
    and Co.

Harcum, E. R.   1966.   Visual hemifield differences as
    conflicts in direction of reading.   Journal of
    Experimental Psychology 72: 479–80.

Harcum, E. R., and R. D. L. Filion.   1963.   Effects of
    stimulus reversals on lateral dominance in word
    recognition.   Perceptual and Motor Skills 17: 779–
    94.

Harcum, E. R., R. Hartman, and N. F. Smith.   1963.
    Pre– versus post–knowledge of required reproduction
    sequence for tachistoscopic patterns.   Canadian
    Journal of Psychology 17: 264–73.

Harcum, E. R., and N. F. Smith.   1963.   Effect of pre–
    known stimulus–reversals on apparent cerebral domi-
    nance in word recognition.   Perceptual and Motor
    Skills 17: 799–810.

Lasch, C.   1978.   The culture of narcissism: American
    life in an age of diminishing expectations.   New
    York: W. W. Norton and Co.

Ortony, A.   1979a.   Beyond literal similarity.
    Psychological Review 86: 161–80.

––––––.   1979b.   The role of similarity in similes and
    metaphors.   In Metaphor and thought, ed. A.
    Ortony.   Cambridge: Cambridge University Press.

Sherald, J. L.   1982.   Dutch elm disease and its manage-
    ment.   U.S. Department of Interior, National Parks
    Services Ecological Services Bulletin, no. 6.
    Washington, D.C.: U.S. Government Printing Office.

U.S. Congress.   Office of Technology Assessment (OTA).
    1982.   World population and fertility planning
    technologies: The next twenty years.   Washington,
    D.C.: U.S. Government Printing Office.

Weymann, R. J.   1978.   Stellar winds.   Scientific
    American 239(2): 44–53.

Appendix D

The Scientific System: Author-Date Form

A. General Information

The author-date form of documentation is widely used in social science books and journals, and it is the documentation form that *The Chicago Manual* recommends for all the natural sciences and most of the social sciences. The author-date system is the form also recommended by the American Psychological Association (APA). If your instructor has asked you to use the APA style, this author-date form is the form you should use.

In the author-date form, you will not be using footnote numbers nor footnotes to acknowledge the sources you have used in your paper. Instead, you will let your reader know the source of information and/or ideas you have used by giving the last name of the author or authors of a work, and the year in which the work was published, right in the body of your paper.

```
Smith and Jones (1976) have found that . . .


Several studies have been done on the effects of DMSO

on the human body (Aaron 1976; Clark and Jones 1978;

Smith 1984).
```

At the end of your paper you will have a reference list, which will include full bibliographic information about each of these sources you cite in the body of your paper. Using the names and dates you give in your text, your readers can turn to the reference list and find out all the information they need about each source.

In this appendix I will discuss only the form you will use for citing sources in the body of your paper. However, as I have just said, this documentation system is not complete without a reference list. So you will have to use Appendix C to find out how to put a reference list together properly.

B. Specifics of the Author-Date Form

The author-date system of documentation will work properly only if the citation you give in the body of your paper matches up with *only one* entry in your reference list. Therefore, the first step you must take is to write out the complete reference list you will be using for your paper. To do that, please turn to Appendix C for guidance.

When you have a finished reference list that includes all the works you will refer to in your text and in which all entries are in their proper form, you are ready to fill in the citations in the body of your paper. I would recommend that you follow these steps in filling in your citations in your text. Follow steps 1 through 3 for each reference.

1. Find the appropriate notecard for each reference. Check what you have said in your paper against your notecard to be sure that what you have in your paper is correct. Check quotations carefully.
2. Find the source of this information/quotation in your reference list to see that you have the appropriate author(s) cited correctly in your reference list.
3. In the body of your paper, write in the author and date in the proper form (see section B.1 and following for more information).

You can cite more than one source in the same citation in your paper; see section B.7 for more information.

1. Basic form for the author-date citation

Each reference to a work in your reference list must give the author or authors of that work and the date of publication of the source. If you are quoting the words of an author, or if you are referring to a specific part of a long work, you will also give page numbers or the number of a section or chapter.

The basic forms of the author-date system look like these examples:

```
Austin and Smith (1980) argue that behavior modifica-

tion techniques can be used effectively to enable peo-

ple to lose weight.



Behavior modification techniques have been used success-

fully to enable people to lose weight (Austin and Smith

1980).
```

Notice that if you mention the name of the author(s) in the sentence you have written, all you need to add is the date. But you must include the names of *all* authors listed in the entry in your reference list.

When you don't mention the name(s) of the author(s) in your sentence, it is preferable to put the citation at the end of the sentence, especially if the citation is long. However, it is acceptable to put a citation after a noun or noun phrase to which the citation refers.

Acceptable
```
Investigations of anorexia nervosa (Jones and Smith

1973, 1974, 1977a) indicate that this self-starvation

is an attempt to gain control of one's environment.
```

Better
```
Investigations of anorexia nervosa indicate that this

self-starvation is an attempt to gain control of one's

environment (Jones and Smith 1973, 1974, 1977a).
```

As you can see, the author-date system is really very simple. However, it is critical that you give the correct names and dates, or else your reader will not know to which entry in your reference list you are referring. And you will remember that I have said that each documentation system has its proper forms for giving necessary information about a source. Therefore, study carefully the forms I give in the rest of this section. As I have done in Appendix C, I am here following the form suggested by *The Chicago Manual of Style;* if and when it differs, I also give the APA form.

There are two basic differences between Chicago and APA citations. In the Chicago form, there is no comma between the author(s) and date, and Chicago prefers the word *and* to be used to join authors' names. In the APA form, there is a comma between author(s) and date, and APA expresses *and* with an ampersand (&).

Chicago
```
(Jones 1978)

(Jones and Smith 1980)
```
APA
```
(Jones, 1978)

(Jones & Smith, 1980)
```

2. Two sources in which the authors have the same last names

If your reference list contains works by two different authors who have the same last name (Frank Smith and Carl Smith), you will have to use the author's first initial to distinguish the two.

Chicago

```
C. Smith (1980) has argued that the side effects of
DMSO are negligible; other researchers draw different
conclusions (Albertson 1976; F. Smith 1974).
```

APA   Add commas between authors' names and dates.

3. Source with two authors

```
Jones and Welsh (1970) have suggested that . . .
```

Always spell out *and* when you use the names of authors as part of your sentence. When the authors' names are in parentheses, the form is

Chicago `There is evidence that . . . (Jones and Welsh`
          `1970).`

APA `There is evidence that . . . (Jones & Welsh,`
     `1970).`

Even if two authors have the same last name, both names must be repeated.

```
Robertson and Robertson (1969) tested . . .

Such investigations (Robertson and Robertson 1969) . . .
```

If you *know* that these two Robertsons are members of the same family, in the body of your paper you could write "The Robertsons (1969) tested . . . "

4. Source with more than two authors

Chicago

Three authors. Use all three names.

More than three authors. Use the name of the first author plus "et al." (Latin abbreviation for "and others"). Thus, Green, Short, Maximillian, and Witherspoon becomes Green et al.

APA

When citing works by three or more authors, give the complete set of names the first time you refer to the work. In subsequent references to this work, use the last name of the first author, followed by "et al."

FIRST REFERENCE IN YOUR PAPER
```
Green, Short, Maximillian, and Witherspoon (1980)

have found . . .
```

```
This conclusion has been questioned (Green et al.,

1980).
```

```
Green et al. (1980) have shown . . .
```

But you must be careful with the "et al." form.

Before you shorten any citation to the Green et al. form, check your reference list. If you have more than one work by Green and any other co-authors, the citation "Green et al." could refer to any of these works. Because such a shortened form could confuse your reader in this case, no citations to Green should be shortened in your paper.

5.   Source with corporate author

For more information on corporate authors, see Appendix C, section C.2.c. In your citation, use the name of the agency, corporation, or institute that appears first in your reference list entry. Remember that your readers must be able to go from your citation straight to the correct entry in your reference list. If your paper includes references to many agencies or institutes with very long names, consult *The Chicago Manual* for suggestions about cross-listings and abbreviations.

6.   Citations that include specific pages or sections of a work

Whenever you quote directly from a source, you must include the page number(s) in the citation.

Chicago
```
The results have been called "poppycock" (Wilson 1980,

70).
```

```
Wilson (1980) has argued that these results are

"poppycock" (p. 70).
```

When quoting from a work that is part of a multivolume set, you will have to include the volume number. Separate volume number and page number with a colon.

```
(Jones 1976, 3:197)
```

APA
```
(Wilson, 1980, p. 70)
```

```
(Jones, 1976, vol. 3, p. 197)
```

If you are referring to a specific portion of a book or a specific table or figure in a work, your reader would appreciate it if you would include this information in your citation. Use an accepted abbreviation for the material (chapter, section, figure, table) to which you are referring.

Chicago
(Jones 1979, sec. 18.5)

(Wilson 1972, chap. 5)

(Clark 1984, fig. 5)

APA
Separate author and date with comma.

7.   Citations that refer to two or more sources

If you are citing more than one source by different authors at the same time, arrange the works alphabetically according to the last name of the first author, and separate the references with semicolons.

Chicago
(Hall and Smith 1982; Kingston, Leonard, and Pepperdine

1976; Weinstein 1954).

APA
(Hall & Smith, 1982; Kingston, Leonard, & Pepperdine,

1976; Weinstein, 1954)

If you are referring to several publications by the same author(s), list the dates chronologically and separate with commas.

Winston (1966, 1970, 1972a) has investigated . . .

8.   Citation of a reprint of an older work

Some works, especially those that are considered classics, are frequently reprinted long after their original publication date. Similarly, a work may be translated into English years after it was published in the author's native language. Because the date of publication indicates when the information in a work was made available to the public, it is important to give your readers an original publication date if the original date is appreciably older than the date of the reprint or translation.

Chicago
(Freud [1928] 1961)

APA
(Freud, 1928/1961)

For full examples of reprints and translations, see Appendix C, sections C.2.e and C.2.i.

9. Citation of a source referred to in a second source

As I pointed out in Section 4, subsection C.1, true scholars and researchers always seek out works that are referred to in another source. However, if you wish to use information that has been mentioned in one of your sources and you have not been able to locate the original work, here's the way you should make such a citation.

▶ In your reference list, enter the work in which you found the material.
▶ When you cite this material in the body of your paper, give the author of the original work first, then cite the work in your reference list.

> YOUR REFERENCE LIST
>
> Smith, C. E. 1968. <u>The mechanisms of behavior</u> . . .
>
> CITATION IN YOUR PAPER
>
> Johnson (cited in Smith 1968) found . . .

10. Citation of interviews and other personal communication

For the proper form, see Appendix C, section E.

C. Explanatory Notes

Once in a while you may feel the need to add information that is not documentation information, nor information that is central to the argument you are developing in your paper. You may include such explanations or commentaries in explanatory notes. However, before you add such explanatory notes to your paper, be sure they are appropriate. An explanatory note should never include information that is central to your readers' comprehension of your ideas; this information belongs directly in the body of your paper. Nor should you use notes to add information that you think is "interesting" but not relevant. Notes are distracting, and they take your readers' attention away from the argument of your paper.

If you decide that you have a legitimate reason to add a note, here's the procedure you should follow.

▶ In the body of your paper, at the end of the relevant statement, place a number, raised one-half space above the line. Notes should be numbered consecutively throughout the paper, beginning with number 1.

> . . . Freud's concept of the ego.[2]

▶ The note itself may be written at the bottom of the page on which the note number appears or on a separate sheet of paper headed "Notes" at the end of the paper, before your reference list. If, in your note, you use information from a work listed in your reference list, use the same mode of citing this work that you would use in the body of your paper. If you have questions about the way your notes should be placed and the way they should look, check the physical format of notes in the humanities system, Appendix B, section L.

Appendix E

The Scientific System: The Numbered Reference List Form

A. General Information

The numbered reference list form is not as popular as the humanities form or the author-date form, but it is used in some scholarly journals in the natural sciences. Do not use this system of documentation unless your instructor has asked you to use this form.

The numbered reference list form could be called a combination of the humanities and the scientific systems. It resembles the humanities system in the sense that references to sources in the body of the paper are indicated with numbers (in parentheses or brackets). But, whereas the numbers in the humanities system refer to notes at the foot of the page or the end of the paper, the numbers in the numbered reference list form refer the reader directly to entries in a reference list, comparable to a bibliography, at the end of the paper.

There are two variations of this numbered reference list form.

1. In the first variation, the works in the reference list are numbered according to the order in which they are cited in the body of the paper. If, later in her paper, the author refers to a work she has already mentioned, she simply uses the number of that earlier citation. This variation, however, can be cumbersome and it is not used very often.
2. The more popular variation uses a reference list that is first ordered according to the last name of the author of a work and the publication date of the work. Then the completed list is numbered. This variation is the one I will explain in this appendix.

The effect of this system is to remove the intermediate step of notes, and it takes the reader from "note" number directly to the "bibliography"— which is what a reference list represents in scientific papers. The numbered reference list system should not be confused with systems, found in many journals in the natural sciences, that use numbers in parentheses or brackets

216

in the body of the paper but which refer to footnotes at the bottom of the page (see Appendix C, section F).

B.   How to Set Up the Numbered Reference List Form

1.   Setting up the reference list

The first step in using the numbered reference list form is to put together your reference list. Make a stack of all the reference cards for the sources you intend to refer to in the body of your paper; then alphabetize according to the last name of the first author given. I cover in detail the way to set up a reference list and the proper form for entries in a reference list in Appendix C. You should now turn to Appendix C and put together your reference list.

When your reference list is complete, assign a number to each entry on the reference list, starting with the first work on the list. You could save time by typing the final draft of your list as you assign numbers. Type your list on a separate sheet of paper headed "References" or "Works Cited." At the left-hand margin, type the number of the entry. Be sure to indent the second line and all subsequent lines of an individual entry; the readers need to be able to spot the entry number at a glance. See Appendix C, section G, for proper form of the finished list.

2.   Citing sources in your paper

The next step is to insert the proper number or numbers of your reference list entries at those points where you have used information from a source. I would suggest that you follow these steps:

1. Go through the body of your paper, beginning on page 1. Stop at each sentence where you've indicated that you have used one or more of your sources.
2. Double-check the information in the body of your paper against your notecard to be sure the information in your paper is correct.
3. Find the number of the source or sources in your numbered reference list, and insert this number in the body of your paper.

a. Form of citation

You may put the number in parentheses or in brackets. The number may appear in regular type or it may be underlined. You may choose which of these forms you like, but once you make your choice, you must use the same form throughout your paper.

b. Placement of citation

The number should be placed after the name of an author if you mention the author's name in your sentence.

```
According to Jones and Weston (12), . . .
```

If you do not give the name of the author, the number should be placed after the statement that includes the information you have taken from this source.

```
Reduction by ZT3 produces salt and iodine (4).
```

If you wish to cite more than one source, list the entry numbers in chronological order, separated by commas.

```
Investigations have revealed that . . . (1, 12, 17).
```

If you give two pieces of information in one sentence that come from two different sources, place the numbers of the appropriate sources directly after the statement that includes the information.

```
PQR was extracted from the solution (6) and quantified

by the Smith—Jones method (14).
```

C.   Explanatory Notes

Once in a while you may want to give your readers further explanation of a term or procedure you have used, or you may want to comment on something you have said in the body of your paper. The procedure for such explanatory notes is to put a footnote number in the paper at the end of the relevant sentence. Obviously, this footnote number must look different than your reference list numbers or your readers will think you are referring to a work in your reference list. The normal form for a footnote number is a number raised one-half space above the line.

```
. . . in this procedure, reactive CH4 was used.²
```

The note should then be placed at the bottom of the page on which the number appears, separated from the body of your paper with a line. In Appendix B, section L, you will find more information about the proper placement of footnotes.

Be very careful about explanatory notes. If you decide you want to use an explanatory note, you should ask yourself why you need this note. If the information in the note is critical to the readers' understanding of the point you are making, the information should be in the body of your paper. If the information is interesting but not really relevant to the paper, it probably should be omitted. Footnote numbers are very distracting. They encourage the reader to stop reading the text and look down to the bottom of the page. If you interrupt your readers too often, or if you interrupt the readers to give them irrelevant information, they will not be following your paper properly and may become very irritated with you. If you feel you should include more extensive information about data you have used or procedures you have followed, and this information is inappropriate in your text, consider placing it in appendixes at the end of the paper. You will find information about appendixes in *The Chicago Manual of Style* or Kate Turabian's *A Manual for Writers of Term Papers, Theses, and Dissertations*.

Appendix F
The Final Manuscript of Your Paper

Once you have documented your sources, you have only three steps left:

▶ to copyedit the final rough draft
▶ to type your paper
▶ to proofread the typed copy

When you type your final draft, you should be doing only what professional typists do—transcribing exactly what is in the rough copy into finished, typed form. If you try to type and to copyedit and to proofread all at the same time, you can slow your typing down to a crawl and you can get yourself into a great deal of trouble. I remember times when I allowed myself to start rewriting my paper when I was supposed to be typing it. I'd change one sentence and then realize that this change would mean that I would have to change another sentence. Suddenly I was faced with stopping and doing a major revision or having a paragraph in my final paper that was a mess of disjointed statements. It is wiser, therefore, to plan to take the time to copyedit the complete rough draft first, to make a clean, easy-to-read final rough copy that you will then simply type. A pair of scissors and glue or transparent tape make it easy enough to create such a clean, easy-to-read manuscript. If you have asked someone else to type your paper for you, it is very important to give your typist a clean, easy-to-read manuscript if you expect an accurate typed copy in return.

A. Copyediting

Copyediting involves reading your paper, from beginning to end, focusing on one paragraph at a time. The following list indicates the type of stylistic and mechanical features you want to pay attention to.

▶ Be sure each sentence leads the readers clearly from one idea to the next.
▶ Check your word choice. Be sure the words you've used are words that precisely reflect the ideas you are trying to convey. Eliminate slang and expressions that are too casual for formal papers.

▶ If you are using numbers in your paper, you should be aware that the commonly accepted style is to spell out numbers if they can be expressed in one or two words and to use numerals if more than two words are necessary.

> one hundred books   1,512 subjects
> a million dollars   412 ships

You should not begin a sentence with a numeral. If you are writing a scientific paper in which there are many numbers, check Turabian, the APA *Publication Manual,* or *The Chicago Manual of Style* for their recommendations about the proper style for numbers.

▶ If you want to use abbreviations in your paper, be sure you have told your reader what the abbreviation stands for. The first time you refer to the company, chemical compound, or organization, give the full name first and put the abbreviation after it in parentheses.

```
Dimethylsulfoxide (DMSO) is a chemical compound . . .


A leader in this field is International Business Ma-

chines (IBM), a corporation that . . .
```

▶ To be sure your quotations are in a proper form, check Section 6, subsection B.4.

▶ Be sure titles in your paper are in their proper form. The rule of thumb is very simple. If a work was published originally as an independent, separate unit, the title should be underlined. Thus the titles of books, journals and magazines, record albums, films, operas are underlined. If a work was originally published within a larger, independent unit, these titles are placed in quotation marks. Thus, if a poem was originally published in a magazine, the title of the poem will be placed in quotation marks. Similarly, the titles of chapters of a book, the titles of essays and articles, the titles of songs or cuts on a record album are put in quotation marks.

A note on punctuation and quotation marks
Commas and periods are always put *inside* quotation marks.

```
Marble and other cold objects are central images in his

poem "Death."


Describing the loss as "overwhelming," General Smith

promptly resigned his post.
```

Semicolons and colons are placed outside the quotation marks. Question marks and exclamation points are placed inside the quotation marks if they are part of the quotation; if they punctuate your sentence, they are placed outside the quotation marks.

```
The speech ends with a question: "What is real?"

Did anyone hear him say "I give up"?
```

A note on capitalization in titles

The Chicago Manual gives the following guidelines for capitalizing words in the titles of works:

Capitalized	*Not capitalized*
the first word in title	articles (*a, an, the*), unless first word in title or subtitle
the last word in title	
all nouns	coordinate conjunctions (*and, but, or, for, nor*), unless first word in title or subtitle
all pronouns	
all adjectives	
all verbs	prepositions (*from, including, to, at, of,* etc.), unless first or last word in title or subtitle
all adverbs	
all subordinate conjunctions (*because, since, unless, before, after,* etc.)	the *to* in an infinitive (*to be, to go, to work,* etc.)

▶ Be sure the grammar of each sentence is correct.

  ▷ Do pronouns have antecedents? Do the pronouns agree with their antecedents? (. . . the company. It . . . ; Scientists. . . . They . . .).

  ▷ Do subjects and verbs agree in number?

  ▷ Is the base tense of your paper consistent? If you are treating an event or events as if they occurred in the past, always refer to these events in the past tense; if you are treating an event or events as if they are occurring now, always use the present tense. What you want to *avoid* is referring to such events in the past tense in one sentence or paragraph, and then switching to the present tense in another sentence or paragraph.

```
        Hamlet was very upset by his father's death, so

upset that he contemplated suicide. . . .

        In this play, Claudius and Gertrude are unwitting

villains. They act as if they are concerned about

Hamlet's welfare, at least at first. . . .
```

▶ Proofread; correct all errors in spelling and punctuation.

▶ If you have used the humanities form of documentation, be sure that note numbers in the text correspond with the correct footnote or endnote.

If you have questions about stylistic issues that I have not covered here, check Turabian or an appropriate style manual.

B.   Typing: The Format of the Paper

If you have taken a look at one of the Turabian books or other authoritative style manuals, you know that much of the material in these books is related to the appearance of the final paper. Because these manuals are written for authors preparing manuscripts for publication, some of this information may not apply to a paper being prepared for a class. For example, most style manuals advise you to double-space everything in a paper because double-spacing makes it easier for the compositor to set the manuscript into type; however, since you don't have to worry about a compositor, I have recommended that you single-space block quotations, notes, entries in bibliographies and reference lists. In this section of this appendix, I make some recommendations about the format of your paper. With some exceptions (like standard margins), these recommendations are only recommendations. Obviously, if your instructor has asked you to follow another format, that is the format you should use.

You want to make your paper as easy to read as possible. I suggest that you use medium to heavyweight typing paper (sixteen- or twenty-pound). Don't use flimsy paper like onionskin and try to avoid erasable paper that smears when you run your finger over typed lines. If you are using a cloth typewriter ribbon, be sure it is fresh; as a teacher I can tell you that it is very irritating to try to decipher a paper typed with a ribbon that died several papers ago.

Title and title page   Your research paper should have a separate title page. The title of the paper itself should give the reader a clear picture of the content of the paper, even though you may consider such a title boring. Clever titles are fun to create, but they may be very frustrating to the reader, as you yourself may have learned when you were using indexes and the card catalogue.

> **Frustrating**
> ```
> Fun and Games
> ```
> **Better**
> ```
> Using Game Theory to Analyze the
>
> Ethiopian-Somalian Conflict
> ```

There is no one proper form for a title page. If your instructor has no specific format he or she prefers, I recommend this format.

▶   Center your title about one-third of the way down the sheet of paper. Capitalize only the first letters of central words (see note on capitalization in titles on page 214). Then, place the following information, in block form, in the lower right-hand corner (start about 3½ inches from the bottom, beginning each line about 3½ inches from the right-hand edge):

your full name
the number and title of the course
the full name of the instructor
the due date of the paper

Margins   The standard margins for pages in a manuscript are 1¼ (or 1½) inches on the left and 1 inch on the other three sides. Remember that footnotes must be placed within these margins. Often the first page of the manuscript begins about 3 inches from the top of the sheet of paper.

I have found that the easiest way to be sure that my pages are all within the proper margins is to make a margin-rule sheet. Using an opaque piece of paper, I draw in the standard margins with a heavy black felt-tip pen. Inside the left-hand margin I draw a second line, five spaces from the left-hand margin, to indicate where to begin new paragraphs, block quotations, and other indented material. When I am typing, I can see these black lines through the sheet of paper on which I am typing.

Page numbers   As a teacher, I prefer that students put page numbers in the upper right-hand corner of the page, and I like to see the student's last name typed before the page number.

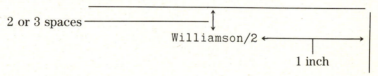

If you begin the first page of the paper 3 inches from the top of the sheet, put this page number at the bottom of the sheet, centered, two spaces below the bottom margin. The numbering of nontextual material (endnote pages, bibliography, appendixes, etc.) varies; I would recommend simply numbering all pages in your paper consecutively. Thus, if the last page of your text is page 14, the first page of your endnotes would be page 15, and so on.

Headings and table of contents   If you are doing a primary research report, you will use headings in the body of your paper (see Section 5, subsection B). A table of contents isn't really necessary. If you have written a secondary research paper, whether or not you separate your paper into divisions and subdivisions signaled by headings will depend upon the length and nature of the paper. Headings break the readers' attention, signaling a major transition. Thus, headings would be obtrusive in the middle of a tightly organized argument. On the other hand, if your paper is very long and the argument is rather complex, headings can be very helpful to the reader. If you are not sure if it would be appropriate to use headings, consult your instructor.

If you decide that headings are appropriate for your paper, your outline should suggest what headings you should use and where they should be inserted. All headings should follow the parallel-structure rule: express all headings in the same grammatical form (all phrases, or all sentences). For more information on headings, I recommend that you consult *The Chicago Manual.* If your paper is divided into a number of divisions and subdivisions, a table of contents might be useful to the readers. *The Chicago Manual* or Turabian's *Manual* can give you more information about the format.

Tables, charts, and graphs   If you are giving your readers statistical information, charts and graphs are a very useful visual aid. To be most effective, such charts and graphs should be placed in the body of the paper at those points where you refer to the information on these charts and graphs. In Turabian's *Manual* you will find a very helpful chapter on this subject.

Appendixes   An appendix is what we might call a very long explanatory note. If you wish to include detailed information relevant to some part of your paper, information that does not belong in the text of the paper, you may place it in an appendix, which will be put at the end of your paper. Raw data used in a primary research paper are often compiled in appendixes; in secondary research papers, you will sometimes find documents, like letters or legal documents, reproduced in appendixes for the readers' information. If you decide that you have material that should be put in an appendix, you will find more information about the format of appendixes in Turabian's *Manual.*

C.   Proofreading

The last step is to proofread the final typed copy. I realize that by the time you have finished typing your paper you never want to see it again. On the other hand, any error that appears on this final copy is, in the eyes of your readers, an error for which you are responsible and errors will detract from the paper. Think about how far you have come since you started this research project months ago. Do you want to risk having all your hard work graded down by your instructor because the paper is full of typos? Ideally (and I realize that I am talking about ideals) you should put the typed copy aside for a day, or at least a few hours, before you attempt to proofread it. Under any circumstances it is hard for a person to proofread what he or she has written; we tend to look at a sentence, say "I know what that says," and not look carefully at the spelling and punctuation (which is what proofreading involves). It is almost impossible to proofread directly after typing a paper. The best solution is to try to type the paper before you go to bed, then to proofread it the next morning, before you turn it in. Correct all errors neatly in pen (black ink looks best). Pages with a large number of errors should be retyped.

Two Sample Research Papers

Julius Caesar

Act IV. Scene iii:

Theme Through Structure

In an army tent temporarily staked out in the plain
near Sardis, Brutus and Cassius meet. They heatedly discuss
a bribery charge against Lucius Pella and plan for the next
day's battle; they part in uneasy reconciliation. Brutus
prepares for bed, weighed down with thoughts of the battle
at Philippi on the morrow, the death of his wife Portia, his
disagreement with Cassius over policy—all overshadowed by
the ghost of the dead Caesar. In Act IV, scene iii of Shakespeare's Julius Caesar the plot is not advanced beyond
mention of the next day's battle (lines 196–225, 307–09).
Yet the scene is not extraneous. In it, more clearly than
in any other in the play, the audience is brought face to
face with the play's theme. Here is strong evidence of the
disorder which results when a country's leader is overthrown
by force. And as Adrien Bonjour has pointed out, overpower-
ing the idea of national sin, which pervaded the Henry te-
tralogy, is the theme of personal reparation which must be
demanded of Brutus for his murder of a dear friend (13).
The sense of tragedy is increased as Brutus and Cassius,
shorn of their armor and their public personalities, show
their degraded characters; the sense of the tragic fate of
Rome is traced in the attitude and actions of these men who
felt worthy enough to illicitly take her leadership (Wilson
xx).

The emotional tone of the scene reflects the disorder of the state and of the mind of Brutus. The angry ten-

229

sion of quarrels (lines 1-123, 196-229) and bitter words
(lines 133-43) is artfully interspersed with weary pauses.
Oh, let this quarrel end, begs Cassius, "for Cassius is
aweary of the world" (line 95), and Brutus's bitter words to
the poet are explained in his acknowledgement that "I am
sick of many griefs" (line 144). It is a mood of meditation
and sorrow, the artificial glow of candles and wine, that
surrounds the announcement of Portia's death (Charney 12-
13). And the closest harmony which the scene achieves--the
sleep of Lucius, Varro, and Claudius--is rudely broken by
the cry of Brutus just as, Bonjour notes, the thrust of his
knife had broken the natural harmony of the state (56-57).

The actions of the two main characters of this
scene, while they do not further the plot, allow the audience to judge the effects of Caesar's murder. The strong-
minded Cassius--who, as Moulton says, represented force in
the rebellious movement (172)--now fawns on the favor of
Brutus, avowing that "I cannot drink too much of Brutus'
love" (line 162) and peevishly insisting that "When thou
didst hate [Caesar] worst, thou lovest him better/Than ever
thou lovedst Cassius" (lines 106-07). And, still demonstrat-
ing that weakness which he displayed earlier, he allows Brutus to overrule his suggestions on strategy (line 224).

But in the character of Brutus a more important
change has taken place. Charney points out that here, in
the privacy of his tent, on the uneasy eve of battle, "the

personal, domestic, and unheroic world of Brutus opens before the audience" (12). It is bare and simple, as Charney
notes, reflecting the Roman influence as much as does the
clear and uncluttered verse (16). We quickly see that this
is not the same Brutus that Cassius accosted on the Luper-
cal. His defensive outbursts of anger, his sleeplessness,
his bitter words point to a mind in the turmoil of doubt and
disillusionment, on the verge of admitting to itself that it
has made a grievous error. When Brutus determined that "it
must be by his death" (II.i.10) he made a moral choice--a
choice which, following the tradition of the English morality plays, was wrong (Ribner 53), but a choice which had to
be made (Bonjour 41-42):

> There is a tide in the affairs of men
>
> Which taken at the flood leads on to fortune;
>
> Omitted, all the voyage of their life
>
> Is bound in shallows and in miseries. (IV.iii.218-21)

       Early in this scene, Cassius touches the quick of
the deep-seated infection of Brutus' mind, and Caesar's
dearest friend slaps down the intruding hand:

> Did not great Julius bleed for justice' sake?
>
> What villain touched his body that did stab,
>
> And not for justice? (lines 19-21)

Here Brutus is asking two strong rhetorical questions, questions which ironically cry out with an undercurrent of un-
certainty. He is begging Cassius to assure him that Caesar

was struck down for justice's sake; he wants Cassius to tell him that all the conspirators acted on noble motives, for, according to Bonjour, he has come to doubt their motives (49). In the bribery case of Lucius Pella, is it not now clear that "the name of Cassius honors this corruption" (line 15)? Brutus knows the answer is yes when he asks

> . . . shall we now
>
> Contaminate our fingers with base bribes,
>
> And sell the mighty space of our large honors
>
> For so much trash as may be grasped thus? (lines 23–26)

MacCallum contends that Brutus is also close to admitting that perhaps the effects of the murder have not been the desired ones (qtd. in Furness). During the bitter argument which follows Brutus' castigation of Cassius for stooping to bribery, Cassius in exasperation says to Brutus, "Do not presume too much upon my love; I may do that I shall be sorry for," to which Brutus retorts, "You have done that you should be sorry for" (lines 64–65). Ostensibly Brutus is referring to the bribes, but there is more here. Their argument has been filled with references to Caesar and honor, and Brutus' retort could perhaps be a response to his earlier questions. Cassius has already done something he should be sorry for in his involvement in Caesar's murder. It would follow, then, that Brutus, too, should be sorry for his own involvement in this deed. But Brutus cannot openly

and directly question his own role in the assassination.
Instead, he surrounds himself with a barrier of justification. When he contemplated Caesar's murder, it was with the
thought of what power Caesar might abuse with the crown;
here Brutus implies, so Dover Wilson argues (175), that the
actions of Caesar had warranted his murder: "Did not great
Caesar bleed for justice' sake?" (line 19). The closest he
comes to admitting his error is in the acknowledgement of
the fate which he realizes awaits him: "We, at the height,
are ready to decline" (line 217).

The anxiety, the force of the moral implications of
his deed have quite changed Brutus. It is a mistake of
reading Plutarch into Shakespeare to suspect Brutus of know-
ingly sharing funds which were gained illicitly (lines 69–
75). Yet although he retains his strict honesty in the case
of Lucius Pella (line 6) and defends himself against bribery
charges (line 67), as Wilson contends, Brutus' honesty lacks
its former nobility, just as Brutus has lost the noble Portia (176–77). The residue of his honesty seems no more than
what Moulton calls an habitual scrupulosity (182). There is
no better illustration of the degeneration of Brutus' nobility than the ironic juxtaposition of Brutus' unwarranted ac-
cusation of Cassius' involvement in the bribery case and his
implication, in the next breath, that Caesar died for justice's sake!

Many critics list among Brutus' newly acquired

habits the vice of hypocrisy, basing their charge on Brutus'
reaction to Messala's announcement of Portia's death. Those
who hold this theory, according to Smith (114), maintain
that Brutus, already aware of the death of Portia (line
147), pretends ignorance of any news of his wife and then
affects a Stoic acceptance at the news, an act commented
upon by Cassius (lines 194-95). However, I feel that this
view is not in keeping with the tone and action of the rest
of the scene. There is little cause for Brutus to feign
Stoicism when he has been chided by Cassius earlier for no
longer observing the practices of his philosophy (line 145);
there is no other evidence of conscious hypocrisy on Brutus'
part in this scene. Technically, Messala is in a position
to overhear Cassius when he moans, "Portia, art thou gone?"
(line 166). Moreover, in the fawning actions of Cassius
thus far, there is no preparation for his facetious comment
on Brutus' act (lines 194-95).

Other critics, basing their theory on the fact
found in Plutarch (1195) that Portia's death was falsely reported to Brutus and noting in the text that the figures
which Messala gives on the number of dead senators does not
agree with that given to Brutus earlier (lines 174-76), sup-
pose that Brutus falsely hopes that his earlier report that
Portia is dead is false (Smith 115). There is little tex-
tual evidence for this theory and it certainly would have
been too abstract to have been grasped by the audience. I

234

tend to agree with Dover Wilson and Granville-Barker in sup-
posing that Shakespeare first wrote lines 179-93 and later
wrote lines 141-56, intending to delete the original set
(Wilson 179-80). It is not unusual in Shakespearean texts
for passages to be mistakenly printed, e.g., Sonnet 146,
lines 1-2. Such a view would take care of an explanation of
Brutus' Stoic acceptance of the news and the sentimentality
with which Moulton explains Cassius' lines: "Brutus has been
heart broken by the loss of Portia, [and] Cassius is forced
to give way and acknowledge Brutus' superiority to himself
even in his own ideal of impassiveness" (173).

Most striking, however, in the change which one
notes in Brutus' character is his growing resemblance to
Caesar. He is arrogant and cruel to Cassius--in Dorsch's
words "an Olympian god chiding an erring mortal" (xli)--ar-
guing his worth as a soldier (line 51), overruling Cassius'
suggestions as he did before, but now with a superior air
(line 198). He is overbearing with the poet (lines 134-38).
Like Caesar, Brutus no longer follows the dictates of his
religion (line 145). And Cassius mentions Caesar time and
again in the course of their conversation (lines 58, 106-
07). All too well does this illustrate Ribner's point of
how tightly bound up with the tragedy of Rome are the trage-
dies of Caesar and Brutus (53). As the audience is allowed
that last step into the inmost depths of Brutus' being and
his guilt, we see what Dover Wilson calls the mounting cli-

max of the inevitability of Caesarism (xx) as it is illustrated by the spiritual authority of the ghost of Caesar
which steps forth from the mind of Brutus (Moulton 200–01).
It is the last and most profound statement of the upset of
harmony and order achieved by his murder.

Bonjour, Adrien. The Structure of Julius Caesar. Liver-
     pool: Liverpool UP, 1958.

Charney, Maurice. Shakespeare's Roman Plays. Cambridge:
     Harvard UP, 1961.

Dorsch, T. S., ed. Introduction. Julius Caesar. By
     William Shakespeare. Arden ed., 6th ed., rev. Cam-
     bridge: Harvard UP, 1955. i–lxxiv.

Furness, Horace H., ed. Notes to IV.iii.28–29. Julius
     Caesar. By William Shakespeare. Variorum ed. Phila-
     delphia: Lippincott, 1913. 205.

Moulton, Richard. Shakespeare as a Dramatic Artist. Ox-
     ford: Clarendon Press, 1929.

Plutarch. The Lives of the Noble Grecians and Romans.
     Trans. John Dryden. New York: Modern Library, n.d.

Ribner, Irving. Patterns in Shakespearean Tragedy. New
     York: Barnes and Noble, 1960.

Shakespeare, William. Julius Caesar. Shakespeare: The Com-
     plete Works. Ed. G. B. Harrison. New York: Harcourt,
     1952. 809–44.

Smith, Warren D. "The Duplicate Revelation of Portia's
     Death." Shakespeare Quarterly 4 (1953): 153–61. Rpt.
     in Shakespeare's Julius Caesar. Ed. Julian Markels. A

Scribner Research Anthology. New York: Scribner's,

1961. 113–19.

Wilson, John Dover, ed. Introduction and Notes to IV.iii.

Julius Caesar. By William Shakespeare. Cambridge ed.

Cambridge: Cambridge UP, 1949. vii–xxxiii, 175–83.

A Primary Research Report
[Author-date—APA style]

Comparative Study of Diving Bradycardia

in the Common White Rat and

the Leopard Frog (<u>Rana pipiens</u>)

Astrid Furniss and
Linda Nixon
Environmental Physiology
Dr. David Martinsen
Biology Dept.
Spring 1984

Physiological responses to water submersion have been documented in numerous animals. Several changes have been found to occur, including apnea, temporary cessation of respiration; ischemia, redistribution of blood; peripheral vasoconstriction; and the slowing of heart rate, or bradycardia (Anderson, 1966). In birds and mammals, diving bradycardia due to cardiovascular changes is of particular interest as a mechanism of O_2 conservation.

Recent studies on diving bradycardia have involved vertebrates including birds (diving and nondiving), frogs, rodents, muskrats, man, and dogs (Jones, 1966; Scholander, 1963). Lin and Baker (1975) have reported that comparatively, when taking into consideration a number of variables, the diving response of a rat is similar to the diving response of marine mammals and birds, with both being natural reflexes. The diving response in these animals is an immediate and sustained bradycardia. This has been found to vary from the cardiac response in amphibians, although it has been found that the recovery period is similarly rapid for all (Jones, 1966). Experimentation by Lund and Dingle (1968) has shown that bradycardia in restrained diving frogs is achieved in two forms. Depending upon temperature and season, the heart rate either decreases rapidly, indicating a reflex mechanism under vagal influence similar to that of other vertebrates, or it decreases slowly, indicating a non-reflex mechanism.

It is our intent to compare the dive reflex of a frog (<u>Rana pipiens</u>) to that of a common laboratory rat in an effort to substantiate previously recorded data of other researchers. In particular, we will examine the type of bradycardia shown with respect to the period of onset and the degree of bradycardia attained. While temperature has been found to influence the response of frogs, little study has been done on mammals in regard to this variable. The effect of temperature on the rate is thus of interest in our study.

MATERIALS AND METHODS

Six female white lab rats were obtained from the Oregon Health Sciences University, Portland, Oregon. They were approximately 2-3 months old and ranged in size from 250-300 grams. Three leopard frogs (<u>Rana pipiens</u>), approximately 28 grams in size, were purchased from Pet & Pond in Tigard, Oregon. One specimen of bullfrog (<u>Rana catesbianca</u>) was caught at Mollala State Park in Canby, Oregon. The rats were maintained in a room at approximately 23°C. The frogs were kept in a sink with approximately 1 centimeter of water. The rats were fed science diet plus a mixture of seeds on occasion. The frogs were not fed.

Experimentation on the rats was performed over a three-week period. The rats were lifted from the cage by their tails and maneuvered head first into the restrainer. The subjects were placed in a standard plastic rat restrainer,

using tape to secure the gates (Figure 1). Hypodermic needles (25 gauge) were placed just under the skin at the midventral region on each side of the rat. Leads from the Carolina model ECG recorder were attached to the needles and
time and event were recorded. The rat was allowed to adjust
to the situation for several minutes. Throughout the experiment, we had difficulties with the equipment. A control
was performed by placing the rat in a container without water and measuring heart rate. A control for a response to
tilting was also performed. Approximately 4 inches of de-
ionized water was placed into a glass (and later plastic)
container. The rat was lifted into the container and submerged (whole body) in water, keeping the restrainer parallel to the table surface. The lengths of the dives ranged
from 10 seconds to 30 seconds and temperature varied from
15°C to 30°C. The rat was then lifted out of the water and
placed on the table. Recovery heart rate was obtained for
several minutes. In one trial the rat was set on top of the
tank instead of on the table because of electrical interference.

[FIGURE 1: "Rat Restrainer" placed here]

Experimentation on the frogs was carried out over a period of approximately one week. After the death of one of
three specimens of leopard frog, the remaining two were
moved from a shallow tank to a deep sink. For restraint of
the frogs, a piece of corkboard (5″ × 7″) was obtained.

String was looped over the frog's limbs, drawn through holes in the corkboard, and tied down (Figure 2). The frog was able to move somewhat, but no better form of restraint was available. Electrodes (shortened, 25 gauge) were sterilized by heating and then placed under the skin. One was located at the midventral line of the right side and the other was placed on the left upper thigh near the pelvic girdle. Jerky movements of the frog made electrode placement difficult. Electrodes were hooked to the ECG equipment, as for the rats, and time and heart rate were monitored for several minutes. The frog was then lifted into 23°C water (in a glass tank). Problems were encountered with the sinking weights falling off the corkboard. The frog remained in water for 20 minutes, during which time he freed one leg and ripped his side, causing bleeding. Excessive movement resulted in problematic data and a dive shorter than the desired 30 minutes. The frog was removed from the water and recovery was monitored.

[FIGURE 2: "Frog Restrainer" placed here]

Unsuccessful attempts were made to restrain a bullfrog using similar apparatus to that described above. Later, the bullfrog was anaesthetized by placing it in 100 ml. of 1% solution of Ethyl m-aminobenzoate methane sulfonic acid (tricaine) for 10 minutes. The bullfrog was hooked up to ECG equipment, but attempts to obtain heart rate were unsuccessful. The same procedure was successfully performed us-

ing the same Rana pipiens as used in previous experimentation. The length of the dive was increased to 35 minutes in
23°C water, with the frog remaining under anaesthetic for the
duration.

RESULTS

Analysis of heart rate data was particularly difficult
to carry out due to equipment flaws, extreme sensitivity of
recording to animal muscle movement, and electrical interference from the room. It was necessary to make some assumptions in measuring heartbeats per minute during pre-
dive, dive, and recovery periods. The heart rate of the
first 5 seconds on each rat dive was calculated, as well as
an average heart rate for the overall dive, because heart
rate recording was most free of muscle static during this
time period. In order to calculate beats per minute, a 5-
20-second period was blocked off and the number of sharp
vertical lines (strokes) during this time was counted (Table
1 for all data).

[TABLE 1: "Effect of submersion in H_2O upon heart rate of rat (varied H_2O
temperature); and TABLE 2: "Effect of submersion in 23°C H_2O upon heart
rate of leopard frog" placed here]

Rat control. The rat's heart rate response to being
lifted and lowered into a tank without water and then removed was essentially no change. The heart rate decreased
by 1% of normal heart rate during the no-water dive and increased by approximately 5% (of normal heart rate) on recovery. The heart rate obtained on tilting the rat was 122% of

resting heart rate. The rate returned to normal when back in the horizontal position. From these results, we concluded that experimental error could be reduced by holding the organism parallel to the surface rather than tilting it.

Rat experimental. For all dives, regardless of temperature and length of dive, immediate and pronounced bradycardia was established upon submersion. It was noted that during the first 5 seconds of the dive, there was a greater decrease in heart rate. During the rest of the dive, the average heart rate was found to be somewhat higher, with slight irregularities in rate at points. Recovery to near-normal heart rate was immediate in all animals. At times normal heart rate was found to be significantly different from heart rate just prior to dive (pre-dive rate). It was decided that normal (resting) heart rate should be compared with overall dive rate, whereas the pre-dive heart rate should be compared with the rate during the first 5 seconds.

The original data were collected at 23°C, with temperature being introduced as a variable late in the experiment. All dives at 23°C ranged in length from 10 to 15 seconds (Figure 3). With the exception of one dive, all dives showed similar results. That is, overall dive heart rate was found to be from 24% to 28% of resting normal. In the remaining dive, the heart rate was 39% of resting normal. We omitted the abnormal dive when averaging the data, since the others were all so close. Reproducible results were obtained when a second dive was performed several minutes after a first dive. Normal and pre-dive heart rates for the same animal tended to vary from day to day, but no effect on the degree of bradycardia was observed.

[FIGURE 3: "Heart rate of rat during submersion in 23°C H₂O" placed here]

During performance of dives at 15°C, both temperature and dive length were introduced as variables (Figure 4). Two 15-second dives and two 30-second dives were performed. Generally, the heart rate started out at a higher rate than the dives performed at 23°C. The overall dive heart rate was found to be 24% to 25% of resting normal during 15-second dives. This is similar to that found at 23°C. For 30-second dives, the percentage of resting normal attained during the dive was quite variable, ranging from 21% to 30%. The percentage of pre-dive heart rate during the first 5 seconds of the dive, however, was the same for all dives at 15°C, and was found to be 17% to 18%. For 15-second dives, the heart rate returned to normal immediately, while in 30-second dives, removal from water resulted in tachycardia and profound muscle movement for a short time.

[FIGURE 4: "Heart rate of rat during submersion in 15°C H₂O" placed here]

Dives carried out at 30°C lasted 20 seconds. An assumption was made here, based on results from above, that limited increase in length did not significantly influence the degree of bradycardia experienced (Figure 5). The initial resting heart rate was quite variable in all three trials. One rat displayed an extremely fast heart rate of 552 b.p.m., while the others were at 396 and 444, well within the average of previous trials. The percentage of normal heart rate reached in the dives ranged from 16% to 20%, which is lower than that obtained at other temperatures. The percentage of pre-dive heart rate attained in the first 5 seconds of dive was also found to be quite low, at 14% to 15%. Recovery from warm-water dives did not reflect as sharp an increase in heart rate immediately after removal from water as did recovery from cooler water dives.

[FIGURE 5: "Heart rate of rat during submersion in 30°C H₂O" placed here]

Frog control. Lifting the organism and putting it into an empty tank tended to increase heart rate due to increased movement. A full dive-length control was not performed because of time involved and noncooperation of the frog.

Frog experimental. During experimentation with the leopard frog, an unintended variable was introduced after the first trial. Because of difficulties in restraining the frog and recording ECG due to frog movement, it became necessary to anaesthetize frogs in later trials. Only one organism served as a subject for dives because of problems with other organisms and also for purposes of comparison (unanaesthetized vs. anaesthetized). In both trials, a gradually developing bradycardia was found to occur.

In the unanaesthetized frog, a heart rate 58% of resting rate (44% of pre-dive rate) was established after the frog had remained in 23°C water for approximately 15 minutes

248

(Table 2 and Figure 6). There was a sharp increase in heart rate during the first minute of recovery. However, it was not possible further to measure recovery because the frog had worked himself loose.

[FIGURE 6: "Heart rate of unanaesthetized frog during submersion in 23°C H₂O" placed here]

The anaesthetized frog showed dive rates of 78% of resting heart rate and 72% of pre-dive (Table 2 and Figure 7). Furthermore, it took 24 minutes instead of 15 minutes to reach the lowest level. During recovery, no increase in heart rate was found in the first few minutes, but then a rapid increase to near pre-dive level was noted. For both dives (unanaesthetized and anaesthetized), recovery heart rates were intermediate to resting and pre-dive rates.

[FIGURE 7: "Heart rate of anaesthetized frog during submersion in 23°C H₂O" placed here]

DISCUSSION

The results of our experimentation with rats have shown that rapidly achieved bradycardia does occur in response to forced submersion. Comparison of data with the results of previous experiments indicates the reproducibility of this response. Although using a slightly different diving meth-odology, Lin (1974) and Lin and Baker (1975) found dive heart rates and percentage decreases similar to the results we obtained. Their results indicated pre-dive rates of ap-proximately 401 and 411 b.p.m., and dive rates of 114 and

118, while our averages were a pre-dive rate of 416 and a dive rate of 107 at 23°C (Table 1).

When looking at temperature effects on degree of brady-cardia, results were obtained that did not coincide with our predictions. On the basis of experimentation with muskrats (Thornton, Gordon, & Ferguson, 1978), in which increasing temperature of water caused a decrease in degree of brady-cardia, we predicted that this might be the case for rats, also, since both are homeotherms. Apparently, in the musk-rat, water temperature of 2°C resulted in more pronounced bradycardia (24% RHR) than warmer temperatures of 20°C (34% RHR) and 35°C (50% RHR). The temperature effect is explained by compensation in heart rate due to differences in the amount of vasoconstriction, the cutoff of blood flow to the periphery, experienced at varying temperatures. (Vasocon-striction will be discussed later.) Our results did not follow this muskrat pattern. The lowest rates as well as the largest heart rate drops were evidenced in the 30°C dives, while the extent of bradycardia in 15°C and 23°C dives was rather variable. Generally, less bradycardia was expe-rienced at 23°C. Observations of rat behavior when submerged in warm water suggested that increased temperature had a calming effect on the rat. Heart rate readings were thus more readable. The decreased struggling may also explain the lower heart rates obtained.

Further control of temperature and use of more organ-isms would be necessary to make a more conclusive statement.

However, our evidence, as that of Thornton, Gordon, and Ferguson, indicates that thermal factors do have some effect on the diving response in mammals. This would be an interesting line of research to pursue.

One important variable that needs to be taken into consideration in interpreting our results is the role of psychological elements in the rats' physiological responses. For example, during one of our trials, the rat displayed a highly elevated pre-dive heart rate of 552 b.p.m., while during a trial performed earlier in the day, the pre-dive rate was 408. Conversely, another rat showed a heart rate of 448 on one day and a lower rate of 378 on a later date.* As Lund and Dingle (1968) have suggested for frogs, such factors as "experimental procedure, training, temperament, fright, previous diving, and anticipation of diving" may significantly affect the variability of response during dives, even in the same animal (p. 266). Undoubtedly, conditions in the laboratory are not the best. Drummond and Jones (1979) have shown that in the muskrat there is a significant difference between unrestrained voluntary dives and restrained forced dives, with larger drop in heart rate found in the unrestrained animal. Frequent struggling during restrained dives increases heart rate. Admittedly, the muskrat is a true diving mammal, whereas the rat is a non-

---

*For specific dive data, see lab manual.

diver. However, a similar effect on heart rate cannot be ruled out.

Furthermore, restraining animals for dives may not be indicative of "natural" response. A recent review article by Butler (1982) has indicated that bradycardia and vasoconstriction are not a characteristic of most of the short dives performed by diving birds and mammals, but rather the "exercise" response of increased heart rate and blood to the muscles is experienced. Longer dives, however, do show bradycardia. In our study, length of dive did not seem to have an effect on the degree of bradycardia, though dives were only seconds long rather than minutes. However, in recovery it was evident that a longer dive of 30 seconds produced an initial tachycardia and profound muscle movement on emergence from water, probably due to an O_2 debt.

The occurrence of diving bradycardia in rats, as in other vertebrates, has been shown to accompany redistribution of blood flow to favor the heart and brain with reduction of flow to the periphery. A fourfold increase in peripheral resistance was noted on onset of apnea in forcibly submerged rats (Lin & Baker, 1975). Blood pressure changes resulted in bradycardia, a 71% reduction in heart rate, and a concurrent 68% decrease in cardiac output. Tracing radioactive metals to tissues clearly showed that nonvital organs received less blood during diving.

The vagal reflex nature of this response has been established using vagotomy and atropine injections, which block the parasympathetic nerve fibers to the heart (vagal), and propanolal injections, which block the sympathetic nerve fibers (Lin, 1974). The study showed that atropine effectively eliminated bradycardia. Without atropine, Lin found that during diving there was a greatly suppressed sympathetic tone and 300% increase in parasympathetic tone. Baroreceptors, which decrease heart rate in response to increasing blood pressure, have been suggested as a causal factor in diving bradycardia due to their sensitivity to rate of pressure change as well as blood pressure levels (Anderson, 1966). Lin (1974) disregards baroreceptors because bradycardia was induced during falling aortic blood pressure in reserpine-treated rats. Also Huang and Peng (1976) report that chemoreceptors in the carotid sinus region of the heart, rather than baroreceptors, are responsible for initiation of bradycardia, with denervation of chemoreceptors eliminating the response.

Bradycardia is a response which appears not only in rats, but has a universal nature among birds and mammals (Scholander, 1963). The benefits of bradycardia following vasoconstriction to an animal entering an environment in which ability to attain oxygen is reduced are clear. Only organs needing O_2 are supplied, allowing the heart to decrease its work load and thus further preserve O_2 stores. Interestingly, Lin (1974) notes that the pattern of response in the rat is more similar to that of diving mammals, which show a more immediate and pronounced bradycardia, than to that of other nondivers such as man, who has a slowly developing bradycardia (Scholander, 1963). The more pronounced bradycardia, as seen in the diving mammal the muskrat, most likely serves a protective purpose on the heart exposed to frequent periods of hypoxia (in water). Depletion of ATP in the heart myocardium results in cell damage, while lowered heart rate conserves ATP (McKean & Landon, 1982).

The heart rate response to diving of an amphibian serves as an interesting comparison to that of a mammal. Frogs are cutaneous breathers and therefore do not experience the same degree of O_2 debt as birds or mammals do upon submersion. A bradycardiac response with vasoconstriction would not be adaptive in these animals because respiration requires circulation to the skin. Some degree of cardiac hypoxia, however, would eventually occur and this would lead to a gradually developing reduction in heart rate (Heath, 1980). Usually, however, dives in nature are not long enough for levels of O_2 to become a problem.

The results of our experimentation with frogs have shown that a gradually occurring bradycardia is found in accordance with the results of previous experiments (Jones, 1966; Jones & Shelton, 1964). The time that it took for full bradycardia to be achieved in an unanaesthetized frog was found to be approximately 15 minutes, whereas numerous researchers have found it to take 15 to 30 minutes. Although slightly different diving methodologies were used, including type and attachment point of electrodes and the

species of frog (<u>Rana temporia</u> rather than <u>Rana pipiens</u>),
Jones and Shelton (1964) found frogs in 13°C to 15°C water to
attain a heart rate 60% of the initial rate in air during
bradycardia, with the initial rate being 40 b.p.m. Our
results showed an initial heart rate in air of 57 b.p.m. and
a reduction to 58% of normal rate during submersion in 23°C
water. However, it must be noted that most research has
been done using fully aerated water, whereas the water we
used was bound to become depleted of O_2 and could result in
ours having a more pronounced bradycardia, although it was
at a higher temperature.

While a slowly developed bradycardia seems consistent
with skin respiration in frogs, Lund and Dingle (1968) have
described two types of dive response in frogs: a rapidly attained bradycardia similar to other vertebrates and a slowly
attained bradycardia as in that found by Jones and Shelton
(1964) and ourselves. Vagotomy and atropine treatment re-
vealed that rapid response increased under vagal influence
and varied with temperature and season. Slow bradycardia
seemed to be a passive response to lack of O_2, rather than
being under vagus control. Apparently in July, vagal inhi-
bition could be reduced or eliminated at higher temperature
than in September, showing seasonal dependence of dive response. A slow response was only found during restrained
dives in July at low temperatures (10°C). Perhaps the season
(spring) in which we performed our experiment had some effect on the frog, but it would be necessary to study more

animals in order to document this. It is noted that the
method of restraint may be influential in the type of bradycardia established. Again, more results are needed to test
this.

After trouble encountered with the unanaesthetized
frog, it was discovered that Ethyl m-aminobenzoate methane
sulfonic acid (tricaine) could be used as an effective anaesthetic to render the frog more complacent to experimentation. Tricaine has been found to work as a general anaesthetic in poikilotherms. Its influence on the skeletal
muscle and neuromuscular junctions has been tested by Fried-
man et al. (cited in Wayson, 1978) and found to have no de-
pressant effect on neuromuscular transmission in "the dose
range used for anaesthesia in poikilotherms" (p. 68). This
seems to coincide with the findings of Jones and Shelton
(1964) that a frog lightly anaesthetized with tricaine
showed no difference in diving bradycardia compared to the
unanaesthetized frog.

However, these were not the results that were obtained
during our experimentation. This can be explained by a number of reasons. The major reason is that the doses used
seemed to be more in the range of "near lethal dose" rather
than "lightly anaesthetized." Tricaine is found to dissi-
pate rather rapidly when the frog is submerged. In our
case, the frog remained anaesthetized for the entire length
of the dive (40 minutes) and was still under the anaesthesia
when we placed him back in the sink. Further evidence that

dosage was "near lethal" comes from the fact that the heart rate in the bullfrog was barely detectable, although he too was removed just at the point of going under the anaesthetic. It may also be the case that had we run more trials, it would have been found that the anaesthetized frog was in the range of the unanaesthetized frog, showing that the anaesthesia may indeed have no effect on the degree of bradycardia attained during submersion.

Jones and Shelton (1964) performed experiments in an effort to show that the slowing of the heart during forced submersion was not produced by the artificial circumstances of the dive. The frogs experimented with were allowed to roam freely in a tank of fully aerated water, being attached to the recording apparatus by only a few wires. Results showed that the heart rate tended to be quite low, although occasional increases were found due to periodical surfacing of the organisms. This did not prove that the degree to which bradycardia was attained was not influenced by forced submersion, for Lund and Dingle (1968) have stated that resistance to the restraining apparatus or discomfort during experimentation could have an effect on both metabolism and heart rate, and thus be reflected in an "increased need for physiological adjustments" when diving (p. 266). Rather, it qualitatively showed that some degree of bradycardia in fact is attained, regardless of the dive situation.

It seems clear that the appearance of bradycardia in frogs is due to a shortage of O_2 in the organism. However,

Jones and Shelton (1964) have suggested another factor which they believe to be just as important as lack of O_2 in changing metabolic rate and causing a decreased heart rate. Their experimentation has shown that the "cessation of rhythmic breathing" could be of great importance in the response to forced submersion (p. 422). They have found that the act of breathing has a stimulating effect on the heart, and that the influence of breathing movements on heart rate must be an effect mediated by the nervous system, i.e., vagal influence. Bringing the frog into pure N_2 after submersion caused a tachycardia similar to the effect of bringing the frog into air, and therefore rhythmic movements must not be ruled out as a mechanism, although we have no data to support this.

ERRORS—PROBLEMS

Although our data is found to be quite similar in certain respects to the work of others, many sources of error could have had an influence on our results. The most blatant source of error is that of heart rate readings taken off ECG. The equipment used was quite archaic compared to the equipment most likely used by others. We had numerous problems with equipment failure and found that there was much interference in the readings, especially that of muscle movement. Also, the timing mechanism of the machine was quite erratic. Sometimes it would work, sometimes it would not. When it was working, the 1-second markings were often not the same distance apart, even though in any given trial the speed control was not changed. This situation was circumvented somewhat by trying to time the dives accurately, although for a variety of reasons this was not always possible. Also, it was discovered too late in our experimentation that static interference was often coming from the table on which experiments were performed. Perhaps conducting experiments in a sound-proof chamber would improve accuracy of results.

A further source of error was encountered in the handling of specimens and in inefficient apparatus. Especially with the rat, it was often found difficult to maneuver the organisms into the small tank because there was minimal room for the experimenter's hands. The major problem with the frogs was that the weights attached to the bottom of the corkboard became detached. It would have been much less disruptive in both instances had some sort of lowering device been used.

Other sources of error were undoubtedly due to the apparatus and experimental methodology. During the first trial performed on a frog, one digit of the specimen's right leg was injured when he struggled as the strings were being tied down. Furthermore, he was able to work one leg loose while submerged. As a result of the movement, the electrode slightly ripped the right side of the frog, although the needle remained intact. Both the movement of the frog and the presumed trauma caused by the wounds may have had an effect on our results. Movement may also have played a role in experimentation with rats, for, although they were restrained, some movement was still allowed within the restrainer.

SUMMARY

1. Pronounced bradycardia was achieved upon submersion in water in both rats and frogs, although the length of time until full bradycardia was reached differed.

2. Bradycardia in rats seems to be influenced by temperature, although further studies are necessary to determine its role.

3. Restraint methods, as well as use of anaesthesia in the frog, are suggested as influential factors in the development of bradycardia.

4. Occurrence of bradycardia in the rat may be an effective method for O_2 conservation, although the adaptive significance is not entirely clear in the frog.

5. The study was more accurate on a qualitative level as opposed to quantitative level because of small sample size studied, as well as inaccuracy of equipment and other sources of error.

We would like to acknowledge the help given by Professor David Martinsen, Martin Munsel, and Larry David in connection with this project.

References

Anderson, H. (1966). Physiological adaptations in diving vertebrates. Physiological Reviews, 46, 212–243.

Butler, P. (1982). Respiratory and cardiovascular control during diving in birds and mammals. Journal of Experimental Biology, 100, 195–221.

Drummond, P., & Jones, R. (1979). The initiation and maintenance of bradycardia in a diving mammal, the muskrat (Ondatra zibethica). Journal of Physiology, 290, 253–272.

Heath, A. (1980). Cardiac responses of larval and adult tiger salamanders (Ambystoma tigrinum). Comparative Biochemical Physiology, 65A, 439–444.

Huang, T., & Peng, Y. (1976). Role of the chemoreceptor in diving bradycardia in rat. Japanese Journal of Physiology, 26, 395–401.

Jones, D. (1966). Factors affecting the recovery from diving bradycardia in the frog. Journal of Experimental Biology, 44, 397–411.

Jones, D., & Shelton, G. (1964). Factors influencing submergence and the heart rate in the frog. Journal of Experimental Biology, 41, 417–431.

Lin, Y. (1974). Autonomic nervous control of cardiovascular response during diving in the rat. American Journal of Physiology, 227, 601–605.

Lin, Y., & Baker, D. (1975). Cardiac output and its distribution during diving in the rat. American Journal of Physiology, 223, 733–737.

Lund, G., & Dingle, H. (1968). Seasonal temperature influence on vagal control of diving bradycardia in the frog (Rana pipiens). Journal of Experimental Biology, 48, 265–277.

McKean, T., & Landon, R. (1982). Comparison of the response of muskrat, rabbit, and guinea pig heart muscle to hypoxia. American Journal of Physiology, 243, R245–250.

Scholander, P. (1963). The master switch of life. Scientific American, 209, 92–106.

Thornton, R., Gordon, C., & Ferguson, J. (1978). Role of thermal stimuli in the diving response of the muskrat (Ondatra zibethia). Comparative Biochemical Physiology, 61A, 369–370.

Wayson, K. A. (1978). Selective toxicity and comparative pharmacology of tricaine methanesulfonate. Unpublished doctoral dissertation, Oregon Health Sciences University, Portland.

Planning Ahead: Developing a Work Schedule for Your Research Project/Paper

Begin with the date on which the paper is due, and work backwards.

Date

☐

☐

☐

☐

☐

Stage in the process
Due date, the date on which you will give your paper to your instructor

Polished final draft ready to type (1 to 3 days before due date: be realistic about the amount of time the typing will take, and allow time for proofreading the typed copy)

First rough draft (10 days to 2 weeks before due date)

If you are working on a critical paper, the date on which your research is essentially complete and you begin to develop the thesis for your paper; if you are working on a primary research project, the date on which you have all the necessary data from your tests/experiments in your hands (at least 2½ weeks before due date)

Date on which you begin the research process by selecting an area of investigation, developing your research question, and starting your Researcher's Notebook (at least 6 to 7 weeks before the due date; the sooner the better)

Index

Index

Notes